Coaching Skills

Fourth edition

Coaching Skills: The Definitive Guide to Being A Coach

Fourth edition

By Jenny Rogers

Open University Press

Open University Press
McGraw-Hill Education
McGraw-Hill House
Shoppenhangers Road
Maidenhead
Berkshire
England
SL6 2QL

email: enquiries@openup.co.uk
world wide web: www.openup.co.uk

and Two Penn Plaza, New York, NY 10121-2289, USA

First published 2004
Second edition published 2008
Third edition published 2012
First published in this fourth edition 2016

A catalogue record of this book is available from the British Library

ISBN-13: 978-0-33-526192-5
ISBN-10: 0-33-526192-2
eISBN: 978-0-33-526193-5

Library of Congress Cataloging-in-Publication Data
CIP data applied for

Typeset by Transforma Pvt. Ltd., Chennai, India

Fictitious names of companies, products, people, characters and/or data that
may be used herein (in case studies or in examples) are not intended to
represent any real individual, company, product or event.

Praise for this book

"If you can afford to buy only one book about coaching which has to cover the field, buy this one; if you can afford to buy a thousand, buy this one first, as it's the very best. Jenny Rogers is right up to date with the latest research, but keeps the book still resolutely practical, and very much in the real world. Compassionate, thorough, fun."

Anne Scoular, Managing Director Meyler Campbell

"This book is most certainly the 'definitive guide to being a coach'. Of all my coaching books, this is the one that sits dog-eared and littered with post-it notes on my desk. It is a coaching 'bible' that I keep coming back to; it provides a very strong foundation of principles and values on which to build your coaching expertise, a wide range of ideas with relevant case studies, immense practical advice and coaching theories from the foundations to the most modern thinking. Jenny's engaging style provides support, pragmatism and encouragement with a good splash of wit. It is an essential handbook for all coaches whether starting out or raising your game."

Jacqui Fairbrass, Executive Coach,
Trafalgar Personal Development Ltd

"Jenny Rogers' handbook on coaching skills is a classic, owned and read to destruction by a generation of coaches. The author's experience, compassion and wisdom shine from every page. She combines the wisdom gained from decades of experience with the erudition from being widely read in the field. The result is a guide that is clear and easy to read, packed with relevant examples and supported by evidence and recommendations for further reading. This fourth edition, Coaching Skills: the definitive guide to being a coach, brings the work up to date by showing how a number of recent publications about the workings of the mind are relevant to coaching practice. Throughout the book there are new stories and new insights. For new coaches, this is a must-buy. For owners of earlier editions, consider an upgrade: this one is the best yet!"

Professor Lis Paice OBE, visiting professor at
Imperial College London

"This fourth edition of a classic coaching primer remains as practical and accessible as ever; and it still has value for experienced coaches, too."

David Clutterbuck, EMCC special ambassador, UK

"A lifetime of experience and passionate reflections about coaching are distilled into a book which is sophisticated yet beautifully easy to read. This book says all the really important things that there are to be said about what it means to be a coach. It gets to the heart of the underlying principles as well as the practice of coaching. Jenny suggests that the best coaching should be infinitely fascinating, challenging and enjoyable. The experience of reading this book is all these things and more. Every coach, from novice to expert, should read it."

Kim Morgan, Managing Director Barefoot Coaching Ltd, UK

"Coaching Skills is a gem of a book for beginner coaches. Jenny Roger's authority, underpinned by years of real experience as a coach, gives her a matchless writing style that results in a convincing and dependable text. I recommend this book to all my students and welcome this updated edition."

Dr Elaine Cox, Director of the Postgraduate Coaching & Mentoring Programmes, Oxford Brookes University and Founding Editor of the International Journal of Evidence Based Coaching and Mentoring.

"A complete must for anyone learning or refining their coaching skills - this book is both immensely practical and informed by a wealth of knowledge and experience. Rogers gets to the heart of what makes coaching transformative and empowers both client and coach. She demystifies the disciplined craft, paying meticulous attention for example to different kinds of questions and their impact. Alongside this, her exposition of trust and her approach to challenge in the coaching relationship open the door to the real artistry of this work: the intuition and human connection that underpin it at its best."

Professor Helena Gaunt, Vice Principal and Director of Academic Affairs, Guildhall School of Music & Drama

"Coaching skills in its previous editions has been a must have book for coaches as they begin their career and look for ways of building their confidence and skills. This new edition speaks as much to the coach who is wanting to extend their boundaries through new material on neuropsychology, how to work with the client's life story, working with trauma and when it's OK to stop asking questions and offer

advice. There is no more authoritative, practical and readable writer on coaching skills than Jenny Rogers'."

Carole Pemberton, Career Coach and author of Resilience
(Open University Press, 2015)

"Drawing on a substantial amount of practical experience, Jenny has produced a very clear and no nonsense account of the wide range of coaching skills and techniques. The book, which is written in a very engaging and accessible style, provides some helpful further reading of some interesting texts and offers a substantial guide to the practicing coach."

Professor Bob Garvey, York St John University
Business School

"Jenny's Definitive Guide is a beautifully eloquent and engaging evolution of her earlier Coaching Skills: A Handbook, *which has been our principle text, forming the backbone of our coaching practice in the elite sport environment since 2010. The fourth edition sees new chapters that encourage us to look at some of the more challenging aspects of practice and develop the subtle skills required for effective and genuine coaching. As ever, the content is brought to life by Jenny's extensive experience which she conveys to the reader with wonderful humility, humour and wisdom. An absolute go-to book for new, developing and experienced coaches,* The Definitive Guide *demonstrates Jenny's continued commitment to the subject and provides an incredibly pleasurable and inspiring read, which will continue to have a profound impact on our coaching training and development at the EIS."*

Joanna Harrison, Head of Performance
Lifestyle at the English Institute of Sport

"Jenny Rogers' Coaching Skills was the first book on coaching I ever bought. It has been read, referred to and loaned so often that it is almost in pieces. I couldn't wait to get my hands on this fourth edition and it didn't disappoint with new coaching topics (such as giving information coaching style), new case studies and the same elegant and hugely enjoyable writing style. I recommend this book to everyone interested in using a coaching approach in their work and life. It is both authoritative and engaging. From the first chapter you know that this author doesn't just know about the theory of coaching. She clearly practices it and really understands both the joys and the challenges of working with real clients on real issues. If you only buy one book on coaching, buy this one."

Jane Cook, Head of Coaching Linden Learning, UK

"Coaching Skills *is a comprehensive yet succinct overview of the coaching field. It combines wisdom gained from coaching practice with insights culled from a wide selection of the latest literature. The section on neuroscience makes a compelling case for why coaches should take this subject seriously while also providing sensible warnings about the tentative nature of neuroscientific knowledge. A judicious approach that characterises the whole book.*"

Martin Vogel, founder of Vogel Wakefield, the counter-consultancy.

"*This book is a masterpiece and a joy to read for anyone with an interest in executive coaching. Jenny is one of the pioneers of business coaching and in* Coaching Skills *she distils her extensive practical experience and combines it with a wealth of well researched and accessibly described theory. Jenny writes with elegance, humanity, and refreshing frankness about the reality of being coach.* Coaching Skills *is deservedly on the essential reading list for many coaching certification programmes and is a great way for practising coaches to refresh their thinking and take their learning to the next level.*"

Betsy Kendall, AFBPs, COO & Head of
Professional Services at OPP Ltd.

"*Rogers' book has been on our required reading list for our certification program for years and her latest edition keeps great pace with the growing sophistication in the field of coaching. From her new and nuanced case studies to the practical new chapter examining when and how to provide information and advice in a coaching style to her — she covers new territory with a clarity that serves coaches from novice to masters.*"

Pam McLean, Ph.D., CEO, Hudson Institute of Coaching, USA

"*The new 4th edition of* Coaching Skills *will be a welcome addition to the bookshelves of coaches both new and experienced. Jenny Rogers writes in a clear, engaging way as she shares her wealth of knowledge and experience gleaned over decades. For the newcomer it's a helpful introduction to coaching and the thinking that is currently shaping it. For the established coach it's a great repository of wisdom and experience, a present help in times of doubt and uncertainty. I recommend it highly.*"

Mark Wakefield, Vogel Wakefield, the counter-consultancy

"Coaching Skills *is a comprehensive and beautifully written exploration of the practice, art and newly emerging scientific basis that underpins the success of effective coaching.*

Of equal value to those new to coaching and to the experienced coach, this excellent book provides a detailed and practical framework for coaching, aided by numerous illustrations drawn from the author's extensive experience.

Highly readable, practical and informative Coaching Skills *deserves to be the reference text all practitioners."*

Dr Gregory Ward, Medical Practitioner,
Associate Postgraduate Dean and Coach

"I have read the fourth edition of Jenny Rogers' Coaching Skills: The definitive guide to being a coach *with invariable curiosity and pleasure. Jenny manages to grasp and adequately describe the most important issues that coaches tackle with in our quickly changing world. In this edition she adds new models (such as OSCAR or the Prochaska and DiClemente model of change), chapters (such as giving information and advice in coaching or dealing with tears and trauma) and refers to the essential contemporary matters we all face such as working across cultures or coaching by phone. It all makes the fourth edition an up-to-date and comprehensive coaching manual, whereas numerous case studies and author's reflections, sense of humour and distance make it a fascinating book that you can't put down. I have recommended this book for years both to beginners who could find here key concepts presented in a clear and convincing way as well as to experienced coaches who could be reminded of how complex coaching is and therefore how crucial it is to keep learning and reflecting."*

Dorota Porażka, Vice-President of the Board,
DORADCA Consultants Ltd, Poland

"Wow, what a wonderful resource. Packed full of tips, ideas, tools and techniques for new and experienced coaches. Jenny Rogers gives a very clear and appropriately detailed description of the delights and challenges of being a coach providing "useful guidelines not rigid instructions". There are lots of case examples that illustrate the theoretical points and demonstrate the skills required to manage the coaching relationship productively while avoiding the pitfalls. There is a concise introduction to other models and methodologies like Neuroscience, Clean Language and Immunity to Change that will excite coaches who are seeking to refresh their practice. Importantly there are sections on Ethics, Boundaries and Psychological perspectives that is a must for all coaches to digest."

John Leary-Joyce - President AoEC, author
Fertile Void, Gestalt Coaching at Work

"A bang up to date look at all things likely to cross the paths of today's executive coaches, including a useful summary of the impact that neuroscience is having on the way we work. Of all the many 'how to' coaching books out there this stands out as the one which demonstrates why coaching is simple but not easy. With deserved authority and confidence, Jenny busts a few coaching myths and reinforces the non negotiables sharing her knowledge, common sense and wisdom gathered from her own experiences as one of the UKs leading executive coaches."

Liz Macann, Director, Macann Coaching Consultancy

"The beauty of Jenny's work is that she combines her formidable knowledge of the topic with years of practice, to give the reader a wealth of references, theories and techniques all elegantly brought to life with real examples. In this fourth edition, Jenny talks candidly about some of the edgier aspects of coaching, such as how to challenge with purpose and skill, and trauma in the coaching room. Here Jenny shines a light on the importance of developing character, courage and judgment as a coach, and in this definitive guide we get to see what truly masterful coaching looks like."

Maria Fay, Executive Coach

Contents

How to do it respectfully and in ways that do not raise resistance

Handling strong emotion in the coaching room. What to do if clients cry. Stress and mindfulness. Working with people who have experienced trauma. Suicide myths and reality. Developmental disorders, severe psychological problems: when and how to refer clients for specialist help

Introducing differences of pace and mood to a coaching session by using a variety of approaches and techniques, eg 'brainstorming', 'empty chair' techniques, role play, shadowing, observation and guided visualizations

Ethical dilemmas. Cross-cultural and multi-cultural coaching. The role of supervision: what it can and can't do. Note-taking and legal risks. Identifying high-quality training, getting accredited. Assessing the effectiveness of coaching

Why good coaching is more than just using a toolkit of techniques. Getting beyond anxiety and trusting the coaching process

A template for running the first coaching session

The advantages and challenges of coaching by phone. How to overcome the disadvantages

Introduction

Like many others who got into coaching in its early days, coaching found me. Several decades ago, I was newly back in the BBC, running its management development programmes. Soon, I began to get tentative phone calls: 'I've done all the courses, but now I'm in a new job and I need to get to grips with this or that issue – can you help?' Or, 'I've got this editor in my team. He's too senior for a course but he urgently needs help with his leadership style. Anything you could do?' Some of these queries had the air of 'Psst! I need help – but don't tell anyone!' Others just assumed that it was only right and proper that tailored and time-effective help was going to be available for some of the most senior people in the organization. Significantly, there was no accepted word then for the process that people were requesting. I believe we referred to it as 'one-to-one sessions', fumbling for a phrase that would accurately describe what would happen.

This book represents the material I wish had been available to me then at a time when there was no training for coaches and I literally knew of no one else who was doing it – though unknown to me many other pioneers and early-adopters were also learning their craft. Knowing then what I know now would have saved so much time and spared clients so many of my well-intentioned but clumsy early attempts at coaching.

I have written the book with a number of different readerships in mind, but they are all united by one theme: a wish to understand how coaching works and how to do it well. You could be an experienced coach looking for an affirming benchmark and a reminder of why coaching is so challenging. You could be in a different job or role but are wondering what coaching is and whether you could make a living at it. You could be a trainee coach, resolutely committed to the idea of improving your practice. You might be a therapist or counsellor, considering turning your existing skills to a different kind of clientele and asking what that would mean for you.

Writing this book has emerged from a number of strands of experience. First, I have now had many thousands of hours of coaching experience with many hundreds of clients from a wide variety of sectors. My experience has been as an executive coach – that is, I work more or less exclusively with senior people from organizations – but the basic principles I look at here will apply whatever type of coaching interests you.

All this has been hugely enriched by two decades as a teacher of other coaches and working as a supervisor/coach-mentor. It's so easy sitting placidly in your chair, listening to another coach, blithely free of the need to make those split-second decisions that the coach has to make. The wrong turnings are so much more obvious than when you are in that hot seat yourself. It is also humbling – working with naturally gifted coaches who need little in the way of direction. However, mostly this experience has reminded me what the common difficulties are and has given me insight into the approaches that will work – and I regard myself as the most immediate person to benefit from this, as despite my many years of practice I am constantly aware that being a coach is never as easy as it may look.

I am often asked what it takes to be a good or even a great coach. There is a quick answer and a slower, more thoughtful one. The quick answer is that as a good coach you have a self-confident fascination with how people achieve their potential and a wish to go with them on that journey; unbounded curiosity about people; intuition into what makes them tick; a high degree of self-knowledge; the self-discipline to keep yourself out of the way, and the ability to resist giving advice or wanting to be right.

The slower answer is that you can't become a great coach by wishing to become a great coach. You will be trying too hard, an understandable and common trap for newer coaches. Coaching well means managing a constant state of ambiguity. You have to have curiosity about people, yet know when that curiosity is coming from your agenda and not the client's. You have to have intuition and yet know when to hold it back. You have to be able to resist giving advice and yet know when it is not only appropriate but vital to do so. You have to keep yourself out of the way and yet you have to be fully there and a real presence for your client – you are not a coaching cypher, self-restrained to the point of disappearing. You have to like people and yet be able to control much of your need to have them like you because you will often have to challenge and be tough. Coaching is a serious business, and yet, as one of my colleagues once pointed out, you will continually hear boisterous laughter emanating from a coaching room.

This is the territory I have covered in this book. I assume your own curiosity and commitment. I discuss and describe coaching techniques, but the best coaching transcends techniques; it has a seamless, flowing quality. Observing outstanding coaching seems like witnessing the only conversation that could ever have happened on that topic – and yet another coach could have had another quite different and equally effective conversation.

Anyone writing this kind of book hits the problem of how to represent client experience. I want to bring the experience of coaching to life and the best way to do this is through real case studies. Yet, as a coach, I promise my clients confidentiality. I have resolved this problem through a rigorous and wholehearted process of disguise, often blending more than one client's story while staying true to the real-life themes. When in doubt, I have checked the disguise with the original client.

Many of the influences which have gone into writing this book have probably disappeared into an internalized set of assumptions about human behaviour, going right back to my good fortune as a postgraduate student in encountering thinkers such as Henri Tajfel, Michael Argyle and other social psychologists of the 1960s. The great Kurt Lewin, with his insistence on turning theory into action-centred research, has been a constant source of thought-provoking ideas. My thinking has also been profoundly affected by the work of the early exponents of psychoanalysis such as Sigmund Freud and Carl Jung; by the humanistic-existentialist writers and practitioners such as Viktor Frankl and Irvin Yalom; by the Gestalt school; by Albert Ellis, by Carl Rogers and his Person Centred Therapy; by Transactional Analysis; and by Gerard Egan's Skilled Helper model. The discoveries of neuropsychology are a fascinating and newer source of enlightenment. All of us in the coaching field also owe a debt to the Coaches Training Institute in California for beginning the process of synthesizing coaching practice into a workable and elegant model. I have acknowledged these and other specific sources throughout the book wherever I am aware of them, which may not be in every case. My own blend of these and other ideas is eclectic, opinionated and personal. This is not a textbook.

As in the first three editions I have tried to convey the real-life flavour of coaching with all its typical ups and downs. Many books on coaching, perhaps unwittingly, give the impression that coaching is a kind of fairytale. The client is puzzled or miserable, the coach waves a magic wand, the client lives happily ever after. Beginner coaches who read these books are often secretly dismayed by the stubborn refusal of their actual clients to behave like the ones in the fairytales. The reality is that however experienced the coach and however willing the client, sometimes you will have triumphs and sometimes you will make hideous mistakes; there are semi-successes, but no discernible happy endings; sometimes there are florid failures – or even worse, in some ways, there is no proper ending at all. The same is surely true of every other profession, so why should coaching be any different? It is also true that there can be much learning from a flop, as long as you know why it occurred. I hope this book will help you identify the likely reasons for noble failures as well as for glorious successes.

In the years since I wrote the first edition of this book, coaching has changed dramatically. Where there was once just a handful of pioneers there are now tens of thousands of coaches. Coaching has become a second, third or fourth career for people who want to step off the conventional career ladder, making it much harder for buyers of coaching to distinguish effective from ineffective practitioners. Where you once had to explain patiently what coaching is, now it is a much more readily understood. Where there were no training courses or qualifications there is a now a market of jostling providers. Coaching was once a special and sometimes a secret process offered to a few; now it is openly and routinely offered to many – for instance, as a follow up to a management development programme. This is not always a benefit as it can result in resentful or otherwise reluctant clients who have not had a choice about whether or not they need and want a coach.

However, it is still the case that to be a coach is to have a wonderfully privileged job. I find that it is never less than demanding and never dull. Clients ask you to walk with them at key moments in their lives and careers, sharing their triumphs and disappointments, their vulnerabilities, their hopes, their dreams. The discussions have an openness, candour and directness that few other conversations are likely to have. The Chinese sage who pronounced that 'What we teach is what we most want to learn' was completely correct. As a self-development process *for the coach*, you can't beat coaching, and yet you will never get to the end of it. As William Zinsser, the celebrated author of , *On Writing Well*, wrote in the thirtieth anniversary edition of his book (2006): 'The product that any writer has to sell is not the subject being written about, but who he or she is' – and writing the various editions of this book has represented my own learning journey. This edition, as with all its predecessors, represents my current understanding of what I need to remember at all times when I am working with a client. Even now I am capable of making a clunking mistake that the most naïve beginner would spot immediately. There will never be a point for me, nor I predict for you, where it is possible to stand back and say, 'Well, I made it – I'm now the complete and perfect coach.' That is one of many factors which will make your likely learning lifelong, as mine has been.

I invite you through this book to learn how utterly stretching, fascinating and enjoyable this process is.

1   Defining coaching

A few years ago there was an international conference of the great and the good in the coaching world. One of their remits was to find the final, definitive, once and for ever answer to the question: *What is coaching?* This conference found it tremendously difficult. There seemed to be as many definitions as there were eminent persons in the room. In fact the task more or less defeated them. If this was the case for such a distinguished group, what hope is there for the rest of us? This chapter looks at what coaching is and how it is like and unlike some of its close cousins such as therapy, consulting or motivational interviewing.

It doesn't help that the word *coach* is so loosely used. 'Coach' may suggest a teacher earning extra money by helping your reluctant children through a loathed physics or French exam. Or it may suggest the pushy parent in tennis who also acts as coach and manager to a prodigiously talented child. More attractive images may be from other kinds of sports coaching. Here a coach may be a clever, sophisticated and highly paid guru figure whose tantalizing and competitively sought coaching secrets are eventually revealed in books and newspaper articles.

This idea is still clearly alive and well, as I discovered to my dismay when I called one client's office to hear his colleague shout, 'John! It's your guru on the phone!'

In some organizations, even now, having a coach is unusual and is reserved for senior people with performance problems where the intention can therefore be frank corrective training; to need coaching is then, understandably, seen as being a sign of shameful failure. 'Is this outplacement in advance?', one client asked me suspiciously. This was at a time many years ago when I was relatively new to the field. Alas, I came to see that in her case it probably was outplacement in advance, and that her company was seeking to show that it had done everything it reasonably could before sacking her. In this case I had been manipulated by the organization as much as she.

In other organizations, a mystique has grown up around coaching. In one such, where I had been working as an executive coach for many years, it was widely believed that coaching was a special privilege reserved for a secret list of high-flyers and that you had to wait to be invited to join it, although I knew for certain that this was a myth.

While these are recurrent concerns and confusions, it is probably much more common to be troubled by an underlying comparison with psychotherapy ounselling. Many potential and actual clients ask worriedly about this. a few weeks ago a client asked me if coaching was 'just therapy for well people'. The inclusion of the word 'just' was telling. When coaching is described to them, clients may say, with visible suspicion, 'this sounds just like counselling'. In spite of much more enlightenment in the way we view mental health, there are still many hugely unhelpful clusters of association with needing help in this area of our lives. The thrum of underlying belief is that we 'should' be able to deal with such difficult issues on our own. These are not rational worries. They have to do with fearing the power of our own emotions, of losing control, of the veneer of 'grown-up-ness' being ripped away.

The themes that unite all of these concerns are basic to understanding what coaching is. Take it as axiomatic that all clients, whoever they are and however grand, successful and important, fear two things: vulnerability and loss of control. They are right in these fears because coaching is about change, and to change you do make yourself vulnerable and you may indeed not appear to have the degree of control you want over your life while the changes are happening.

The role of theory

This is a potentially confusing field. Psychology emerged as a branch of philosophy. Psychotherapy was originated by doctors who were psychiatrists. It was presented originally as a science. These early beginnings are still significant. Essentially psychotherapy and counselling are part of the health sector, whereas executive coaching is a branch of management development, and life-coaching an approach to personal development closely paralleled by the popularity of the many thousands of self-help books.

Coaching, by and large, is a pragmatic trade drawing on borrowed theory. The best current summary is in the book edited by Leni Wildflower and Diane Brennan (2011), *The Handbook of Knowledge-Based Coaching*, where it is clear that our theoretical base comes from an extremely eclectic range of ideas. Currently, practice leads theory by a long way and you may hear coaching described as *a-theoretical*. Depending on your point of view, you can see this either as a strength or as a weakness which needs addressing. Perhaps it is both.

The flowering of coaching as a discrete activity in the last two decades of the twentieth century had much to do with the so-called *Human Potential* or *New Age Movement* of the early 1970s, where Erhard Seminars Training (EST) – founded by Werner Erhard – involved many of those who became pioneers of what we now call coaching. EST became Landmark Education in 1991, and

still trains many thousands of people a year. But the actual origins of c
have tangled roots in all of the following: psychology, psychiatry, me\
physics, systems theory, linguistics, therapy, hypnosis, management dev\
ment, anthropology, leadership theory, organization development, traini..g,
selling, religion and philosophy – among many others. Coaching, whether
dignified by the label or not, must be as old as human society. There is, for
instance, a case for pointing out that Socrates was doing a form of coaching
2400 years ago in Greece when, according to Plato, he seems to have claimed
that his only knowledge was of his own ignorance and that his role as a philosopher was analogous to that of a midwife: you do not give birth yourself,
but you play a vital role in enabling the mother to do so. The Socratic Method
involved solving a problem through forming a question. In doing so you would
be forced to look at your own beliefs, questioning their validity, essentially as
coaches do today.

The history of coaching is carelessly understood by many of us now
practising its art. Leni Wildflower's entertaining book, *The Hidden History of
Coaching* (2013), is well worth a read if much of this is new to you.

A definition of coaching: choice in action

My definition is a simple one that conceals complexity:

> Coaching is the art of facilitating another person's learning, develop-
> ment, well-being and performance. Coaching raises self-awareness
> and identifies choices. Through coaching, people are able to find
> their own solutions, develop their own skills, and change their own
> attitudes and behaviours. The whole aim of coaching is to close the
> gap between people's potential and their current state.

Behind this definition there are six foundation principles which help differen-
tiate coaching from some other apparently similar disciplines.

Principle 1: The client is resourceful

The client has the resources to resolve his or her problems. The client has
not come to be *fixed*, though there may be others in the client's world (for
instance, a more senior manager paying the bill) who believe that this is the
purpose of the coaching. Clients may share this belief sometimes: 'If you were
me, what would you do?' Only the client can really know what to do because
only the client knows the full story and only the client can actually implement
the action and live with the results.

Principle 2: The coach's role is to develop the client's resourcefulness through skilful questioning, challenge and support

It follows from the first principle that the role of the coach is not advice-giving. When you give advice you imply that you know best and that the client is a lesser person. When you do this you will most probably get sucked into the 'Why don't you?' . . . 'Yes, but' game:

> Why don't you lose a bit of weight?

> Yes, I agree I should but I can't do it yet . . .

Advice-giving also leads to dependency – the opposite of what you are trying to achieve as a coach. There is more about this in Chapter 2. The coach's role is to ask the penetrating questions which take clients into territory they have never previously considered. In doing this, clients will build on their own resourcefulness. This does not preclude you from offering the client information, but there is an art in doing it in coaching style (see Chapter 10).

Principle 3: Coaching addresses the whole person – past, present and future

Coaches working in the corporate field sometimes see their role as strictly being about work. I believe that this is a mistake. My experience is that difficulties in the professional lives of clients are usually paralleled by difficulties in their personal lives. Also, relationship patterns formed in early life always have a bearing. Coaching is not psychoanalysis, but unless you know a little about early life and issues in current life beyond work, you are unlikely to be able to work with the client as fully as is possible when you and the client take a more rounded view.

Principle 4: The client sets the agenda

There is no set agenda with coaching. The coach may indeed have a mental model of, for instance, effective leadership, but if this is not a concern for the client, then it should not appear on the agenda of the sessions. The agenda is set by the client. When the client agenda is exhausted, then the coaching must stop, even if only temporarily. I have occasionally had enquiries from potential clients who have heard that coaching is 'interesting' and want to try it, but when they learn that they have to provide the agenda, their interest wanes.

Principle 5: The coach and the client are equals

The coach and the client work together as equals. The model is colleague–colleague, adult–adult, because it is based on unequivocal respect. If a client regards you with awe, or vice versa, it will be difficult to work together. Suspending judgement is essential. Where you cannot respect a client for some reason, or where the client does not respect you, it is unlikely that your coaching can be effective and it will be better to end or not start at all.

Principle 6: Coaching is about change and action

Clients come to coaching because they want something to change. The core purpose of coaching is to increase self-awareness, to make choices explicit, and to close the gap between potential and how things are currently. The role of the coach is to help them achieve this. It follows therefore that you cannot coach a client who does not want to change – so third-party referrals should always be regarded with initial caution. Equally, if a client says they want to change, but seems to be unable or unwilling to do so in practice, then the coaching may have to stop – or you could consider referring the client to another coach.

As coaches, we are dealing with both the 'being self' and the 'doing self', as seen in Figure 1.1.

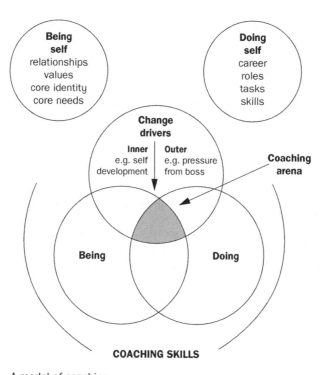

Figure 1.1 A model of coaching

The 'being self' is the inner personality and the sum total of the experiences, attitudes and roles that we play, or have played, in our lives. It is about core values and beliefs – who we are, rather than what we do.

The 'doing self' is the externally focused person with tasks to accomplish and skills with which to do them. It is usually the doing self which initially presents for coaching. For instance, 'Please help me become more effective in my work'; 'Show me how to run a meeting better'; 'Help me write a proper CV' – and so on.

The request for coaching is triggered by change. If there is no need for change then it is unlikely that you have a genuine client. The change could be internally triggered – a being self area. Birthdays with a nought or a five on the end may well be cause for reappraisal of life and direction. So may a serious illness or a major change in personal status such as marriage, having children, the death of a parent or a divorce. Alternatively, or often in addition, there is externally imposed change: the organization may be losing or gaining staff; the client's role may have changed through promotion or restructuring. Skills that seemed perfectly adequate before may not look so impressive now. There may be a new boss who demands a different kind of performance with consequent pressure for change in individuals. The client may have actually lost their job or be threatened with losing it. The crossover area in the middle of the diagram creates the agenda for coaching.

This is why it is essential to take a whole-life perspective and to accept the client's initial agenda as merely the starting point for the coaching. The inexperienced coach often fails to act on the instinct which tells him or her that this is the correct way to go. As a new coach myself I was sometimes far too overawed by the seniority of my clients to ask them what felt then like impertinent questions about their background and childhood. I quickly discovered what a mistake this was and now ask routinely about early life experience.

What happens in a coaching session: an overview

Typically coach and client will meet on the coach's premises for a series of ninety-minute or two-hour sessions. The length of coaching programmes varies enormously. I have clients I see for a single session, usually because they want coaching to prepare them for a job interview, and others where I am in my third year or longer of meeting them monthly for two-hour sessions. Goals may take two forms:

- *Dilemmas*: Which of two or three paths should I follow?
- *Puzzles*: How can I make something or someone more comfortable, work better, be more focused, get past a block?

Examples might be:

- improve an important relationship
- manage my time better
- make more money
- decide what I want to do as the next step in my career
- tackle performance problems in my team
- plan my entry into a new job
- restructure my organization
- learn how to make more convincing presentations
- acquire the skills I need in a new role
- launch myself into a freelance career
- tackle the stress in my life
- get a better balance between work and home
- leave full-time work and decide whether retirement is something I want.

Normally there will be two or three topics in each session. The client will leave with a plan of action around each of their goals. The first part of the next session reviews how the 'homework' has gone. So a typical framework might be like this:

5 minutes	What has happened between the time we last met and now?
10–15 minutes	How did you get on with the action points we agreed last time? What have you tried? What have you learnt?
5 minutes	What items do you have for our agenda this time? • What priority do those items have in terms of their potential for impact on your life? • How much time would you like to devote to each during this session? • How does each of these items link to the overall goals we agreed for the coaching?
90 minutes	Coaching on the agenda items
5 minutes	What 'homework' will you be doing between this session and our next?

As coaching grows in popularity and familiarity, it is developing a number of distinct branches.

Life coaches concentrate on whole-life dilemmas: personal relationships, work–life balance, planning for the future.

Advisory services: people who offer all kinds of familiar advisory services are now describing what they do as coaching, so debt counsellors may now be *debt coaches*, acting tutors offer *audition coaching* and marriage guidance has sometimes been repackaged as *relationship coaching; learning coaches* work in schools.

Sports coaches increasingly work from the core coaching principles I describe in this book rather than from the do-it-my-way expert perspective of the recent past.

Executive coaches' work is generally concentrated on the most senior executives in large or medium-sized organizations. Clients expect familiarity with and a track record in management and a deep understanding of organization behaviour. Potential topics for coaching include everything in the life-coaching agenda plus any and every aspect of running organizations. As with life-coaching, executive coaching is also developing its own niches – new leaders, managing the first 100 days in a new job, retirement planning for older leaders, stress and burnout, finance, careers, finding a new job after redundancy, interview preparation, presentation skills, voice, image, strategy, and many others. Executive coaches may also work as *team coaches*, where they apply the same principles to whole teams. Fees for executive coaching are generally many times higher than fees for life-coaching.

As well as types of coaching defined by client groups and their concerns, coaching is also developing rival schools and philosophies. So you may encounter coaching described by these words and many others: *Non-directive; Performance; Ontological; Gestalt; Systemic; NLP (Neuro-Linguistic Programming); Psycho-synthesis; Psychodynamic; Psycho-drama; Solution-focused; Speed; Narrative.* The majority have been influenced by particular schools of therapy which have seen that there is a market in coaching and have branched out to embrace it by offering training courses. Coaching conferences usually give the opportunity to sample a range of these approaches and many have suggestions that are worth integrating into your own repertoire. Be sensible and realistic here. Some of these ideas may involve unattractively rigid notions about asking particular questions in a particular way. This may be a method that works for the founder of the school with his or her uniquely charismatic and evangelical personality but mysteriously fails to work for others. As one colleague commented after attending a workshop run by one such celebrated speaker: 'I trudged home very disheartened, wondering why I couldn't make it work the way he does.' It is unlikely that any one school of theory and practice has the whole answer, and all the research into the efficacy of therapy suggests that the theoretical orientation of the therapist is far less important than the ability to create an alliance of equals through warmth and rapport. The same will doubtless prove true of coaching.

Differences between coaching and other disciplines

There are many other disciplines with close resemblances to coaching and also with significant differences. Sometimes you may work from more than one of these roles, depending on the circumstances.

Coaching and psychiatry

A psychiatrist is a doctor trained in treating severe mental illnesses. Entry to the profession is strictly controlled by licensing after lengthy training, and practice is monitored and audited. If your licence is withdrawn, you cannot practise. Continuous updating is mandatory.

You might see a psychiatrist if your family doctor believes you could benefit from stabilizing medication prescribed by a specialist or if for some reason you feel you have temporarily lost your way in some form that feels serious. Psychiatrists also deal with disabling forms of mental illness such as schizophrenia, severe post-natal depression, drug and alcohol dependency or a chronic depression.

Successful therapy often involves drugs as well as a 'talking cure' where the patient would typically be referred to a psychotherapist. Psychiatry has increasingly been influenced by the understanding that the patient needs to be a full participant in their treatment and it has in fact been profoundly influenced by the success of coaching. The 'Recovery Approach' is increasingly common. It assumes that patients can take control of their lives and that *recovery* is not something done *to* the person but something that they manage for themselves because they know their own condition, their own life, and what they really want better than any clinician can. This means that it is the patient who defines their goals, not the clinician. The clinician's role is to facilitate recovery, not to coerce or control, and ideally the relationship becomes a partnership, much as it is in coaching.

Coaching and psychotherapy

The boundary with psychotherapy is probably the one that worries coaches most.

In Colin Feltham and Ian Horton's excellent *Handbook of Counselling and Psychotherapy* (2000: 2) the activity is defined as:

> addressing psychological and psychosomatic problems and change, including deep and prolonged human suffering, situational dilemmas and crises and developmental needs, and aspirations towards the realization of human potential.

There is a huge spectrum of approaches to psychotherapy and a number of rival 'schools' using different models. Some people in the field claim that there are as many as 400 different schools of therapy. This probably accounts for the widely varying levels of effectiveness reported.

My own experience reflects this in a small way. Some years ago a personal crisis left me needing psychotherapeutic help. I could not shake off the overwhelming anxiety which haunted me for months afterwards. My world seemed to be dissolving. In seeking psychotherapeutic help, I experienced first a very poor and then a profoundly helpful experience of therapy.

My family doctor referred me first to Dr X who operated out of an elegant private medical practice. I probably alienated him from the start by asking if his doctorate was a medical one. This was a bit naughty as I already knew it wasn't, but I was by now annoyed by the grandiosity of the way I had been kept waiting and treated as a petitioner. He sat at a 'world domination' desk, sideways on, while I sat on a very much lower sofa on what felt like the very far side of the large room. It was a smart, black leather sofa, but in sitting so much lower I couldn't help but feel that I was meant to be literally sitting at his feet. He asked me about my 'symptoms' (*sic*) and dispensed a good deal of platitudinous advice, all of which I had heard before, and ended the session 20 minutes early. I paid for an hour, but received 40 minutes. I did not go back.

Instead, I sought help from a fellow coach who also operates as a therapist. Her steady, calm exploration of feelings and mutual exploration of practical strategies for dealing with them were just what I needed. If proof were required that a high price is no guarantee of high quality, her charges were a quarter of those demanded by Dr X.

Where is the boundary with psychotherapy?

In some of my recent work as an executive coach I have encountered these situations with clients: a finance director wanting to re-enter work after recovering from a severe episode of bipolar disorder; a chief executive whose most pressing issue was her marital problems; a banker whose misery at work meant that he was visibly upset through a great deal of the session; a marketing executive in a fast-paced internet-based organization who was finding it increasingly challenging to deal with the stress of a harsh and ultra-competitive environment.

You may read of these clients with a shudder of dread: surely these are just the sorts of situations where a coach should keep well out of the way and refer the client to a therapist? If so, I disagree. I believe that that the squeamishness of so many coaches is unjustified and unnecessary. This fear is reflected in much of the literature on coaching, sometimes suggesting, for instance, that any deep exploration of feelings is inappropriate, that any topics connected with personal life should be avoided in executive coaching, or that somehow 'everyone knows' where therapy is needed. In the first edition of this book, written in 2003, I dutifully went along with this even while I was privately wondering if it were true. My belief now is that the boundaries with therapy are extremely shadowy and that I am content that this should be so.

Some coaches worry a lot about these boundaries. Their fear is of 'getting in too deep', or of 'doing harm'. Discussing these ideas also reveals many common misconceptions about therapy – for instance, that it is a monolithic discipline, always about the past, involves the therapist as interpreter, goes on for years, and is somehow mysterious and unfathomable and therefore 'dangerous'. These stereotypes fail to represent the reality of vigorous and mutually antagonistic squabbling between different types of therapy, the thinness of the line between many kinds of therapy and coaching, and also the additional reality of 'brief therapy' – a short programme, often as little as six hours (less than many coaching programmes) because funding and therefore access to therapy is rationed.

The naïve view of therapy is heavily influenced by film and TV, where the therapeutic model implied is most often psychoanalytical, the earliest form of therapy, and still being practised, where it is common for therapist and client to meet frequently and for a lengthy period.

Some people are suspicious that coaching is just therapy-lite, though I privately believe that coaching is therapy-plus. However, there is a common view among some of our potential clients that therapy is something that is for gullible wimps, so as coaches we do indeed need reassuring and honest answers to these challenges. The debate has also been stoked by attacks from therapists asserting their own version of the stereotype, this time that coaching is superficial, short-term, ridiculously expensive and conducted by charlatans or by people who have failed in other careers. For a view of this sort, see Steven Berglas's article (2002) in the *Harvard Business Review* where exaggeratedly good psychotherapy is compared with exaggeratedly bad coaching to (unintended) comical effect.

The truth is that without therapy there would be no coaching, though I find that many coaches seem to be unaware of this debt. Most strands of theory and all of our techniques have descended from therapy one way or another. I am shamelessly eclectic in my own choices here, lifting ideas and approaches from the humanistic, psychoanalytical, Gestalt, Transactional Analysis and many other traditions. If it works, I will use it.

Much of the muddle about therapy and coaching starts from the false assumption that human beings are rational. So, allegedly, coaching deals in rationality and therapy deals in emotion. In fact, as so much recent research in neuropsychology (see Chapter 4) makes abundantly clear, the limbic system of the human brain, its emotional centre, is far more powerful than the prefrontal cortex – the seat of thinking and reason. Decision-making is emotionally, not rationally led. How can it therefore make any sense to ex emotion from our work with clients? It is true that much executive coaching starts with work issues because these are safe to declare and the organization is paying. But problems in work life are always affected by what is going on in private life, and vice versa. Banning the discussion of personal issues results in thin, lopsided coaching, and no problem worth looking at in coaching is without an emotional dimension. Concentrating exclusively on work issues and on so-called 'performance coaching' results in an overemphasis on the behavioural approaches which have dominated our first 40 or so years as a profession. These may be useful as far as they go, but their impact is often limited and superficial.

Some differences between psychotherapy and coaching

In general, when you compare psychotherapy and counselling with coaching you will tend to see a number of differences. The most important is the probable mental state of the client. A client for psychotherapy or counselling is far more likely to be in a persistently distressed and disabling state than a client for coaching. Feltham and Horton's definition, quoted above, refers to 'deep and prolonged human suffering'. Many psychotherapists still refer to their clients as *patients*. Where this is the case, the underlying model is the medical one of doctor–patient and not the partnership of equals that I describe above as Principle 5.

By contrast, most experienced coaches will assume that clients have robust mental health unless proved otherwise, and look to work with clients on functional rather than on severe psychological problems. All schools of psychotherapy stress that therapy is a partnership. In practice this critical difference in assumed mental state will almost inevitably lead to a profound imbalance in power, which makes a genuine relationship of equals a lot less likely in a therapist–client relationship than in a coach–client relationship. For instance, psychotherapists may be motivated by a sincere and profound wish to *help*, and by feeling pity for the suffering of their clients. They will describe their work as a *helping* discipline. The helper, almost by definition, feels as if they are in a stronger place than the helpee. Coaches are more likely to describe what they do as *working with* a client.

With executive coaching there are some further tweaks on the power relationship which are significantly different from therapy. These coaching clients are generally well paid and powerful people and they – or their employers – are paying premium fees for their coaching. By contrast, therapy and counselling may sometimes be provided free or very cheaply to the user (for instance through an insurance scheme, the National Health Service, a voluntary agency, or an employer through an Employee Assistance Scheme) and are potentially therefore subject to the peculiarly corrosive tendency to see such users as petitioners, lucky to get their rationed treatment.

Not all, but much psychotherapy looks to the past to explain the present, and the therapist is interested in answering the question 'Why?' Insight into cause and effect and the origins of emotions is a strong feature of some (though not all) schools of therapy. The coach may look briefly to the past but is more interested in the client's present and future and is probably more concerned with the question 'What?', as in 'What to do?', than in the question 'Why?'

There are also some differences in practicalities and mechanics. Coaches will see clients for an average of six two-hour sessions, probably spread over a period of months. Therapists will tend to suggest seeing their clients for a 'fifty-minute hour' every week. This gives a distinctly different timbre to the experience for both sides.

Psychotherapists have considerably longer and more thorough training than is the case for most coaches and the barriers to entry are set a great deal higher. There is more regulation and qualifications are taken a lot more seriously.

My colleagues and I have trained many therapists in how to become coaches. We find that large numbers of the skills overlap. We also find that therapists may bring as many prejudices and assumptions about coaching as coaches may hold about therapists. While therapists may assume that coaching is 'superficial' (it's not) compared with therapy, coaches may allege that therapists glory in the distress of their clients, or enjoy 'wallowing' in the past. None of these stereotypes is true. Our therapist trainees often comment on how much more overtly goal-focused coaching is compared with therapy and that it does move at a much faster pace with more future focus. I describe this, again as anecdotal evidence, with no assumptions that lack of goal focus makes therapy inferior or that a faster pace is necessarily 'better'.

Coaching and counselling

Counselling is sometimes described as the 'shallow end' of psychotherapy, though it is also sometimes used as a synonym for psychotherapy. As with psychotherapy, heroic efforts have been made since the mid-1960s to control the quality of counselling through better training and accreditation.

Counselling and psychotherapy are often used as interchangeable terms, but by custom and practice the word counselling seems now more likely to mean a short-term engagement around a particular crisis. Often, the client will have been managing perfectly well until the onset of this crisis. Typical examples would be trauma counsellors who work with survivors of a rail crash; relationship counsellors who work with couples (the 'marriage guidance' area); spiritual counselling offered by religious groups; police officers who counsel rape survivors or the families of missing children; specialist nurses who counsel people newly diagnosed with life-threatening illness; or priests who counsel the bereaved.

More than any of the other approaches described in this chapter, counselling has come to carry with it an emphasis on the powerful comfort of non-judgemental listening in the moment. This means talking it through extensively, without either counsellor or client feeling any of the obligation to *action* which both coaching and psychotherapy may imply.

Note: Chapter 11 has more ideas on handling strong emotion in the coaching room and advice on when and how to refer a client for therapy or counselling.

Coaching and mentoring

This is an easier one.

The word *mentor* comes from the Greek myth of the king who asked Mentor, an older, wiser man, to look after his son during the king's absence. Pure mentoring still has this implication and is how the word is most often used.

In practice there are two distinctly different forms of mentoring. One is best described as *sponsorship mentoring*. This means being a career friend, someone who knows the organization, is extremely senior and influential and can act as patron. The implication is that the mentor takes a keen interest in the career of the mentee, passes on useful hints and tips and, when the time comes, may influence promotion decisions on behalf of the mentee. The other form of mentoring is *development mentoring*. Here, the mentor may or may not be in the same organization, though probably is in the same sector, and may be only a little older or more senior. The aim is different: to develop the mentee's confidence and skill. Formal mentoring schemes in organizations can be powerful ways of developing the next generation of leaders. This depends in practice on investing significant time and money in training the mentors and in running the scheme, conditions that, sadly, often seem to be lacking with many organizations grossly underestimating the skill and effort needed to make it a success.

In practice, mentoring does have the overtones of implying that the older and wiser person will be passing on their advice. Where this is so, mentoring is a different activity from coaching. Where coaching principles apply, mentoring and coaching are synonyms for the same process. In practice, *mentoring* is coming to seem like an older-fashioned word for *coaching*.

Coaching and consulting

There are consultants who act like coaches and coaches who act like consultants. The word *consultant* has itself been appropriated much like *coaching* has by people in a wide range of disciplines, but mostly people associate the word consultant with management consultancy. Here there are some significant differences from coaching.

Typically, the management consultant has technical expertise: systems and processes, change, organizational culture, tax and audit, leadership – and many others. There is a focus on objectivity, on solving problems, gathering data, analysing the data and making recommendations. Consultants do not normally work on implementing their recommendations (though some do) because if they do, they become in effect substitute line managers and lose their impartiality and therefore their usefulness. The focus of consultancy is usually on organizational issues and you see its end product in externally evident matters such as changed systems, hierarchies and staffing levels. Measurable business results such as increased output and lower costs are generally expected by the client who commissions the work.

By contrast, coaches have expertise in human relationships and focus on personal and internally generated issues and are as likely to work on their client's strengths as on their weaknesses. Analysis of problems is a collaborative effort and coaches do not generally make formal recommendations. The focus is more personal and more intense because it is on the client's deepest motivation and on assuming that the client has the resources to make their own choices. Specifically, a coach is much more likely than a consultant to look at what holds clients back from making the changes that they say are desirable, yet about which they mysteriously dither and procrastinate. It is much harder to measure the results of coaching because its focus is on areas that are far less tangible.

Many consultants now incorporate a coaching approach into their work, for instance consciously building an alliance with their clients with the aim of transferring their technical skills, and there are many coaches whose clients hire them because of their technical as well as their psychological expertise, so this an increasingly greyed area.

Coaching and training

If coaching is about learning, and it is, then how is it different from training? There are some major and some subtle differences.

A trainer has a set curriculum and presents as an expert in his or her subject. Some trainers behave more like lecturers than coaches, doing a lot more of the talking than any coach would consider appropriate. There may be externally agreed standards involving accreditation or assessment which the trainee is expected to reach and on which, by implication, the trainer is assessed. So, for instance, in schools, Standardized Assessment Tests (SATs) *grade* the pupil but *assess* the school and its teachers against nationally agreed norms. On many training courses, the participants have been enrolled against their will, whereas coaching has to be entered into voluntarily.

A coach has no set curriculum and would rarely talk for more than a few minutes at a time, but may be an expert in his or her subject – for instance,

ng, leadership, life-planning or human relationships generally. There
ivalent of SATs in coaching.

As with mentoring, training is far more effective as a learning process
when it proceeds from coaching principles.

Line manager coaches

Interest in coaching as an alternative to command and control is growing.
This is because in a non-authoritarian society, people reject command and
control. Developing a 'coaching culture' has become a desirable aim for many
organizations.

Here coaching is an approach to performance management which
emphasizes the manager's role as *developer* rather than as *controller*. Line
managers use a *coaching approach*, encouraging team members to develop
self-confidence, resourcefulness, skills, belief in the value of their own decision-
making and so on through a process of accelerated learning. However, the
line management responsibility puts a significantly different slant on how
the line manager coach can work. As a boss, it is entirely probable that you
are part of whatever problems your coachee has, and this can be challenging
to see let alone to acknowledge. Also, it is always more difficult to promise
confidentiality, encourage or expect complete disclosure, set aside your own
considerations, or remain detached from the possible outcomes. As a boss
you have a stake in the outcome, whereas when you are purely a coach you
do not. My book *Manager as Coach* (2012) explores these differences in the
line management context, making the case for coaching as a powerful way of
increasing staff engagement and improving business results.

Motivational interviewing

Motivational interviewing (MI) developed in healthcare at much the same
time as executive coaching was taking root in organizations. Both were
powerfully influenced by the Human Potential Movement. MI was originally
seen as a way for healthcare practitioners to work with patients on topics
such as giving up smoking, and at its heart was the acknowledgement that
human beings are ambivalent about change. We know that we should change
a particular behaviour, yet we hesitate to do it. MI has broadened its scope
considerably since its early days. It is a very close cousin to coaching, sharing
many of the same values, principles and methodologies. The most important
difference in practice is that the motivational interviewer will usually have
an agenda and an overall aim: the patient really should give up smoking,
should drink less, should exercise more. This will almost always mean that

there are power differentials in the relationship of a kind that we do not see in coaching.

'Situational' coaching

Anne Brockbank and Ian McGill's book, *Coaching With Empathy* (2013), offers an especially useful way of understanding the nuances of coaching. Theirs is a sociological perspective, written by a husband and wife team with backgrounds in psychotherapy, sociology and action learning. It asks: *Whose view of 'reality' prevails here? Who owns the purpose?* Is it subjective, that is, the individual's own view, as opposed to some assumed-to-be-objective view? Secondly it asks: '*What is the* (often unspoken) *purpose*? Is it to preserve the status quo, or is it transformation? If you follow this matrix it makes no difference whether you call the activity *coaching, training* or *mentoring* or whether you are talking about line management coaching or life-coaching.

Quadrant 1: Performance coaching

Unspoken aim: maintain the status quo, get people to fit in.
This is the traditional apprenticeship model and is what people often mean by the word *mentoring*, but it can apply to coaching just as readily – for

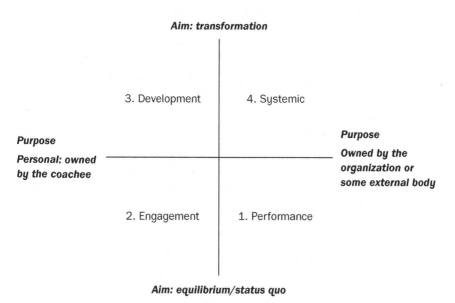

Figure 1.2 'Situational' coaching

instance, if you are asked to take on a client whose performance is about to derail (and in effect doing the work that should be done by the line manager). The assumption is that there is an objective reality out there – for instance, a competency framework or a set of professional standards – and that these are fixed benchmarks. It is useful for demonstrating 'the way we do things around here', for instance as part of an induction process. It reinforces the existing power relationships and what Brockbank and McGill call the 'power horizon' remains invisible and the Taken for Granteds (TFGs) are never challenged. The individual's view is not considered to be that important. Coaching as a line management activity often has this flavour because coachee and manager are assumed to share the organization-set agenda.

Quadrant 2: Engagement coaching

Unspoken aims: minimize opposition to change, improve performance.

Here, the individual's subjective view is taken into account, but essentially the aim is to maintain the status quo. It is useful when an organization needs to train people in acquiring an unpopular skill such as conducting appraisals or giving feedback. The power relationships are unchanged and still largely invisible. When coaching is undertaken here it is to 'correct' the 'mistaken' ideas of the individual but to do it respectfully. As external coaches, we may be asked to undertake coaching as a way of developing a high-flier, but again, ultimately what is expected is behaviour change and conformity to the organization's norms. With both Performance and Engagement coaching, the focus is on work and work skills – in my model it is entirely about the Doing Self. Personal life is not on the agenda and organizational clients may be surprised by or even opposed to the idea that it could be. Coaching may have this flavour where the emphasis is on skill-development and where it therefore has more of the feel of one-to-one training.

Quadrant 3: Development coaching

Aim: explicit transformation. The coachee is expected to take responsibility for their own learning and life. Their agenda is what matters.

This is the approach I endorse: my Being/Doing model is another way of expressing the same beliefs. The coach may be a fully trained internal coach who has a day job in another department, or an external executive coach. The coachee's goals are the foundation of the work, although in executive coaching the line manager's and organization's goals are also fed into the agenda; values are explicitly explored. It encourages questioning and challenging, including taking a cool look at 'the power horizon' – how decisions are actually taken as well as the things that are Taken-for-Granteds. The work is holistic: both work and private life are explicitly on the agenda. The rock-bottom assumption is that people are infinitely resourceful. It is always possible that the coachee may leave the organization as a result of the work. Questions such as life purpose, the quality of relationships (work and home), feelings, career, health may all be explored legitimately. Techniques used here have a more obvious debt to psychotherapy and are linked in a clear line to humanistic psychotherapy – for instance, to the work of Carl Rogers.

Quadrant 4: Systemic coaching

Aim: transformation of the organization.

Here the aim is the ambitious one of transforming the organization so that it embraces a 'coaching culture' where all relationships, whether with staff, suppliers or customers, are governed by coaching principles. Peter Hawkins' book *Creating a Coaching Culture* (2012) gives a comprehensive guide to what is involved, pointing out that to succeed, this noble aim must link with the organization's strategic objectives.

I find this model a valuable way of reminding myself what kind of coaching I am engaged in at any one time. So, for instance, when I am doing career coaching I am somewhere on the crossing point between Quadrants 1, 2 and 3. I have information about how to handle a job interview, which assumes that there are useful rules about interview behaviour which I need to pass on to the client. My purpose is transformation, and the client is setting the agenda ('help me get that job'); but to help the client get there I need to offer information and advice which comes from my view of the world and from principles I have found that interviewers expect, rather than the client's view of the world. When an organization asks me to coach a problem performer, I am aware that they are asking me to operate out of Quadrants 1 or 2, in other words to get the client to fit into organizational norms and to deal with their potentially disruptive or challenging behaviour. My whole-person approach may therefore not be the right fit and I need to raise this explicitly at the outset.

Where organizations offer coaches, mentors or 'buddies' to newly hired staff, the intention is almost always to offer support that falls squarely into Quadrant 1 because it is entirely about how to fit in – for instance, how to learn the hidden rules of the culture quickly. Line manager coaches are virtually always operating out of Quadrants 1 and 2 because their role is essentially to manage performance and to accustom their teams to inevitable change.

The Brockbank–McGill matrix draws attention to the importance of understanding what it is we are doing and why, rather than obsessing about what we call it or how, exactly, to define it – and also makes it plain that there is a legitimate place for all four kinds of activity.

When done well, all the approaches in this chapter have a great deal in common. When done badly, all make similar mistakes. So there are mentors who act indistinguishably from the best coaches and coaches who can fall into the traps of the worst mentors. There are coaches who do psychotherapy without labelling it as therapy and therapists who might as well be coaches. There are management consultants who work on organizational issues and yet also forge a close and trusting relationship with the chief executive where, in effect, they are also working as a coach. To be successful, all depend on unforced respect for the client – the foundation stone of which is what Carl Rogers, one of the most significant thinkers of the twentieth century in this area, called 'unconditional positive regard'. All require the practitioner to create and sustain an extraordinary degree of rapport and to act from the highest ethical standards. All need an extraordinary degree of self-awareness and self-management. All demand extraordinary levels of listening and questioning ability plus the capability to challenge appropriately – and an infinite curiosity about and interest in people.

2 Creating trust: foundation values and practices for coaches

A coaching conversation is unlike most other discussions. It involves a high level of trust and candour on both sides. Creating and sustaining this unusual environment is what gives coaching its power. To do it as a coach involves abandoning many of the normal conventions of conversation in our society and replacing them with high-level, alternative skills, all of them about communicating acceptance and respect. This chapter looks at the foundation principles that are necessary to create that trust.

The concept of choice in coaching

One of the ground precepts of coaching described in Chapter 1 is a belief that the client is resourceful, can make choices, and is responsible for him or herself. Underneath this belief are the fundamental principles of choice and self-responsibility. Making these principles explicit has been the great gift of mainstream twentieth-century psychology to the world. They are the foundation, for instance, of the Transactional Analysis (TA) school: that whatever misery and dysfunction there is in your life, you can transform yourself through conscious choice. Its underlying assumption is similar to many in other schools of psychological thinking: human beings, uniquely among animals, are able to look to the future, therefore we are not the prisoners of our past.

The American psychologist Will Schutz, developer of the personality questionnaire FIRO-B™, also skilfully articulated these principles, though from a different perspective. Schutz took the concept of choice to its ultimate in his book *The Truth Option* (1984: 18): 'I choose my whole life and I always have. I choose my behaviour, my feelings, my thoughts, my illnesses, my body, my reactions, and my spontaneity.'

Schutz's philosophy was that choice is not a moral concept, only one which has consequences. If you assume that you can make choices, then you take responsibility for your life. You bring areas that are unconscious into the areas of consciousness. For instance, you may feel afraid of your own violent or sexual feelings but your overtly expressed values do not allow you to admit this to yourself. You conceal your fears in hearty condemnation of people who do indulge their violence or sexuality.

Similarly, if you express fear of your boss or a colleague, there may be no objective reason at all for the fear; your real fear is of being unable to cope. If you see others as the cause of your fear, then you will spend a lot of time and energy criticizing, trying to change others or avoiding them. Equally, your life may be filled by anticipation of being humiliated, ignored or rejected, regardless of whether this is actually likely or not. Once you see that the fear is in you, you can work on your ability to cope: a very different strategy, and one that is at the heart of coaching.

Avoiding the principle of choice always involves a pay-off. For instance, if I take a lofty line on people who abuse their power, then my pay-off is that I hope to be seen as morally superior. If I claim that the organization is causing me hideous stress by overworking me, my pay-off is that I am a victim and will attract sympathy, attention and possibly financial compensation as well. If I claim to be confused, then people may excuse my inability to make a decision. Schutz stressed that accepting the principle of choice does not involve blame, either of yourself or others. At its heart it involves taking responsibility for yourself.

You cannot take responsibility for others. I sometimes challenge clients to show me how they could actually *make* someone else happy or unhappy. No client has yet been able to show me how this could happen. We all choose how we respond to any stimulus, often at an unconscious level, but we choose none the less. When you take inappropriate responsibility for others, you will quickly get to burnout – something familiar to all experienced coaches whose clients describe the stress that accompanies believing that you have to do everything yourself.

If you really accept that people are resourceful, then you have to believe in the concept of choice. It follows that you can't be a victim, or be brainwashed or manipulated. As Schutz commented, 'Nothing is stressful to me unless I interpret it as stressful.'

This concept has never been more powerfully illustrated than by the Austrian psychiatrist and neurologist Viktor Frankl in his moving book *Man's Search for Meaning* (1959). Frankl was imprisoned in Auschwitz and other camps during the Holocaust in conditions that were at the most extreme edge of anything human beings can be asked to bear. He did not know whether his wife and family had survived (his wife, mother, father and brother in fact all died in the camps). He had been imprisoned purely on grounds of his Jewishness and stripped of his professional identity, his clothes and even the hair on his head by his Nazi captors. He was ill, cold, malnourished, surrounded by desperate and dying people, forced to do brutally hard physical work and in constant fear of being murdered. Yet in his book he describes feeling that although his captors had physical liberty, he had more freedom:

> .. there were always choices to make. Every day, every hour, ffered the opportunity to make a decision, a decision which deter- ined whether you would or would not submit to those powers

which threatened to rob you of your very self, your inner freedom; which determined whether or not you would become the plaything of circumstance.

(Frankl 1959: 87)

Frankl chose to separate himself mentally from his surroundings. At one stage he had a vision of himself after the war, giving lectures and writing about his experiences. This sustained him and saved him from the 'give-up-itis' described by the Allied soldiers who eventually liberated the camps. They observed that many former prisoners simply lost their will to live. In Schutz's terms, they chose to die. Viktor Frankl chose to live. After the war he founded a still-thriving Institute devoted to his own version of psychotherapy, 'Logo-therapy', wrote many more books, and died full of honours in 1997 at the age of 92.

Realizing that we have choices is in itself powerfully motivating, rather than assuming that the default choice (do nothing), of which we are often unaware, is all that is possible. At the same time, never underestimate how frightening this idea can be when you have hidden inside a belief that some-how others are responsible for your happiness. Most of us secretly or overtly want to have at least a little or a lot of dependency on others and simultane-ously want at least a little or a lot of autonomy. If you feel you have cracked this conundrum you are lucky indeed, because few of us have.

You insist, I resist

Coaching is about drawing out this intrinsic human resourcefulness. It follows, then, that if you do genuinely believe in the resourcefulness of your clients, you will have to find alternatives to giving advice. So the first step to estab-lishing trust is to abandon advice-giving as a coaching tactic.

This is easy to say and to write, but it is probably the single most dif-ficult task for a coach. Many people who become coaches have had earlier jobs where they have been paid to give advice. Their professional training has positioned them as specialists and a great deal of their professional identity is invested in being an expert. So when confronted with the messy and sprawling issues that clients bring to coaching, inside, the new coach is thinking:

> It's my job to find the solution for this client – I'll have failed if I don't.

> I can't bear this client's pain and confusion. I need to help her by telling her what I think she should do.

> It's so obvious – he needs to do x or y.

If advice worked as a helping tactic, it might be possible to make a case for it as a prime approach to coaching. However, in most circumstances, it doesn't.

Think for a moment about something you do which is generally acknowledged to be unwise. This might be something like smoking, drinking more than the recommended number of units of alcohol a week, driving too fast, eating unwisely, being over- or underweight for your height, not taking advantage of health-screening services, or getting too little rest. Now imagine a good friend is giving you advice on the topic.

This is what typically happens:

You:	I'd really like to give up smoking, but it's so hard!
Helpful friend:	Yes, you should you know, it's the one way we can reduce the risks of heart disease – and think of the money you're wasting!
You:	Yes, I know, but it's so hard to do.
Helpful friend:	The best way to do it is to go cold turkey.
You:	Mmm, I tried that four years ago and it didn't work so I don't think I can do that.
Helpful friend:	You could! My friend Emma went to a wonderful hypnotherapist and she stopped straight away. Has never had a cigarette since.
You:	Yes, but that's Emma. It may have worked for her but I don't think I could do it just like that.
Helpful friend:	Yes you could.
You:	Well I'm not ready yet.
Helpful friend:	(Gives up in exasperation.)

In this example, you and the helpful friend are playing the 'Yes, but' game. The friend makes a suggestion and you say, 'Good idea – but . . .' The chances that you will give up smoking on the basis of this conversation are nil.

The reasons are that, first, however well meant the advice may be, being the recipient of it is probably making you feel angry and guilty. No one enjoys being told to change something they already know they should change, so all your energy is going into repelling the advice. When you feel you are being told what to do, your first response is virtually always to defend your existing position. It becomes impossible to listen carefully to what the other person is saying, however sensible it is.

Second, it is most unlikely that you will not have heard this advice before, as the reasons that people continue to smoke have little to do with ignorance of its long-term effects. The tone of the conversation precludes any real honesty on your part. It will guarantee that you withhold the most important aspects of the issue for you. It neither gets to the reasons why you smoke nor taps into any of the reasons that you might want to stop. Most seriously, the conversation implies that your friend is a well-adjusted human being whereas you are a bit of a sad addict, so, however well meant, the conversation could undermine your confidence.

Furthermore, you have to live with the results of the advice, not your friend. If you do take your friend's advice and it all goes wrong – for instance, days of cold-turkey-hell where your relationships temporarily collapse under the searing anger and misery of withdrawing so suddenly from nicotine, the friend is a handy scapegoat: 'He/she made me do it.' If the advice turns out well, then it reinforces the notion that other people have more willpower, are cleverer, more able and more decisive.

Even at its most apparently straightforward, advice-giving actually runs a significant risk of being ignored. Doctors are respected professionals who complete a long training before being let loose on us, their patients. Their advice carries genuine authority. Yet research has shown that at least a third of all prescriptions are either never taken to the pharmacy or remain in the patient's bathroom cabinet.

Some advice-giving is about control. Think about the most recent time when you passed on a piece of advice and ask yourself how far it was really an attempt to control the other person through the apparently benign process of giving advice. Advice-giving can feel generous. It can come from a warm heart. When a client expresses misery, it can be tempting to take refuge in expressing fellow feeling through describing something similar that happened to you. Reading your own biography into a client's concerns is dangerous for any number of good reasons. Most obviously, you are not the client. However similar your situations may appear, the client's history, personality and circumstances are totally different, so his or her responses and choices will be different. Also, the client may very well have held back the most important aspect of his or her situation. Here is an example:

Penny (coach) and Michael (client)

Penny was coaching Michael, a middle-manager client inside her organization. He came for help on how to move his career on. By the end of their second session, Penny was becoming increasingly puzzled: he said he wanted another job, yet he seemed reluctant to think broadly about the possibilities. Penny knew the organization and the whole sector well. She could see that Michael had considerable ability and was outgrowing his current role. She told him that in her own career she had hit a similar plateau, saying that in her case she had made a sideways move in the same organization but in a different city. This had worked for her, so surely it would work for him?

The coaching ended after its scheduled three sessions with Michael politely thanking her for her help and leaving Penny acutely puzzled. She was aware that the coaching had not been effective. A year later Penny discovered that Michael's wife, also a manager in the organization, had developed motor neurone disease. At the time of the coaching the illness had been diagnosed, but Michael's wife had asked him not to tell colleagues. Staying put geographically was important because they both felt it guaranteed the continuation of the excellent medical care she was receiving.

In reviewing this work with her supervisor, Penny realized that the turning point in the coaching, guaranteeing its failure, was this apparently bland piece of advice-giving, wrapped up as help. She had not been able to establish sufficient trust with Michael to enable him to tell her of his wife's illness. And at the point where this might have been possible she, in her own words, 'blew it'.

Saying 'Something just like that happened to me' can seem like a good idea. It is a disclosure and may therefore seem as if it will create trust. Just occasionally it might. But far more often it seems to be saying, 'This worked for me so it will work for you. Do it my way.' It suggests that you are not really listening because you are queuing to speak – telling your story is more important than listening to the client's. My fellow coach Phil Hayes enjoys recounting an achingly bizarre example of this tendency:

Friend 1:	How are you – haven't seen you for a long time?
Friend 2:	No, I've just recovered from meningitis. It was awful and I've only just come out of hospital. In fact I nearly died.
Non-listening Friend:	Oh – I nearly died once.

Less extreme examples of the same behaviour run the risk of appearing to trivialize the client's concerns by not exploring them. Common responses to other people's distress or worry include clichés such as:

Don't worry, time will heal.

There, there . . .

Buck up – it's not that bad!

You'll get other chances.

Plenty more pebbles on the beach/fish in the sea.

Least said, soonest mended.

. . . and so on.

Coaching as rescuing

The human impulse to care for the vulnerable has obviously been essential to our survival as a species. Human infants with their prolonged period of defencelessness need the kind and skilled care of adults. Adults are programmed to respond to overt dependency with tenderness. Appealing to this instinct is necessary for successful parenting, but it is a false trail in coaching.

If you step in as rescuer with clients, you deny them their ownership of the issue. By rescuing, you actively or by implication behave as if you feel they are too frail to solve the problem themselves. This can happen when clients are overwhelmed by their anxiety. They pour out their hearts, telling you how unbearable it is to be burdened by such problems. The pressure to help by finding a solution for them can feel monumental.

There are two equally unhelpful ways to respond. In the first, the client spills out his or her worries and the coach simply listens and empathizes, without asking the questions which move the client on. This hand-me-down love results in the client skipping away feeling temporarily lighter, though without having increased his or her capacity to solve such problems in the future. The coach, by contrast, feels unbearably stressed: the client has successfully transferred all the anxiety.

Alternatively, the client asks the coach to find a solution. The client implements the suggested solution and becomes dependent on the coach for answers to similar questions in the future. The coach quickly gets to be seen as *managing* the client and the client is subtly demeaned in their own and others' eyes.

Sometimes the client will make an overt request for rescuing. Here is an example:

Maria (coach) and Richard (client)

Maria was coaching Richard, a client who was in dispute with his organization. He had applied for a number of jobs unsuccessfully and was now on its *At Risk* list, meaning that unless he found another job within an agreed length of time, a redundancy process would be triggered.

Richard had also fallen out with his boss and had registered a grievance about the boss's behaviour, alleging bullying.

Maria was finding it hard going with Richard. He frequently broke down in their sessions. When asked to name his goals for the coaching sessions, his replies were vague, essentially amounting to 'I need a shoulder to cry on.' Richard also lavished Maria with compliments – for instance, about how sympathetic she was.

At their third session, Richard asked Maria to accompany him to the informal meeting which would start the grievance process.

'You understand me so well', he said, 'and I don't trust myself to give a good account of all this stuff at the meeting. Will you come with me?'

Maria is in coaching because she likes people and wants to help. She understood Richard's vulnerability. However, she knew that she had to resist because by accepting she would have been colluding with Richard's belief that he was powerless. Agreeing would have implied 'You really are in a bad way'; 'I can step in and look after you.'

Maria wisely refused Richard's invitation, seeing that her true role as Richard's coach was to tackle his lack of self-belief.

You are at risk of rescuing when you find yourself thinking or doing any of the following:

What would they do without me?

I'm not looking forward to this session; it'll be round and round the same loop.

I don't think they are going to get this right – their old pattern is going to assert itself yet again.

Impatience: Why can't they just do what I say?

Making harsh judgements about the client's capacity.

Believing that if you were in their shoes you'd do the job better.

Toying with the idea of actively intervening in the client's system on their behalf.

Rescuing implies that the client is a victim and if you act on the impulse to do it, it will for certain undermine the client. If you do rescue, you may also find that the 'victim' turns on you: 'You didn't rescue me cleverly enough!'

In general, when you lose faith in the ability of clients to solve their own problems, you are losing faith in the coaching process, thus ensuring that it fails. That is why it is so important to avoid all the many ways in which we can subtly dishearten our clients through giving heavy-handed advice, or through its close relative, rescuing.

There is a place for offering carefully calibrated advice and information in coaching and I explore this in Chapter 10.

Authentic listening, rapport and congruence

Genuine listening is about acceptance. Genuine listening is also rare. Mostly what we experience is pretend listening where the other person utters meaningless phrases such as 'I hear what you say', while actually just getting their own statement ready.

Even rarer is a conversation that does not include an opinion. I think here of my dad, no worse in this respect than most other parents of his generation and a loving, principled man, but throughout his very long life, whatever I said about any important decision or opinion, he would have a comment:

Approval: *That's good, I was worried about you.*
Agreement: *This government is run by idiots.*
Anxious enquiry containing a concealed opinion: *But what will that do to your pension?*
Reproach: *But why are you moving to such a shabby area?*
Disapproval: *I prefer it when you wear skirts.*

Neutral comment and neutral questions are rare indeed.

Rapport and 'body language'

Teaching so-called 'body language' has become a cliché of management training courses, often reduced on these events to a trivialized exercise in mimicry of body posture. This is not genuine rapport.

I was reminded of this when I had an introductory gym session with a personal trainer. This young man leaked boredom. He said the right thing and asked the right questions, though only when, it seemed, he had mentally jerked himself awake enough to remember them. His eye contact constantly wandered away from me and over my shoulder. His smile looked false. I knew with absolute certainty that his 'interest' in me was faked and my indignation at his discourtesy intruded unpleasantly into my ability to learn from what he was telling me. He had no doubt been on a course where he had been taught the 'techniques' of rapport. But rapport, congruence and empathy are not 'techniques'. They are *ways of being* with a client.

Real rapport is more than copying body posture, though two people who are actually in rapport will indeed mirror each other in how they are sitting or standing. When you are in rapport, you will be matching the other person: body, voice volume, breathing, gesture, space, language, pace and energy. You are entering that person's world. To an observer it will look like an elegant dance, first one leading and then the other. In an ideal world this would happen naturally. The coach's world is often not ideal because all kinds of intrusions make it difficult to sustain rapport.

Real rapport comes from unconditional acceptance of the client. This is not the same as liking the client, though in practice you will probably come to like the majority of your clients. When you unconditionally accept a client you will be congruent and when you are congruent you will be in rapport.

Unconditional acceptance means that you are curious about the client. You want to know what it is like to walk in his or her shoes. You accept not just the positive things – that is, the admirable parts, the behaviours that spring from values just like your own – but the parts that are less admirable and of which they may feel ashamed or worried. Most of us grow up learning that acceptance is conditional. Some examples might be that love and acceptance depend on: being deferential to people all the time and putting their needs first; being quietly spoken and modest or alternatively lively and entertaining, always smiling; being 100 per cent successful 100 per cent of the time. An important part of the coaching process is to uncover what these inner voices and assumptions are – there is more about this in Chapter 8.

Coaching works when it offers clients the opportunity to discover that they can be valued as a whole – moving past the conditional assumptions that have cramped their growth. The coach will not judge. This is so rare in our society that clients may doubt at first whether they can trust it; hence the cautious feel that many first and second sessions have. It does mean, of course, that as a coach you have to know, deal with and move beyond your own assumptions about what is 'worthy' and what is not. If you cannot, you will find yourself *simulating* congruence instead of *being* congruent – a distinction immediately obvious to any client.

Ten ways that rapport and congruence break down

These are the ten most common reasons for loss of congruence:

Fear
The coach fears not being good enough and fear floods the internal system. Extreme self-consciousness then prevents the coach from managing the rapport at a conscious or unconscious level. There may be some congruence and rapport, but unfortunately it will consist of the client leading the coach most of the time, rather than the graceful *pas de deux* that happens when there is genuine rapport.

Overwhelming need for the client to like you

We all need to like and be liked, but if the wish to be liked gets out of hand, it will prevent you challenging appropriately. This feeling again arises from fear and lack of self-confidence. 'If I challenge, this client won't like me.' In ordinary conversation with friends we may have cheerful disputes, but in general we keep profound disagreements to ourselves – or maybe even select our friends because they share our opinions and prejudices. A coach often has to disagree, but the disagreement comes from the security of knowing that when it is done respectfully it will be totally acceptable to the client and you will maintain rapport and congruence.

Believing that you already know

The client starts their account and the coach immediately jumps to the conclusion that they already know the answer. 'I've heard all this before', or 'I know what he/she should do'. As soon as this thought kicks in, you stop listening.

Judgement

The coach cannot suspend judgement about some perceived aspect of the client – maybe their profession ('I never did like journalists/bankers/estate agents'), their values, their clothing, their nationality, religion or their personality. The sort of disapproval that originates in prejudice will leak out in all kinds of ways and is usually perfectly apparent to the client.

Imposing actual or implied values on to the client

The coach dominates the process with values that overwhelm because they are projected so strongly through their behaviour, normally through showing enhanced or withdrawn attention. This imposes new restrictive conditions on the client so that the client feels, 'I am only valued when I talk about my successes', or 'This coach likes it best when I cry', or 'I feel I have to over-dramatize my problems – that's what he/she seems to respond to.' Forcing the client into incongruity in order to please the coach is one sure way to damage the coaching process.

Psychologizing and interpreting

The coach attributes simple behaviours to some past trauma ('I can see that this reminds you of your abusive father') or to heavy underlying significance, when in fact they are just simple behaviours.

Compulsive explaining

The coach loves to offer the client little box and arrow diagrams which encapsulate his or her pet theories; interrupts the client in order to offer endless potted versions of favourite management textbooks.

The wish to reform the client

The coach sees that the client has certain unhealthy or undesirable habits such as over-eating, working too hard, having an over-dominant management style, not exercising enough and so on – and cannot refrain from offering suggestions about people who might help, or offering new wonder-methods of controlling the pesky habit.

Preoccupation on the coach's part
The coach has so many issues going on in their own life that it is impossible to concentrate on the client.

Unawareness on the part of the coach
The coach does not know that they are fixed in particular ways of talking and communicating. For instance, the coach mismatches the client's pace: the client is languid in style, but the coach is energetic – or vice versa. Another example would be that the client has an unusually quiet voice, but the coach remains loud. Yet another might be that the client's language shows a liking for a particular sort of metaphor, but the coach does not spot it and uses his or her own version of the same words instead.

All of these are bigger and more common traps than you might suppose. Success as a coach always involves high levels of self-awareness and ruthlessly exposing yourself to your own prejudices and assumptions. Here are some examples taken from my experience as a supervisor to three relatively experienced coaches who ruefully discovered that their coaching had been less effective than they had hoped:

> The coach, in her late fifties, had had a highly successful career in banking as one of the few women to make it to the top. Working with a young woman client also in banking, she found herself responding disapprovingly to the client's decision to prioritize a personal relationship with a man rather than ruthlessly pursuing her career.

> An American coach confessed to being lured into arguing with a British client about healthcare systems in the two countries.

> A doctor coach with strongly-held feminist principles was coaching a younger woman doctor for the first time and realized she had felt instant prejudice on the basis that her Muslim client was wearing the hijab.

Real congruence starts with a buoyant and sincere wish to understand the other person – to see the world as they see it. At the same time you have to be self-aware and self-accepting, letting your own barriers down, free of the need to defend yourself. When you no longer fear others you will not feel the need to protect yourself from difference and when you are able to do this you will probably find that everything else follows.

Mismatches

When you mismatch someone, you break rapport. Sometimes it is possible to mismatch without there being any malign intention, but the client may easily misinterpret what they see. For instance, fiddling with your watch, pen or ring may suggest impatience; looking at a clock or watch may seem to imply that you want to move on to something else; staring unblinkingly at the other person can seem aggressive; waggling your foot may suggest nervousness or impatience; sitting back in your chair when the other person is sitting forward may suggest lack of involvement – and many others.

Mismatching may be useful when you want to punctuate a coaching session by moving from one agenda topic to another, or where the client appears to have got stuck in a mood that does not seem helpful. Sometimes this break can be something as obvious as, 'Why don't we get up and have another cup of coffee?', or just a more subtle change in your own posture and energy level.

The three levels of listening

It would be rare to confess to being a poor listener – about as rare as owning up to being a bad driver or to having no sense of humour. However, coaches can't afford the luxury of self-delusion. Ruthless honesty against a very high standard is the only possible tactic.

The framework proposed by the Coaches Training Institute allows for a hierarchy of listening effectiveness, all of which depends on the self-awareness of the coach. It is described in the excellent book by Laura Whitworth, Henry Kimsey-House and Phil Sandahl, *Co-active Coaching* (1998), and like many other coaching concepts it has its origins in psychotherapy.

Level 1

This is the client's level. As the client you are self-absorbed. You don't have to worry about anything except getting your story out. As a client this level is fine. As a coach it is disastrous. You will be thinking about yourself, not the client. Signs that you are at Level 1 include finding yourself asking the client for more facts: 'how many; when; who; what's the structure; what's the history', when the client hasn't mentioned them. You may find yourself wanting to give advice and talking about yourself: lots of *I* and *me*. You may also notice that you are getting flustered, that your inner dialogue is about your own anxiety:

- What can I ask next?
- Was that a good enough question?

- Will this last for the whole session?
- Does the client like me?

Sample Level 1 conversation

Client: I need to get better at delegating. I'm working 70 hours a week at the moment.

Coach: Yes, that's really not a good idea; you'll wear yourself out.

Client: But I can't really see what else I can do, we're so busy.

Coach: You'll probably find the whole way you're doing it is a bit wrong. I've got a really good handout I can show you. It's worked for lots of clients so it should work for you.

Client: Mmm, well . . .

Coach: It starts from an analysis of how you typically spend your day. I've got a sample here. Shall we work on it now?

In this example, the coach is over-concerned to position herself as the expert. She wants to be helpful, but she is not listening because her own agenda is getting in the way and she has resorted to giving advice before she has established what the client wants.

Level 2

At Level 2, coach and client are seamlessly locked into an absorbing and intensely concentrated conversation. They are most definitely in rapport, their body posture, voices and energy levels subtly matched. The conversation will flow, but the client will be doing most of the talking. The coach's questions are skilful, picking up on the language the client has used, working exclusively from the client's agenda and never giving advice. The questions explore, clarify, summarize and probe, always extending the client's thinking and willingness to learn something new. As the coach you hear what is not being said as well as what is. You are listening for the underlying meanings and are aware of your own impact on the client.

If you can remain at Level 2 for most of a coaching session you are doing well: it is the level at which the majority of effective coaching takes place.

Sample Level 2 conversation

Client: I need to get better at delegating. I'm working 70 hours a week at the moment.

Coach: That sounds tough. How should we work on this?

Client: Well, I think I'm doing it OK, but my staff tell me I'm not. I don't know what they mean really.

Coach: What exactly do they say to you?

Client: An example would be that my assistant tells me I'm constantly checking up on her, but how else am I supposed to find out how things are going?

Coach: Checking up . . . So that's her feedback. 'Finding out what's going on . . .' Sounds like there's lots of anxiety there for you. Do you want to stay with this one as a useful example?

Client: Yes, OK.

Coach: So what's this anxiety like, exactly?

Here the coach is following the client's agenda scrupulously, using his words, deepening the conversation and generating useful data for the conversation that follows.

Level 3

At Level 3 you are doing what has been described as 'radio-field listening', aware not just of everything required at Level 2, but also of the emotion, of the risks it might be possible to take in the conversation, of the underlying choices and of what could be at stake for the client. You trust your intuition. You feel connected with the client at an emotional as well as at an intellectual level, even if no emotion has been named. You see the whole coaching relationship stretching out behind and in front of you and it feels special. These are moments of real connection – of a kind that few of us ever reach in a 'normal' conversation with a friend.

Sample Level 3 conversation

Client: I need to get better at delegating. I'm working 70 hours a week at the moment.

Coach: That sounds tough. How should we work on this?

Client: (small silence and a laugh)

Coach: (gently) So? (another pause) That laugh sounds strained.

Client: It is. I can't take this pace. My staff tell me I'm 'interfering', but I don't know how else to keep everything under control. It's ruining my personal life and if I don't watch it my health as well. My wife complains she never sees me and I don't know when I last put our daughter to bed because I'm home so late. I'm awake every morning from 4 am, and then I can't get back to sleep worrying about work. It's an enormous strain.

Coach: So this is an enormous strain and it feels as if there's a huge amount at stake for you, job and home.

Client: Enormous. It's a burden I don't want.

Coach: Burden is a heavy-sounding word! What does that mean for you?

Client: Unbearable – literally, like a load I'm carrying and that I'd like to put down because I can't control it.

Coach: So this is about a burden you don't want and would like to put down. Shall we explore how you might do just that?

Through working at Level 3, the coach has established a whole-life perspective and has focused the client's mind on what is at stake through continuing to work so many hours. She has done this through listening for the silences and hesitations, by listening for the metaphor and for the emotion behind the words. She has left spaces inside the conversation which the client can fill if he wishes. By doing this she makes it clear that she neither condones nor condemns the long working week, but is simply accepting and respecting the position the client finds himself in. She has spotted the underlying need that the behaviour serves. By noticing the negative energy that his stress is creating she has also harnessed a willingness to begin the change process. The therapist Fritz Perls had a succinct sentence when he talked about this level of listening: 'A good therapist doesn't listen to the content of the bullshit of what the patient produces, but to the sound, to the music, to the hesitations' (Perls, *Gestalt Therapy Verbatim*, 1969: 57).

Working from the client's agenda

Implicit in all of this is the assumption that it is the client's agenda that matters, not the coach's. The minute you stray into Level 1, you will be working from your agenda, not the client's. Coaching starts and finishes with the client's agenda. This is because coaching is about change. Clients come to coaching because they want to change their lives and get results which show that change has happened. Clients know their lives in a way that the coach never can, so only the client can say what the agenda for change is.

The coach's role is to ask the questions which uncover the client's agenda and make it explicit, turning this agenda into the goals which the client can work on and safeguarding it as the only agenda for the coaching. The coach links the agenda with the client's core values and beliefs and works with the client to identify and then move past the blocks and fears which are holding them back (Chapters 7 and 8).

Being worthy of trust: a two-way process

As a coach, I ask my clients to trust me. I am always aware of what a huge assumption this is. Why should they trust me? What can I do to accelerate that trust? Equally, my starting place in the relationship is that I will trust them. Where trust is broken, it can of course be repaired, but as with a piece of shattered china, the repair will always be there, even if apparently invisible, and it will never be as strong as it was when unbroken.

Trust may grow slowly, depending on the skill of the coach and the willingness of the client to be open. This is hard for many clients. They have become accustomed to defensiveness and sometimes to performance. Realizing that they do not have to perform for you is often the turning point in the effectiveness of the coaching: understanding they really can trust you with their failures and uncertainties and that you will not condemn or judge. Equally, they learn that you will acknowledge their achievements and their efforts to change. What does trust really involve? The answers must be honesty, predictability, commitment and reliability.

As with so many other issues in coaching, this is a two-way process.

The client's side in creating trust

First, the client is consistent in what he or she says. When the client describes a particular set up, they will describe it in the same way each time. If you get to see the client in action with their team, you will see the situation they have described – plus a great deal more – but the client's tale will still ring true.

When clients commit to coaching, this involves treating the coach as respectfully as they expect to be treated themselves. In a healthy coaching relationship, what the client says and what the client does are one and the same. The commitment to the coaching is more than just words. If we agree 'homework' it is done and, even if it is not done, there will be learning in why it has been put to one side. When clients say that they will continue to ponder some theme we have discussed, they do. When they say they will give you candid feedback, they do.

What is said inside the sessions should be consistent with what is said outside them. Where this is not the case, trust will be destroyed. An example of this happened to one of my colleagues who had coached a senior manager made redundant by his organization and still smarting from the hurt and rejection. My colleague had asked for feedback at the end of each session and the client said that he had found the sessions 'very useful' and spelt out the usefulness in some detail. Yet two weeks later my colleague heard that the client had described the coaching to a third party known to both of them as 'pointless navel-gazing'. When respectfully challenged about this at their next session, the client blustered and equivocated. Not surprisingly, that was their last meeting.

Clients gain my trust and respect where they are willing to give the coaching process a try. Signs that they are willing to do this would be, for instance, that they are willing to explore previously forbidden emotional areas or hear tough feedback and to sit out the resulting discomfort without attacking me as the bearer of bad news. Coaching demands an unusual degree of openness from both client and coach. Clients who are willing to make themselves vulnerable through honest disclosure will earn my confidence.

Lack of commitment is betrayed in many large and small ways. For instance, a client who consistently cancels the date at the last moment for what seem like implausible reasons is indicating for sure that they do not give a high priority to the coaching. A client who arrives for the session late and looking ill-prepared and bemused about the agenda tells you that their mind is on other things. Such clients could be showing that their interest in learning with you is fragile and may be waning.

The coach's side in creating trust

All of these conditions need to be equally present in the coach. The first step is to look at your own assumptions about how far you can trust the client. You don't need to like every client in the way that you would like a close friend – in fact, it is impossible to do so. You will respect the many aspects of the client which are admirable, but will also be curious and interested in the many self-protective barriers which the client has skilfully erected around him- or herself.

Many clients may present initially as disagreeable people. For instance, a client who bullies or manipulates represents a style of management that I particularly dislike. However, I have worked successfully with many such clients, though I would not have lasted a week with them if they had been my boss. At the other end of the spectrum are the clients who lack assertiveness. They may be condemned by their colleagues as 'weak', or, more kindly, as 'lacking toughness'. With these clients, too, I can usually work well, yet if I worked with them as colleagues they might exasperate me.

What is the difference? As clients I am intrigued by their dilemmas and difficulties. I want to know what self-imposed barriers they have created to success. I accept their plusses, their quirks and failings unconditionally. My role is to encourage and challenge. I don't have to like them in the way I need to like a close friend.

As a coach, what you say and what you do have to be consistent. At the simplest level, you must deliver on your promises. If you say you will email an interesting article, you must do it. If you declare enthusiasm for coaching, you must be enthusiastic. You will give the client 100 per cent of your attention in every session, just as you expect 100 per cent attention back. It will be immediately obvious if you are drifting off or coaching on autopilot.

You will refer to clients respectfully outside the sessions, never belittling them with other coaches or saying anything that could identify them as a client, unless you have their specific permission to do so. Where you feel you cannot work respectfully, then the coaching must end. As you expect from your client, you will never cancel or arrive late for a session on spurious or trivial grounds.

You do not need clients to be just like you to be able to work with them successfully. Your assumption might be that you will be able to work with more or less any client until circumstances prove otherwise.

You will strictly adhere to your promise of confidentiality. Any betrayal here will wing its way back to your client in very short order. A colleague once described the most common approach to confidentiality as 'only telling one other person'. As coaches we need to do better than that. There are limits to confidentiality, so tell the client what they are. Clients need to trust that we will not gossip or betray any of the many secrets we hear in the coaching room. This may range from early knowledge of a company takeover, with its potential to buy shares cheap and sell them dear later, to other kinds of insider knowledge about secret love affairs or people's sexuality. We need to be careful about discussing client organizations. It is tempting to pronounce on their characteristics and culture and by doing so to convey our privileged knowledge of their inner secrets. When we do this it comes across as gossip and diminishes the gossiper who will probably strike his or her listeners as indiscreet and disloyal.

Finally, as a coach you will demonstrate willingness to learn from your clients. This is something that is taken for granted by the best coaches in other fields – for instance, singing and sport. An outstanding opera singer will usually have a singing coach. The best theatre companies employ voice coaches, even for distinguished actors. These coaches will tell you how much they learn from their coachees. Similarly, as life or executive coaches, when we stay open to influence from our clients in the same way that we expect them to be open to influence from us, the coaching relationship will be infinitely the richer.

3   The heart of coaching: the coach–client relationship

What actually goes on between coach and client? Why does coaching work? What makes the difference between an averagely acceptable coach and a brilliant one? How far is coaching actually the partnership of equals that so many of us say we create? Where are the limits to coaching?

The intention to help

A colleague and I were assessing would-be coaches in order to fulfil a contract we had won. We set up a process where we observed the candidates through a session with willing guinea pig clients. One would-be coach intruded grossly into her client's physical space, at one point almost sitting in her lap she was so close; she continually pressed her pet solution onto the client; she talked too much.

And yet . . . and yet her client, correctly identifying that we would probably not be offering this coach a job because of this behaviour, said wistfully, 'In spite of all that, I really liked her and it was actually useful. I will do some of the things she suggested because I knew how much she wanted to help me.' I am not advocating this artlessly naïve and unskilled coaching, as I am certain that this coach would soon have floundered helplessly with many of the demanding clients we had in the pipeline. However, the intention to help in this session was so strongly conveyed that some decent coaching did actually take place.

I have come to see that this wish, when accompanied by strongly-conveyed emotional authenticity, can demolish many of the barriers seemingly imposed by lack of technique. In the enjoyable book *Provocative Therapy* (Farrelly and Brandsma 1974), Frank Farrelly recounts something similar where a student therapist was able to break through the casually callous assumptions of more experienced colleagues that a chronic mentally ill patient could be abandoned 'because he could never get better'. Recounting this, furiously and with angry tears, to the patient, the man was amazed that someone could care so much. He comforted the student, ran away from the hospital and got a job, never to return. As Farrelly comments, '[this] reinforced my idea that even though you had no business being *right* or effective, you could be' (Farrelly and Brandsma 1974: 9).

Power in the coaching relationship: the outer signs

Talking about coaching as a relationship of equals has become a mantra in coaching. Working in partnership is what gives coaching its power. How far can this pious hope be true in practice?

When you contrast coaching with other professions, there are some startling differences. Where many of the traditional professions are concerned – accountants, lawyers, doctors – most people would much prefer not to have to consult them. Almost all are associated with an actual or a potential crisis. Coaching clients are always facing change, but they may see this as bracing rather than threatening. Once they get into the swing of it, clients may look forward to coaching sessions rather than approaching them with the dread that a visit to a lawyer or doctor could invoke.

The traditional professions are selling the superior knowledge that their specialism gives them. Sadly, this has often led to conveying an attitude of superiority. The more obviously service-based and possibly more overcrowded professions (think of financial advisors, architects, interior designers) have always had to take a more client-centred approach. Most coaches will go to considerable lengths to *live* equality in the relationship as well as talking about it. This contrasts with the way many people from the traditional professions treat their clients. So, for instance, I have rarely been on mutually first name terms with any doctor to whom I was a patient; indeed, most commonly, I have been talked at as an anonymous 'you' or addressed, uninvited, by my first name while the practitioner expects to be addressed as 'Dr'. By contrast, I work with many doctor-clients, use their first names from the start and expect them to address me likewise. I always offer tea, coffee or water, thus introducing the social nuance of guest and host – also a relationship of equals.

There are some ways in which the relationship favours the coach. Many coaches insist that the client comes to them. When the client comes to us we have already disturbed the balance of power. The client is on our territory and, a bit like being a guest in our home, knows that he or she is expected to play to our rules. We set the method for the coaching, including the method that says the agenda is the client's. We set the time frame for the length of each session. We set the fees.

Against this, we may offset a number of factors that play to the client's power. The client can and often does negotiate fees downwards, depending on the state of the coach's order book. The client may take a more active role than the coach in deciding the appropriate number of sessions. Apart from the initial session, where most coaches will have a well-rehearsed protocol, the agenda for the sessions is entirely in the client's hands. And, as in any overcrowded profession, all clients know that there are many other coaches out there eager for business.

In his devastating critique of psychoanalysis, *Against Therapy* (1990), Jeffrey Masson suggested that even the best therapists cannot avoid creating an exploitative and controlling climate because it is so ingrained in the profession. The critical difference with coaching is that our clients are mentally healthy, and where they are not, their 'symptoms' are normally the ones of familiar minor dysfunction.

Also, certainly where executive coaching is concerned, we are dealing with robustly successful, senior and well-paid people used to having their own way and dealing with suppliers of all sorts as part of their daily lives. For many coaches in the most obviously elevated end of the market, their clients could be earning ten times or more the income of the coach. Many could also be well-known public figures. This makes a difference – the coach will usually approach the client with at least some vestige of the world's respect and may even be unconsciously basking in power borrowed from the client.

There are other, more subtle, ways in which the coach–client relationship is not one of equals. For the most part, as a coach, you set aside a great many of your opinions during the course of the conversation. The client is allowed to express opinions. The coach is willingly more restrained. It is the coach's responsibility to reach out to the client, not the client's to reach out to the coach. The coach is responsible for setting the climate of the conversation – not the client. The client is invested in his or her own learning – not the coach's. The coach has to affirm the client, but the client has no such responsibility towards the coach.

Unconscious processes

Throughout the coaching process, there may be some unconscious processes going on which may explain phenomena which are otherwise inexplicable. For instance, why do you instinctively like some clients more than others (or they like or dislike you)? Why do some clients seem to bring odd expectations to the coaching relationship? Some ideas from therapy may help explain at least some of what is happening.

Projection

As a coach you remain non-judgemental and unattached to your own ideas about what might be good for the client. This is why self-awareness about the phenomenon known as projection can be so useful. Essentially the assumption is that we all have dark sides which we may not acknowledge about ourselves. We say to ourselves, in effect, 'I don't like this about myself. I'll project it on to someone else and that way I can criticize it because then it's nothing to do with me.' The phenomenon of projection may take a number of forms.

At its simplest, we may project an emotion we are feeling on to someone else. This is because we cannot or will not own the feeling in ourselves. So, for instance, I might say to a friend, 'You seem worried', when actually it is I who am worried, but don't want to face my worry. As coaches, we might start thinking, 'This client is hostile to me', when in fact, you are feeling hostility towards him or her. We may see others as the cause of our problems, especially those closest to us. On the positive side, we imagine that another person possesses the ideals and qualities we fail to incorporate into ourselves and our lives, thus creating cycles of unrealistic infatuation which then turn to bitter disappointment in jobs and relationships, leading to cynicism and resentment.

When we criticize other people, what we criticize may be the very thing we most fear could be true about ourselves. Where you find yourself having these judgemental thoughts, it can be a useful discipline to stop and ask yourself, 'Are these feelings or behaviours that are actually true for me?'

Perhaps the most powerful single idea relating to projection is that how we speak about others always says a great deal about how we see ourselves, especially where we are critical.

Transference and counter-transference

Again, these are concepts from psycho-dynamic psychotherapy. The idea is that clients unconsciously project – on to you and the coaching relationship – patterns and assumptions from earlier relationships in their lives. These projections will be distortions – they are preventing the other person from seeing you as you think you really are. Most usually, they may transfer to you feelings they have had or still have about significant figures from their past. So a client who constantly rebelled against an authoritarian father may see male figures such as a coach in the same light as he saw his father, even though the coach concerned is a mild and pleasant person who is totally unlike the father. Older women may create expectations of being *mother* or *teacher* to a client and this could trigger rebellious adolescent behaviour or expectations of being nurtured. A coach who is roughly the same age may evoke early peer friendships or sibling relationships.

Counter-transference may also be going on – that is when you as coach do the same to the client. So a challenge from a client may painfully reawaken ghosts from an early relationship. For that moment, the client is standing in for the ghost and you respond as you might have to him or her in the past.

The more transparent you are in your working with the client, the less likely these phenomena are to derail the process. For instance, Glenda is a client who appears to be resisting delivery on the actions that she and her coach have agreed. Her coach takes up the story:

Glenda

Glenda told me that she just hadn't had time to do her 'homework'. This was our fourth session and in each of the last three the same thing had happened. I said, very calmly, 'Glenda, I'm really puzzled and intrigued. I'm also feeling a bit stuck and wondering if you're not doing this stuff because I'm not coaching you properly or in a way you can relate to. This is the third session where you've said you haven't had time to do the follow up. I'm wondering what's going on here for you . . .' Glenda looked sheepish and then annoyed: 'You aren't my headmistress you know!'

Coach: No, I'm not. But I'm wondering now if I remind you of one you used to know!
[There was a pause, and Glenda's face changed colour.]
Glenda: Well, yes. You're about her age when I knew her and I was constantly in trouble for not doing my homework and when I left I swore I'd never let anyone boss me about again.
Coach: How else do I seem to remind you of her?
Glenda: You don't – except that you seem very confident and together.
Coach: What else?
Glenda: Can't think of anything else!
Coach: What would you like to say to that headmistress if she were here?
Glenda: Please respect me. Don't come down on me like that – it wasn't fair, though I know I was a right little pest.
Coach: In what ways am I different?
Glenda: Far, far more – in fact, you're not like her at all really!

We then had a candid discussion about our relationship and what needed to happen to make it work. I, for my part, was of course quite unable to promise that I would be anything other than myself, including not being like her headteacher. Glenda was able to look at all her troubled relationships with authority in this light. The frankness and intimacy it created were the turning point in the coaching.

Paralleling

Closely linked with the idea of transference and counter-transference is the idea of parallel processes. This can seem like a strange phenomenon: the client reproduces the same behaviour in their session as they did in whatever incident they are describing. This creates a parallel emotion in the coach. An example might be that a client is describing overwhelming stress in her job. She says it shows itself in impatience and irritation with her direct reports. As the coach you begin to experience the same feeling in relation to your client: irritation and impatience. Here is Carly, a relative newcomer to coaching, describing how both paralleling and projection occurred in a session with her client. Carly had been introduced to the concept of paralleling through a session with her supervisor:

Carly (coach)

My client is a 28-year-old woman of Asian origin, the only girl in a family of six children. The family had arranged her marriage but the marriage is not happy, and she is thinking of leaving, knowing how badly this will play in the culture of which she is a part.

She has successfully avoided having a child despite strong family pressure to do so. She had already talked to me about the dominance of her father in the family and her resentment about how being a girl had meant that she was expected to do household chores which her brothers had been and still were spared. The presenting issue for coaching was her lack of progress in her career. I also come from an immigrant family and had a dominant dad, though I had successfully wriggled free.

My client began to complain about her boss, saying that he either ignored or bullied her. After the session when I reflected on it, I realized that I had taken part in a perfect example of paralleling probably with projection and counter-transference thrown in! As my client went on with her story I began to feel that she was whining and complaining. I felt annoyed. I found myself thinking, 'For goodness sake, just ask for what you want! You deserve to be overlooked! Don't be such a wimp.' Although I of course did not actually utter those dreadful words, I know that an edge of impatience crept into my voice. Unusually, I ended the session ten minutes early. I probably came across as much more curt than I normally am. Now my challenge is to spot this stuff and manage it better!

Why does this happen? One cause is that the coach is over-identifying with the client, inwardly looking for similarities as an unconscious way of tapping into the client's issues.

An alternative, or additional, explanation is that the client, again at an unconscious level, wants to recreate the drama and intensity of the issue in order to force the coach into finding a resolution. In practice, while both these forces may be at work, the most likely immediate trigger is the coach's uncertainty and panic about how to respond to the intensity of the client's emotion. In terms of managing these parallel processes, the key is awareness. Notice that it is happening. Physically make a change – for instance, in how you are sitting. Break the trance-like state which has most likely taken hold of both of you. Consciously mismatch the client. Suggest a stretch or another cup of tea. Ask yourself if you are getting so hooked up in the client's issues that you have lost sight of the essentials: that it is the client who has to find the solution, not you. Useful interventions when you notice paralleling happening are questions which will enable you to position yourself consciously outside the client's issues, for instance by saying:

> So, to summarize, the issues are a,b,c. Which of these do you feel is the most important?

> Or

> I'm finding myself a bit overwhelmed in the issue here; can we just take stock of where we are with it?

Being real

In any relationship where helping is involved, there is always a strong possibility of both sides tapping into the deepest roots of human longing. Psychology as a subject has its roots in philosophy, medicine and religion. Alchemy, superstition and mysticism are lurking just around the corner. When something is wrong, we can crave some magic and sorcery, whether it is a wonder-crystal with the power to ward off danger, faith healing to save us from death, ley lines which will explain puzzling events, or an exorcism which will banish evil spirits. The power of such hopes and beliefs can be overwhelming.

It is only 150 years or so ago that mental illness was widely believed to be possession by the devil, and there are some religious faiths where people still believe that. The idea that there are people with special powers seems to be something we can all find potentially appealing. It is comforting, if also a little scary, to think of giving yourself up to someone who can reassure through their links to the Divine, or through their special insight . . . sliding smoothly into *second-sight* and *psychic*.

Beware of letting your coaching become contaminated with the same ideas. It is easy, believe me. I have occasionally heard clients introduce me to colleagues at a social event as a 'witch', or slightly less alarmingly as a 'white witch'. In the light of this I go to some pains to demystify the coaching process. You cannot work as an equal with someone who believes that you are some kind of secular priest or shaman. Clients may not always welcome this at first – it might be more comforting to believe in the wizardry. But long-term this cannot be right.

Several studies have shown that in some cases placebos (pills that contain no drugs) and placebo procedures (for instance, opening a patient's chest and sewing it up again without any other surgery having taken place) can have almost as much positive benefit as conventional drug or surgical treatment. Nocebos can also be powerful – that is, inert substances where the patient is told to expect side effects – and does. Placebos have sometimes proved many times more effective as treatment for depression than the commonly prescribed drugs and also seem to be powerful in pain control. An intriguing US study carried out by the American Council on Exercise showed that runners who thought they were getting a boost from 'super-oxygenated water' (in fact ordinary tap water) ran three 5 km time trials on average 86 seconds faster than a control group. Where alternative medicine is concerned, defenders of homeopathy, for instance, will maintain that it works despite the intrinsic implausibility of the theory that even though no trace of the homeopathic element can be found in the 'medicine', the water retains a 'memory' of it. We may speculate that what does work is that the homeopathic doctor him- or herself believes fervently in the remedy and conveys this to patients who are also willing to suspend their disbelief. This belief on both sides that the 'cure' will work is what may give it its power.

Not correct

If we take the lesson from placebo research it is possible to see that when both coach and client believe in the power of the coaching process, we are likely to elevate its effectiveness many times over. If, as the coach, you are sceptical about whether it 'works', then you will convey this to the client. A client who is sceptical about coaching will immediately limit the chances that it will be useful for him or her. There is power in coaching and you will want clients to believe in that power. However, the power is invested in the relationship itself and in the coaching process, not in the supposed supernatural abilities of the coach.

Research into therapy, including so-called meta-research (research into the research), for instance by David Elkins (2007), shows clearly that success in therapy has nothing to do with the intellectual cleverness of the practitioner or their theoretical orientation. Instead, the common factors seem to be:

1   The ability of the practitioner to create a climate of warmth, acceptance and rapport.
2   The nature of the 'therapeutic alliance' – how the practitioner and client work; the transparency and clarity of the goals.
3   The context in which the client seeks help and whether or not they have supportive people in their lives who are prepared to help them make positive changes.

4   Client and practitioner believing equally in the plausibility of any approaches that are used, including many that are intrinsically implausible, and in their mutual expectation that a positive outcome is possible – in other words, what we might call a placebo effect.

5   The kinds of techniques used.

Of these five factors, the least important seems to be the last, with some researchers estimating that as little as 8–15 per cent of the eventual successful outcome had anything to do with particular techniques. We have yet to see whether coaching-specific research will throw up similar results, but we may guess is that it will. Trust and warmth are the essential cornerstones in coaching, as in therapy.

Permission to be yourself

When I was relatively new to coaching I acted on an unstated belief that I did have to remain in some kind of positively neutral gear throughout the conversation. The client could get upset, but I couldn't. The client could be boring, but I had to simulate interest. The client could give me feedback at the end of the session, but I had to be restrained.

I see now how wrong that was.

In fulfilling a contract for coaching with one organization there was a 'meet the coach' preliminary event at which, unlike three colleagues, I could not be present. I joined the group the next day for the first of their coaching sessions, held within the timetable of a five-day course. One of the managers in the group who had selected me 'blind' to be his coach told me that he had done so precisely because I had not been present the previous day. His reason, he explained, was that he wanted me to be a 'totally neutral coaching machine' and the less he knew about me the better. In my early days as a coach I would have accepted that, but not by that stage. So in discussing this wish for neutrality, it quickly became apparent that this client felt that the more he knew about me, the more he dreaded that I would judge him. I found the idea of being a 'neutral coaching machine' highly distasteful and also knew that this is not how coaching works. In my refusal to stay at the level of personal invisibility, I was able to show him that he could explore his issues with a real person and be accepted for who he was.

Being open to influence: receiving feedback

The feedback process in coaching is two-way. It's not just you offering feedback to the client (page 190). You will also be inviting the client to pronounce on you. Again, this is unusual in virtually all professional relationships. In asking for feedback you will be modelling how sincerely you believe in the two-way nature of the relationship. You can ask about the content and style of your coaching as well as about the relationship:

> How have you found this session?

> What worked especially well for you?

> What worked less well?

> How are we getting on together – you and me?

When people offer you feedback, they may be uncertain how you will receive it, or they may just not know how to do it properly. So the feedback may take any of these forms:

> Apparent attack (criticism) – 'You asked a lot of questions, but I didn't get any of the advice I need.'

> Apparent compliment – 'You're brilliant at seeing beneath the surface.'

> Vague hints – 'You're a bit hard to understand at times.'

Don't get angry, defensive, self-justifying or confess 'guilt'. Instead, repeat and summarize the feedback and ask the client to tell you more. You may get some surprises as well as getting vital information about how to improve your practice.

Humility

I was working with a client who was in long-term remission from cancer. In talking calmly and optimistically about his treatment, he remarked that the single most therapeutic part of his many visits to the hospital were the conversations he had with his oncologist. This woman had acknowledged the limits of her knowledge as well as stressing her confidence in what did work. She adopted the position of treating patients as fellow adults, mixing judicious optimism with honesty about her own and her profession's limitations. This is a hard act to carry off. Do it too much or in the wrong circumstances and you destroy your client's confidence in you. But act all-seeing and all-knowing and you will be too invested in protecting your image. Coaching is full of paradoxes, and this is one of the most profound: we have to be powerful and powerless simultaneously.

The critical test is: Is this in my client's interest? If yes, then:

When you are puzzled, say so:	*I'm feeling puzzled about the connection between what you've said about x and what you've said about y: what's your take on that?*
When you feel confused about where the conversation or session is going, raise it:	*I notice we've spent nearly an hour on what you've done since we last met; we still haven't set any goals for this one! How do you feel about that?*
If you feel caught in a dilemma, describe it:	*I'm in two minds here about what to do,*
	Or
	I'm caught between a number of different ways of responding here.
When you have made a mistake, acknowledge it and apologize:	*When we met for our last session I feel I pressed you too hard on x issue. I did notice that you seemed uncomfortable but I still carried on didn't I? I'm sorry. That was a mistake.*
When you feel out of your depth, declare it:	*I'm not sure I know what to do here.*

Owning up to apparent weakness or uncertainty may have more impact than you realize. As a coach you need to be an expert at self-management. You must be centred, self-aware and with a high degree of all the many intelligences that the role requires: analytical, emotional, spiritual and systems intelligence. Yet, at the same time, you are human; there are things you don't know and areas where you are uncertain. Conveying these to clients whose lives have often been lived in dread of such 'weakness' may have only beneficial effect.

Acknowledging

We are often the only witnesses to enormous acts of courage and learning. What may seem like small steps to others are often huge leaps for a client. So a client who has overcome her genuine phobia and fear of HIV infection to have much-needed electrolysis may only have you to tell. A client who has given up what to him was the scaldingly shameful and lifelong habit of biting his nails may only feel able to glory in his achievement with you. You may be the sole recipient of an email from an apparently confident senior executive who wants to tell you joyfully about having overcome her fear of giving a presentation to her Board. A client who has experienced the death of a profoundly disabled child may not feel able to tell anyone else that although this death was a sad event, it was also welcome, received with relief, and was not the tragedy that the rest of the world assumes.

Acknowledging is yet another way in which coaching is different from a 'normal' conversation. In *acknowledging*, the coach recognizes an important aspect of who the client is, rather than noticing what the client has *achieved*. The coach is acknowledging the being self, not the doing self.

Peter

Peter is a client who has struggled with an enormous amount of personal and professional change. He has had to start a new job, recruit a new team, and get to know a new boss at the same time as coping with three bereavements.

Peter: These last few months have been the toughest I can remember.
Coach: Yes, I'd like to acknowledge your courage and resolution in keeping going.
Peter: [surprised and pleased] Oh, thanks. Gosh. I feel great!

In *acknowledging*, the coach notices and mentions positive qualities in the client: humour, energy, clarity, courage, doggedness, willingness to learn, humility, and so on.

Note that, in acknowledging, we are not giving empty compliments. Lack of authenticity will be immediately obvious to the client.

In the best coaching relationships clients trust us not just with their triumphs but with their moments of utter despair and self-doubt, often in the middle of a grinding, long-running crisis where even the most resilient person can feel their sense of self-worth ebbing away. When this happens there is one further powerful tool you can use. Ask the client what positive qualities they and others value about them. Encourage them to start the sentence, 'I am a person who . . .' So for instance, the answers might be:

I am a person who is a loyal friend.

I am a person who is a dedicated and loving father to my children.

I am a person who serves others.

I am a person who is a highly skilled [name of profession].

As they speak you write down what they say, adding more if necessary, drawing on what you know to be true for that client. You then email this list to the client, suggesting they print it out and keep it where they can look at it frequently. This is not an everyday technique, but when it is right, it has considerable impact. Clients will typically tell you that they treasure this document: 'I have it Blu-Tacked to my mirror,' or 'It's in my file of most personal, most valued papers; I'll never throw it away.'

Talking about yourself

Coaching is a unique kind of conversation. It differs from other close, intimate kinds of conversation in many ways. In a conversation with a friend, we often aim to demonstrate our kinship with the other person by emphasizing that we, too, have had a similar experience. For instance, here is a sample conversation you might have with a friend:

Friend: I'm really worried about my scan results. Perhaps I've got cancer.
You: Oh, don't worry too much about that. I had a similar thing a few months ago and it was nothing to be concerned about. Yours is probably just the same.
Friend: Oh, that's a comfort, perhaps mine will be all right too!

A coaching conversation would be different:

Client: I'm really worried about my scan results. Perhaps I've got cancer.
Coach: Yes, I can understand that concern. Say more about the worry . . .

The urge to talk about your own experience can be strong. It could help create empathy. It could show that we, too, have our vulnerable side and it could help discharge the emotion that a distressed client can create in the coach.

Coaching is about the client's issues, not the coach's. Talking about yourself will readily distract the client into discussing your experiences and concerns – or even trying to coach you. Your experience could trigger a powerful emotional reaction in your client, and not always a helpful one. For instance, the client may, at that stage in the coaching, feel that he or she needs to see you as someone above the hurly-burly of human emotion.

A client once told me towards the end of our coaching programme that the reason she had selected me rather than the other two coaches she had considered was that I had appeared 'very calm and therefore probably a whole person, not a fragmented mess like me'. This client's starting-out issues concerned managing what felt like the turbulent emotions she experienced in her workplace. If I had appeared to burden her with any of my emotion, then it could have implied that there was no hope for her either. Sometimes, the wish to share a client's pain can seem overwhelming, particularly where the client is describing a loss or trauma that you feel is akin to something you have experienced yourself. There are two related points to make here. The first is that you will be making assumptions that your experience is actually a close parallel to the client's – never the case, however similar it might seem. The second is that you may appear to be making a bid to usurp the client's experience – 'My tragedy is worse than yours.' Alternatively, the client may interpret your comment as 'Well I've coped with my difficulty, so you can jolly well cope with yours – forget it – move on!' It will also be harder to re-establish coaching conventions – the conversation may veer towards a low-key friendly chat.

In the initial 'Hullo-and-how-are-you?' part of the session, a client will virtually always politely ask you how you are. Ninety-nine per cent of the time a conventional 'fine' or 'very well' is the appropriate answer. Exceptions could be when you know the client well enough to share a major triumph or upset in your life and feel that the client has the right to know that he or she may observe tiny changes in your usual demeanour. Without hearing your explanation for such changes, the client might well misinterpret your behaviour as being some reflection on him or her. Equally, giving yourself brief permission to talk about it will, paradoxically, help you manage its impact on you.

You may feel that, as in these very rare cases, the benefits of talking about your own issues and experience could outweigh the disadvantages and benefit the client. When there is profound challenge in your life, it must be right to share at least some of it with your clients. In dealing with two bereavements, the death of a beloved young goddaughter in the middle 1990s and the death of my dear husband in 2010, I found that my clients responded with delicacy, tact and fellow-feeling. None recoiled in embarrassment – as far as I was aware – and of course I might not have been aware of any embarrassment they did feel. I believe I did good enough work during these times. It took hugely more effort to do virtually everything in the way of essential preparation or record-keeping. But once I was with my client, I gave myself up wholeheartedly to being there. Contrary to the rule that only by remaining detached can you be helpful, I confirmed my belief that the opposite was true. I took the risk of disclosing some of the rawness of my emotion and asked for some modest support back: empathy, understanding, tolerance. As a result, I increased the amount of empathy, understanding and tolerance I could offer those clients: take some, give some.

Client relationships in coaching are delicate. 'I'm paying you to be nice to me', said one client sternly, 'but I do think you mean it.' They are not purely 'professional' in the sense that I do what one former mentor advocated and forget them the moment they are gone; nor are they friendships. They grow somewhere in that shadowy territory between the two. Turning to clients, however briefly, for a moment of trustful comfort and understanding felt entirely right.

As coach with a client, my basic belief is that we are all in this together. I don't want to be an omnipotent, detached coach. I want to be there in the middle of the human struggle along with my clients.

Managing boundaries

One of the reasons that therapy has acquired a bad name in some quarters is that it has become clear that there are some therapists who have inappropriate sexual relationships with their clients. The current evidence is that those who do so are a very small number, but that they are serial abusers – that is, they do it often. All the regulatory bodies for psychotherapists explicitly warn against it. As with doctor–patient sexual relationships, it is grounds for being struck off. This is because where the relationship is one of healer–afflicted there is a power differential, and to cross the boundary from healer to lover is thus rightly regarded as abusive. Virtually all of the abusers are male. They justify their behaviour as acts of altruism. The relationships take place, they say, out of pity for the client, usually when the female client believes she is unattractive. As with all abusive relationships, the core of the abuse is in the exploited vulnerability of the abused person.

Remember, too, that power has aphrodisiac qualities, and if our clients attribute power to us or we to them, then this dynamic may be at work – see any scandal in which a famous politician's bedroom secrets are revealed. When the press ponders aloud, 'How did someone as physically unattractive as X draw a beautiful woman like Y?' the answer is usually his fame and assumed power.

Although it would be rare indeed for anything similar to happen in coaching, it is still possible. As in therapy, clients may reveal matters to us that they have told no one else. You may know more about them than anyone else except their partners, and sometimes they may share secrets with you that they have not shared even with a partner. Where this is linked through the coaching with permanent and positive change, it is perfectly natural for the client to have feelings of gratitude and warmth towards the coach and for the coach to delight in being on the receiving end of such feelings.

The intensity of the one-to-one relationship in these circumstances may often have some erotic undertones. When you take a whole-life perspective, you will inevitably get to know something about the client's personal life, and this may include his or her sexual relationships. Talking about it puts it on the agenda. So where coach and client get on well, that powerful instinctive drive to love and be loved may well be in the air, especially if one or both of the parties has some sexual dissatisfaction in their lives.

Examples might be a coach and client of the same age and background finding that there is some sexual chemistry between them at a time when both have unhappy marriages. Another example might be an older male client who may not often have the experience of being listened to intently by an attractive younger woman – and in this case she happens to be his coach. An older female client may enjoy being coached by a younger man for the same reasons. There is the same potential for disaster lurking here as there is in therapeutic relationships. Being listened to with unconditional acceptance is a rare event for most people: it is gratifying. Just as in therapy, a woman client whose self-confidence is at a temporarily low ebb, or who has been abused in the past, may believe that sex is her only gift or that a sexual exchange is the reliable way you find affection. An older male coach could in theory be as tempted to 'rescue' a vulnerable young woman client with sexual reassurance as his misguided therapist counterpart could do. Some clients undoubtedly do use seductive behaviour and this can be destabilizing, especially at times of upheaval in your own personal life. Beware especially of wanting to seem attractive to your clients in the absence of feeling attractive to your own partner, friends or family. If you find strong sexual feelings intruding into your coaching, it is time to end the relationship.

In any professional relationship, there may be other possibilities for the exploitation of trust. So there are doctors, lawyers and accountants who steal from their clients or who exploit a lonely client's need for friendship by persuading them to make bequests. Where the professional concerned has acted out of veniality, they are rightly punished. All of this is less likely in coaching where the relationships are more commonly short and finite.

Note that a client may also abuse a coach. This is even rarer than a coach abusing a client. However, it is possible. Just occasionally you may encounter clients whose distress is overpowering and where the coach becomes the target. One colleague describes such a client:

Anna

Anna arrived for her session with the stated aim of getting coaching on finding a new job. She spent most of the first hour crying, telling me that her life was a mess and that she was sure I couldn't help her. As she warmed to her theme of how I couldn't help her she became angry and agitated, shouting at me, telling me that my fees were outrageous, her employer was mad to pay them, and that I was enjoying the spectacle of seeing her cry just as everyone else in her life had done. I assured her that I was not enjoying it, suggested we stop the session if she was finding it distressing, but also offering to carry on once the initial storm had passed. I realized afterwards that I was receiving the displaced vengeance from years of disappointment and sadness. I was probably the first ever target of her rage who just sat still without retaliating.

An American contact once described the ultimate horror: being stalked. The client in this case, through her own well-thought-through decision in work with her coach, had ended her partner relationship. The rejected partner had stalked the coach, blaming her for the decision. Ultimately this man plea-bargained his way to five years on probation and supervised medication, but only after subjecting the coach to over a year of terrifying threats. Clear breaches of the law should always be reported to the police.

The saving grace in coaching, and the reason abuse is bound to be so much rarer, is that the power is so much more evenly balanced. Our clients do not come to us for healing and are therefore less likely to regard us with the awe that could lead to abuse on the part of the coach.

Can we do harm?

If we believe in the power of the coaching relationship, then it may follow that we may be able to harm our clients. A lot of coaches worry about this, but is this worry justified? We may waste a client's time. We may bore clients. We may annoy them. We may deluge them with unwanted and inappropriate advice. We may do embarrassingly poor coaching, but real, lasting injury? There is a case for saying that the psychological frailty of clients, whether for therapy or for coaching, is greatly exaggerated. Indeed, it may also be exaggerated by clients. If part of your way of staying stuck is to erect a mighty wall around yourself labelled, 'keep off – fragile', then this may be an extremely skilled way of manipulating the world around you to ensure that your self-protective delusions and fantasies remain intact. In fact, the client may be tougher than the coach. If you give in to such apparent fragility, you may in effect be handing control of the session entirely to the client.

It is easy to believe so profoundly in the power of coaching that we over-estimate both its power to do good and to do harm. We can only ever work within the limits of the material that clients are willing to give us. Similarly, we work with clients at their own unique stages of their life journeys and with whatever skills we have at that particular time.

In practice, the harm from coaching is more likely to come from unwitting or careless betrayal of confidentiality (for instance, letting slip that you are coaching a client who has asked you to keep this information to yourself, or making disparaging comments about the client's organization) – easy enough to do – rather than from the psychological harm that coaches tend to worry about so much.

Can a client become a friend?

Just occasionally a client may become a friend. Clients are often pulled to us and we to them because there is some essential like-mindedness. With coaching becoming increasingly specialized, this will be even more likely. As coaches we operate most successfully, in the business sense, in the worlds we understand from our own past experience. This is where our networks, contacts and expertise are rooted and this is what gives us credibility with our clients. All of this makes it more probable that some of our clients will be drawn to us because they have a lot in common with us psychologically and by history.

Signs that a client might become a friend include events where the motivation is to spend social time with the person because you like them for themselves, not because it might enhance the business relationship, so this might include: playing sociable games like squash, golf or tennis; sending or receiving a birthday, Christmas or condolence card; sharing gossipy emails which have nothing to do with the coaching; going to major sporting, cultural or other events purely for fun, not because it is 'corporate entertaining'; attending Christmas or leaving parties and weddings.

I have done all of the above with some clients, and enjoyed it. But when this becomes the dominant pattern, you cannot be a coach to that person. They have crossed the line from client to friend. Friendship is a coach-free zone, just as family is. Coaching is about outcomes, learning and change. The client pays for the empathetic objectivity that the coach provides. None of this is true of friendship. When I am with friends I am off duty as a coach – it's what I do all day; I don't want to do it in my leisure time and I hope my friends do not expect it of me. However, rules are sometimes difficult to follow and I bend them frequently. As I write this, I have just entered a date in my calendar to see a former client, now friend, who has persuaded me to give her a one-off session. This woman has generously acted as advocate for me over the years we have known each other, referring dozens of her colleagues to me. In saying yes, I have already reminded her of this, have told her that we will have the session at my apartment and end with a nice glass of wine. She has made it clear that she expects to pay the going rate, but I will not, of course, be charging her for the session, though I may demand a pleasant dinner somewhere that we might both enjoy as my 'payment'.

In general, coaches are less fretful about these boundary issues than therapists. However, we are in grey territory here. As coaching continues, sometimes off and on over several years and through a variety of jobs, you and your client will get to know each other well. Bear in mind that you will probably know the client a lot better than he or she knows you and in fact one sign that it has passed into a friendship is the point where you find yourself disclosing personal feelings and circumstances to a client. But even where this is not the case, real spark, real liking, playfulness, grace, trust . . . all these are likely to grow. There will be a closeness which is unlike the relationship you had at the outset. This was forcibly brought home to me with a distinguished woman client with whom I had worked on and off for five years. I had been well acquainted during this time with her struggles to survive her cancer long enough to enjoy her rich personal life and to get her organization back on track. The news of her sudden death was shocking, though thoughtfully conveyed to me by her deputy before I could be taken by surprise through reading of it in the next morning's newspapers. At her memorial event, attended by about a thousand people, I felt overwhelmed with sadness during the skilfully put-together video tribute made by her colleagues. I still think of her often with a pang of loss and feel privileged to have known such a remarkable woman.

When it is unequivocally clear that a client has become a friend, it is best to draw attention to what has happened and to explain why the coaching relationship cannot continue, rounding it off gracefully. In practice, it is unlikely that the client-friend will want to continue and a bigger danger is that the coaching will just peter out. If there is still a need for coaching, you might want to make a recommendation about another coach, but of course the decision rests with the client. Be chivalrous about your replacement. Don't ask about the coaching and do control any irrational twinges of jealousy you may feel about your successor.

Dependency

Some coaches worry a lot about the possibility of client dependency. Maybe they have been affected by tales of clients who develop unhealthy reliance on their therapists. Possibly, as with so many themes in therapy, this concern goes back to the early days of psychoanalysis where patients were expected to attend hour-long sessions several times a week. The signs to look out for are these: constant pressing for advice, referring every decision big or small to you, exaggerated deference to the coach's view, pushing boundaries by trying to convert the coach to becoming a friend, wanting extra sessions when there is no apparent agenda. All of this is extremely unlikely in coaching. Coaching is not about *curing* or *fixing*, nor, generally speaking, is it about advice-giving or interpreting. It is overtly a relationship between equals. It is not cheap and most clients will have to justify how this expenditure adds value, even if only to a sceptical spouse.

In practice, you might turn this concern on its head by saying that there is everything to be said for healthily close relationships between coaches and clients because this roots it in emotional connection, the only way real change is likely to happen through coaching. I positively encourage contact between sessions by email, text and phone to keep the momentum going. Doing this makes the work so much more productive and enjoyable and does not create dependency. I have never taken an egg-timer approach to my work. On the contrary, I have assumed that for every client who gets time they have not paid for, there will be one who pays for time they never use. I expect clients to play their part in managing our relationship, and by and large they do.

Endings

Coaching is expensive, and most coaching programmes will be limited by what the organization or individual can afford – often no more than six two-hour sessions. How should a coaching programme end? Some coaches find that the client does not take up their full quota of pre-paid sessions. When this happens, coaches can feel guilty and rejected. Where the coach wishes to end the coaching but the client wants to carry on, the client may feel cast aside and hurt. Clients may also feel uncomfortable where they do not really need or wish to carry on, but do so out of fear that they may hurt the coach's feelings. Sometimes both coach and client may continue to meet when both would really like to stop – so, in this way, both end up doing what neither really wants.

Coaching relationships are like all others: they have a natural arc. Often this means a tentative beginning, a period of intensity and then a period of decline. The decline is sometimes hard to acknowledge. It may happen because the client has found solutions to everything they have brought you, or because you have lost interest in them and their issues, or because the client has learnt everything they can from you. Where you sense that you have reached a full stop, always raise it. The client may or may not be prepared to be honest with you.

Roger

Roger claimed to be a highly self-aware person, but he had received what he saw as a crushing disappointment in his career. He had already worked with two other coaches and a therapist. He had told me mournfully that he was not a rich man, and although he had found the therapy helpful he had not been able to afford to continue paying his therapist for the weekly sessions. (Our programme was being funded by his organization.) With the benefit of hindsight I should have taken a lot more time than I did to explore his previous experience of both coaching and therapy. After four sessions of frustration and a strong feeling of no progress, I eventually challenged him and said: Roger, I've reached the end of what I think I can do. We keep coming back to the same point where you seem to be trying to rewrite your history. I think we ought to stop.

'Funny you should say that', said Roger. And then, in a moment of real candour, 'I got to exactly the same stage with Lucy [his therapist] and she told me that unless I was prepared to stop "sitting in my own shit", as she put it, she couldn't go on with me.' I asked him: 'So are you prepared to stop sitting in your own shit?' He replied: Yes, yes, and I'm finding these sessions really helpful.'

I felt rather dubious, but we made another date. Roger failed to show. When I called his office he was apologetic: I'm terribly sorry, I completely forgot about it.'

I told him to call me again when he was ready. He never did.

Another client, whose presenting issues were around how to develop as a leader in his financial services company, set a date with me but cancelled it at extremely short notice, then agreed another which was also cancelled. Then there was silence. My two or three enquiring emails and voicemails were stoutly ignored. It nagged at me. It was unsatisfactory: was it me? Had something major happened in his life? But if so, what? Discreet enquiries among his colleagues led to a dead end. After a while I forgot him. Three years later, I had a call from a senior HR person in his firm based in the US where he was now working. The question was, could I recommend another coach for this man? I took the opportunity to ask if she knew why he had given up on me. 'Ah yes', she said. 'You raised the question of what he might want to do as an alternative to his career with us and he simply couldn't cope with it. He freaked. He'd always assumed till that moment that it was a career for life.' I could never have guessed that what to me was such an innocent question could have had this major effect, and clearly I had not built sufficient trust with this client for him to be honest with me. I wondered how I might have spotted the problem and dealt with it more effectively. For instance, did I take my own advice about probing for feedback at the end of the session in question?

Sometimes the client simply outgrows the coach. This may be partly thanks to your excellent coaching, or because the client has benefitted from other opportunities for rapid personal development. When this happens, it is possible to be taken by surprise, as described here by a colleague, an experienced and respected coach:

> I had worked with Elisabeta for three years, seeing her zoom up the hierarchy in her global tech company. It was enjoyable and also lucrative work and I felt pride in having been some part of her success in such a well-known company. She was always warm and appreciative: it was a delight to work with her. However, on my way to what turned out to be our final session I felt a sense of dread and foreboding – I was not looking forward to it. What a pity I was not more honest with myself about what was going on here.
>
> We had ten minutes of rather formal catch-up chat, mostly about her family, and then Elisabeta told me that she and her company had found her a new coach as part of her promotion to a yet more senior level. She was gracious, she was straightforward. She presented me with a beautiful gift to mark the ending of our work and as a token of how much she had valued it. I was being fired! Did I feel awkward and disappointed? Yes, of course. Did I feel relieved? Yes, very. I knew perfectly well that I had offered her everything I could and that she needed to move on. I was so glad that she had told me face-to-face and had not taken the easy option of email or of just letting the whole thing slide through lack of contact. This was especially so as one of her constant themes in the coaching had been how to be appropriately assertive. As she was dismissing me I couldn't help admiring how very skilfully she was doing it!

Where, as in this story, you are involved in a running engagement – for instance, contracted by the year – it helps to agree an initial set of sessions with a review halfway through, matched by an invoice point. The review will include the mutual opportunity to assess:

- How far have you got towards reaching your goals?
- What tangible evidence is there that there is change in your life?
- How are you and I doing in our coaching relationship?
- How much more coaching do you feel you would find useful?

You may find that clients frequently return when they have new jobs or challenges, or email with their news sometimes years after the formal coaching has finished. However, you may like to mark the final session of any one stage

)king clients to think back to the issues they initially presented and to
at what has changed, including any feedback that they have solicited
from colleagues. It helps to ask for their feedback on the coaching process
and on you:

- What were the real high spots for you?
- What learning would you say you have done?
- What has permanently changed for you?
- What would you advise me to go on doing, adapt and change in my coaching?

Where the coaching has begun with a three-cornered process involving the line manager, repeating the process is another way to round it off (see Chapter 7 for more on this). After that session I will normally email clients with a friendly note, expressing the hope that they will keep in touch. In general, managing and marking the ending is a lot better for both sides than letting it peter out.

4   Brain-wise

As a keen filmgoer, I have noticed the way sci-fi films have changed. Gone are the spaceships, ray guns and green-faced aliens with funny-shaped heads. Instead we have movies where the focus is the human brain. The plots involve creating multiple perspectives, the blurring of dream with apparent reality, the suggestion that thought alone can alter events – and much more. At one level, these films may appear to be mimicking video games. At another, they reflect the rapidly expanding field of neuropsychology. Being able to look into a living brain with functional magnetic resonance imaging (fMRI) scanners has overturned so many of our previous assumptions about how our brains work. Just like the actual themes of these more recent sci-fi films, the questions raised are profound: What does individual identity mean? What is 'reality'? What is human consciousness? How is the mind different from the brain? How far can one human being permanently change the thought processes of another, whether for good or evil?

This chapter summarizes some of the current themes and ideas relevant to coaching about the human brain, but this is now a huge and expanding field and all of the books I reference here are worth reading for the much more detailed treatment they give.

Why coaches need to know about neuropsychology

As coaches we need to have at least some understanding of this material because it is one of the most important recent developments in our field. Overall, the message is that there is a biological basis to human psychology. Our role as coaches is to work with people on the choices and changes that will make a difference to their lives. What the neuropsychological research shows without any shadow of doubt is that emotion drives human behaviour. If we don't understand this, we will work with clients on the assumption that choices are rational, so we will get agreement intellectually, but no profound change will happen. The research also demonstrates that it is safer for the human brain to do what it has always done – 'This has worked so far, so why change anything?' Clarifying and working on the intention to change is an *emotional* not a rational process. The work of the brain is to rationalize, not to be rational, as so many people believe. Good coaching grounds itself in the limbic system, the emotional centre of the brain. This means that erything – and I mean everything – in coaching involves emotion, including the relationship between client and coach. It is why creating a relationship of mutual warmth, acceptance and liking is so very important because without it both we and our clients will be role playing change rather than truly working on it. Warmth, acceptance and liking create trust. Without it, coaching is impossible.

Emotionally-based behaviour has powerful links with coaching. It begins to give proof of much that coaches have previously asserted based on experience and intuition. The same principles will save us from wasting our own and our clients' time with techniques and approaches that are unlikely to work, as well as suggesting many that possibly we underuse or fail to use at all. Bear in mind, too, that we need to know about these principles because they apply every bit as much to ourselves.

The emotional brain

We have named our own species *Homo sapiens* (thinking/wise man), but emotion has far more impact on our lives and in our decision-making than this self-flattering label might suggest. Emotion precedes thought. All our important decisions (whether to marry, buy a house, have a child, change jobs . . .) are made on a feelings basis and later justified with rationality. We can try to suppress emotion, but it will resurface one way or another.

The explanation lies in how the human brain evolved. Like other animals, the so-called 'snake-brain', the brain stem (because even reptiles have it) came first in evolutionary terms. This controls breathing and heartbeat. Then came the limbic system, the emotional centre of the brain. It is responsible for two powerful tools: learning and memory. These allowed all mammals to start forming relationships and so to be able to care for their young as well as to refine their responses to danger, thus increasing their capacity for survival. So for human beings, the capacity to learn would mean avoiding danger another time.

About a million years ago, the brains of mammals, including early humans, added an extra layer of brain cells: *the neocortex*. In *Homo sapiens*, emerging around 200,000 years ago, the neocortex is many times larger than in any other land-dwelling species. This is what makes us so distinctly human. The neocortex is the centre of thinking and allows us to synthesize our ideas. It enables us to do long-term planning and strategizing and to weigh up one path against another. It has also enabled us to nuance our emotional responses. As you go up the evolutionary scale, the sheer mass of the neocortex increases and so does the mass of connections to others parts of the brain circuitry. There is more prefrontal cortex connection to the limbic system in humans than in any other species, which is why we are able to display so many more emotions and so much more subtly than other mammals. The emotional brain is around 100 million years old, but cognition is a youngster by comparison. Contrary to what we like to assume, cognition is the servant of emotion, not its master.

Every single human being interprets the world from an internal perspective. There is no such thing as 'objective reality'. External circumstances are far less important than how we interpret them: some researchers believe that external events are responsible for as little as 10 per cent of our feelings of well-being. It is our internal – and emotional – 'map of the world' which influences us. This is why *reframing* is so important in coaching: the stories we tell ourselves are what influence our mood and behaviour.

The importance of the amygdala

The amygdala (pronounced am–*ig*-dalla) consists of two small almond-shaped parts of the limbic system. It is the brain's alarm system, controlling the fight, flight or freeze response. It also stores memories of previous situations which have aroused strongly negative emotion. When faced with anything that we perceive to be dangerous or difficult, the amygdala sends the stress hormone cortisol to close down the higher brain functions of the prefrontal lobes and diverts all available energy to the back of the brain: the part that prepares us for action in an emergency. So brain functions unnecessary for fighting or fleeing are shut down, and less glucose and oxygen is available for intellectual processing, including memory. The tendency is to generalize, to make more sweeping assertions and to revert to linear rather than to creative ideas. The amygdala is also responsible for phobic reactions which typically resist rational analysis, and for our inability to think clearly when under stress. Because it stores all our negative memories this is why childhood experiences have such a powerful impact, even if we have forgotten the specific circumstances. The 'away-from' approach – that is, resisting change because it is seen as 'dangerous' – is more powerful than the 'going-to', reward-response. The perceived risk that the new may be horrible is often overwhelming, therefore we may prefer the familiar discomfort of the present. Knowing how deep-rooted our commitment to the present is, even when it is painful, is a sobering reminder for any coach of the importance of being realistic in our ambitions for coaching our clients.

Anyone who has felt panic in a job interview will recognize the impact of amygdala activity: even the simplest question cannot be answered, words disappear, you have an overwhelming wish to run away and hide; later on, memory of the event is blurred. So *danger* can mean symbolic danger such as giving a presentation, sitting an exam, or meeting new people. It can also include hearing an opinion we perceive as an attack, so *amygdala attack* or *hijack* can easily happen in a coaching session – for instance, being given advice clumsily or being confronted aggressively will mean that the client is not able to bring the prefrontal area of the brain into play. This justifies why heavy-handed advice-giving is so counterproductive in coaching. The client can no longer think rationally because all his or her energy is absorbed in the indignation of feeling patronized, misunderstood and generally not heard.

The prefrontal cortex

This part of the brain controls activities such as planning, reasoning, speech, empathic communication, insight and moral awareness. The neocortex can integrate emotions and experience, responding to signals from the mid-brain. It can generate positive, optimistic mood. Activity in this region of the brain can mean we can reassess emotional responses, reconsidering the nature of whatever the danger is and therefore control aggression or other impulsive behaviour by meeting such emotion with positive rational argument. The prefrontal regions of the brain make us capable of identifying the split second between emotional stimulus and response. The right prefrontal lobes seem to be the seat of negative emotions such as fear and aggression. In studies of stroke patients with lesions in the left prefrontal cortex, these patients were much more prone to catastrophic worries about their futures.

Human beings can often be puzzled, shamed and alarmed by the behaviour which the limbic system triggers, let alone having any idea about how to change it. I have found that just explaining some of the simple facts of brain functioning to clients can have considerable impact. I also show them the brilliant free app, *The 3-D Brain*, whose clear visuals bring the whole thing alive.

Gil

Gil was a chief executive who fizzed with energy, intelligence and optimism. Appointing a director of operations altered the dynamic of his senior team and, at the time he asked me to work with him, he felt it had changed dramatically for the worse. 'This man is stubborn and won't listen and I no longer trust his judgement', he said. There had been three events where a professional disagreement had become an argument and had then quickly deteriorated into a shouting match, though as Gil admitted, he had done most of the shouting. 'A blinding rage came down on me and I was dimly aware that I was pounding the table.' On one such occasion two secretaries had come running in from their office outside to check that Gil was not actually physically attacking his colleague. (He wasn't.)

Gil's amygdala had 'fired', and he had given way to frustration then anger. These feelings had engulfed him, something he admitted had happened far too often in his life. Cortisol had flooded his prefrontal brain, disabling his usual rational decision-making processes. He did not need me to tell him that such behaviour was highly inappropriate, laying him open to accusations of bullying. Like many other clients, Gil sought help on how to change someone else (the colleague) but soon realized that to have any chance of doing this, he had to change himself first.

Teaching a client like Gil how the amygdala, and the limbic system generally, works can be a first step to controlling it. I often draw this diagram for clients:

Stimulus ⟹ Response

Figure 4.1 Simple stimulus – response

This is how we will describe our emotional reactions in situations where we have behaved impulsively. The response has felt as if it has a life of its own. Thought has apparently not come into it – and indeed it has not.

A better way of functioning is as follows, all of which can happen in a few microseconds:

Stimulus ⟹ Thinking ⟹ Decision ⟹ Response

Figure 4.2 More considered stimulus – response

The more aware you are of how your limbic system works, the more likely it is that there will be at least a fleeting moment of thinking between the stress stimulus and your response. In fact, even the traditional *counting to ten* will work. Saying to yourself, 'I am not physically under attack here and I can keep my prefrontal cortex working' can transform your chances of this happening.

I asked Gil to monitor his emotional reactions on a daily basis for a week, using a tiny notebook to jot down any insights he had into which types of challenge created what types of reaction in him. Here is part of an email he sent me some months later when our coaching programme was nearing its end:

> I soon saw the pattern. The problems were always with men who are peers. If they challenged me in a particular way I saw it as a threat to my status and sense of myself as powerful and competent. After a week of keeping that miniature diary I began to be able to forecast exactly what I needed to watch out for. After that, practising a new kind of response with you made all the difference.

What is happening here is that bringing awareness into play means that part of our middle prefrontal circuits, the uncinate fasciculus, releases neurotransmitters that calm down the amygdala. The cortical area can also release a peptide known as GABA – short for gamma-aminobutyric acid – which, it seems, can override the activity of the limbic region.

These tactics will also work with clients who describe many other types of situation where the amygdala is doing its work. Examples given to me on a weekly basis by my clients include: high levels of generalized anxiety about work, especially in a climate of unpredictable change; worries about facing a difficult meeting; giving tough feedback to a subordinate; giving a presentation at a conference. Gil's story also shows that simply naming an emotion can help release its grip on us. This is because the process of naming comes, again, from the prefrontal areas of the brain and will help the prefrontal cortex do its work of acting as a brake on the activity of the limbic system. So being able to say, 'I am frightened here because I feel I might make a fool of myself', or 'I am angry because this colleague is threatening my self-esteem' is in itself a way of short-circuiting the emotion.

'Journalling'

Writing down your feelings and thoughts about troubling events has also been shown to be effective in creating improvements at a physiological as well as at a subjective level, as it was with Gil, and perhaps for the same reason, that in writing your feelings down and naming them you are acting as a reporter on your own life. This creates some beneficial dissociation. One research project demonstrated that this remained true even when the writer never reread what they had written or showed their jottings to someone else.

Natalia

Natalia was a senior lawyer working for a high-profile City of London law firm. In our first session it emerged that a year previously Natalia had made a serious error of judgement for which she had been reprimanded by her professional body, the Law Society. She had defended herself feistily, had been supported by her firm and was allowed to continue to practise.

At the time I worked with her, the whole incident still haunted her, intruding into her dreams and creating irrational anxiety about inadvertently repeating the error. Telling herself that this was 'silly' was not helping. She had already told me that what troubled her was the knowledge that she had damaged the emotional well-being and finances of her client. I asked her what name she would give to the feelings that were bothering her. There was a long pause where, as she told me later, she was weighing up whether she could bring herself to utter the words. These were, 'I am deeply ashamed of what I did. Even though there was nothing criminal in it, it was just a lapse of judgement, but yes, the emotions are shame and guilt.'

In public Natalia had had to remain self-confident and composed. She had never been properly able to express remorse. I encouraged Natalia to write a private account of the whole episode, including her feelings and her reflections on her learning, and to add to it whenever she felt there was something further to consider. Without any extra input from me, she named it her 'self-forgiveness diary', a document I never saw. Natalia continued her legal career and set up her own firm, something she has done with success.

How we fool ourselves: Systems 1 and 2

Consider this simple problem. Don't pause too long:

> A bat and ball together cost £1.10
> The bat costs £1 more than the ball
> How much does the ball cost?

The Nobel prizewinning author Daniel Kahnemann gives this puzzle in his book *Thinking, Fast and Slow* (2012), the culmination of a lifetime's work on human thinking. I tried it recently at a conference of coaches, asking people to jot down the answer. Around 75 per cent of my audience had written down 10 p. This is wrong. The correct answer is 5 p.[1]

The central premise of *Thinking, Fast and Slow* is that human beings have two systems for thought. These are theoretical not actual physical systems. One is *System 1*: intuitive, fast, associative, emotional and is always on duty. Its role is to jump to conclusions. Most often, System 1 gets it right because it is shaped by experience, instinctively attuned to subtle shifts and changes in its environment. As Kahnemann says, 'it is the origin of most of what we do right' and it is rare for it to be dumbfounded. If you gave 10 p as your answer to the puzzle above, you were deploying System 1. *System 2* only takes over when it is clear that System 1 has got it wrong. In brain terms System 2 is slow, uses a great deal more precious brain energy, believes itself to be in charge when mostly it is not, reluctantly does statistical calculations and effortfully concentrates on rational processes. What is 4 x 4?

Easy, System 1 gets the answer in a trice. But how about 131 x 47? That is going to take a lot more effort – and brain energy. Thousands of experiments have shown how easily we operate on System 1, only seeing what we want to see, failing to spot all the biases that social psychologists have so helpfully named for us: *confirmation bias, hindsight bias, the halo effect, the Hawthorne Effect, outcome bias* – and many others. We believe what we want to believe – so, for instance, as one of many such experiments showed, if we believe a pain-relieving pill costs $2.50 per dose, we will attribute more pain-relieving power to it than if we believe it costs a mere 10 cents, even though in both cases the 'pain reliever' was actually plain old vitamin C.

We don't see what we don't expect to see and ignore patent evidence to the contrary – *confirmation bias*. If you have never tried or heard of The Gorilla Experiment, try it now by going to www.theinvisiblegorilla.com/videos.html. So, for instance, to quote just one of many such investigations, judges, people whose job it is to be rational, turn out to be influenced more by their blood sugar levels than by the facts, making harsher parole decisions depending on whether it was just before or just after lunch. You may want to believe that people paid to manage a stock portfolio know what they are doing, but in fact their performance is no better than could be achieved by chance or by doing nothing. We hugely underrate how chance influences our lives, so managers attribute the good luck of being in the right place at the right time to their amazing skills, when really events were most probably shaped by events over which they had no control. Similarly, we assume that the future will look like the past – we cannot cope with what Kahnemann calls *Known Unknowns* and even less with *Unknown Unknowns*. We are more optimistic than logic would suggest, so we wildly overestimate the benefits of a project and underestimate the time and money it will take to complete. If, for instance, you have recently refurbished a kitchen, the chances are that you will have spent at least double your original estimate and that the whole project will have taken twice as long as you calculated: what Kahnemann calls the *Planning Fallacy* or delusional optimism. Essentially, Kahnemann argues, we don't know ourselves, we are astonishingly easily manipulated by factors that we just don't spot, we have irrational biases that we justify with phoney 'facts', and if we believe we are too clever to be affected by any of this, then we are plain wrong because we are all susceptible.

Generally speaking we do not spot the danger signals when System 1 is operating. Knowing the theory does not make us any the less likely to be unaware of entering a cognitive trap, but an observer, such as a coach, may be able to see what we do not. In every coaching session clients will bring decisions and dilemmas. System 1 will be operating for them and for us. The challenge is how to bring System 2 into play, for instance by spotting and challenging generalizations and flawed thinking patterns (pages 103 and 172) where the questions become:

- What am I/you ignoring here?
- Where might over-optimism be at play?
- How does this proposed course of action reflect my/your bias in one form or another?
- What alternative perspectives might there be?
- How will this look in a year's time? How important will it seem then?
- What are the known facts here that might complicate or change matters?
- What facts are missing that it might be useful to collect?

When a client tells me that they feel 'tired' at the end of a session, which I fondly take to be a compliment, I feel pleased: with luck it may be a sign that System 2 thinking has been deployed; but possibly, if Professor Kahnemann is right, luck might have had more to do with it than any of my own 'superpowers'.

Multitasking and time management

Many executive coaching clients have some kind of a problem with time management. Only a few decades ago, letters were hand-delivered, houses had one telephone and offices had what now seem like quaint landline systems. Goods were ordered by phone or on paper with a promise that they would be delivered within 28 days. A letter could be answered at leisure, and if you were not there to answer a phone call, then the caller had to wait. Today, emails pour in around the clock, friends, family, colleagues all expect instant answers to texts, customers order online and are impatient with waiting. Meetings are punctuated by its members brazenly checking their phones regardless of whether or not this looks rude, and it no longer surprises me when clients tell me that they take their phones to bed with them 'in case someone needs to call me'.

The trouble is that the human brain and nervous system have not evolved to keep up with this barrage. What so many of us try to do is 'multitasking', apparently handling several disparate tasks at once. But efficient multitasking turns out to be an illusion. As Daniel Levitin describes in his book *The Organized Mind* (2014), what we are actually doing is more like madly ineffectual plate spinning than expert juggling. The human brain does not cope well with divided attention, and what is happening is that we are increasing production of two stress hormones – cortisol and adrenaline – both involved in our fight/fight/freeze mechanism, thus creating an inability to think clearly. It seems also that multitasking feeds the attraction of the prefrontal cortex to the new, super-shiny and exciting, which in turn stimulates the production of the neurotransmitter dopamine, the brain's natural reward chemical. (So while I am typing this I am resisting the urge to check on what has happened to my Amazon order for a wearable fitness gadget and I've just heard the ping indicating that a new email has arrived: Wonder who it's from?) The brain works on oxygenated glucose. Forcing it to multitask rapidly burns up its natural fuel. No wonder we feel exhausted after a whole day of it.

Human energy is also governed by ultradian rhythms. One of several such systems in the human body, these are the daily ebbs and flows, for instance, of blood pressure and blood sugar. Overall, energy works in natural rhythms of 90 to 120 minutes, with peaks and troughs. Given the relentless demands of work life, many of my clients describe trying to work at the peak throughout the day, not realizing that this is biologically impossible. You can do it in an emergency, but not on a daily basis.

In working on managing these issues with clients, it helps to share this information with them. Most clients receive it as liberation: they are not 'weird' after all, and it is unlikely that any of their colleagues are any better designed to cope with it than they. Perhaps it is not chance that many of the organizations which demand most from the their staff, for instance Google, Pixar or Facebook, have playrooms, pleasant restaurants, gyms and other ways of enticing staff into recreation. Different solutions work for different people. This client, a busy account executive at an ad agency, describes his relief at making the firm decision to work in a different way:

> My coaching session was a breakthrough. I'd had no idea that I was fighting my brain! I had been feeling that I was going mad, often trying to work on four or even five tasks at once. I started paying attention to mental and bodily tiredness instead of ignoring it and I soon noticed the pattern of a drop in energy roughly every hour and a half. I now, come what may, take a physical break every hour by standing up, stretching and walking around; I go outside for a short walk at least once a day and I have an actual lunch break instead of mindlessly eating a snack at my desk. Jenny also introduced me to the Pomodoro Technique – a crazily simple idea where you divide your work into units of 25 minutes.[2] At first my colleagues had a lot fun at my expense on this but now I notice a lot of them are doing the same. I no longer feel tired. I do better work. I'm off that multitasking treadmill. I see now that I need to focus on managing my energy, not my time.

The SCARF model

One of the themes in neuropsychology is how much of our energy is concerned with basic survival needs that are as much emotionally as physically based. Human beings are social animals. We need to belong, we need approval. These needs to avoid social threat and to seek social reward appear to involve the same brain networks as those involved in physical survival. So, for instance, you are attacked by a mugger and you fear for your life. You are attacked by a colleague in a meeting and told you are incompetent. The brain responds to the physical or the psychological attack in the same way. It also seems that our brains are more finely tuned to see threat than to seek reward and that our need to protect ourselves from threat is never far from our minds, though perhaps not always at a conscious level. The research is summarized by the writer David Rock in the paper (2008) where he also describes his useful model based on the acronym SCARF, standing for Status, Certainty, Autonomy, Relatedness, Fairness: basic needs and motivators.

Status: We need to feel as good as or better than others. We need to know where we stand in the pecking order and the smallest threat to status can trigger uncontrollable emotional responses. So, for instance, I have lost count of the number of times clients have described disproportionately heated wranglings over box-ratings in performance appraisals. 'I marked myself at 4, but my boss marked me at 2! He can go xxxx himself if he thinks I'll ever put myself out for him again!' Being offered feedback of any sort can also create threat to status, which is why when we do it in the coaching room we need to do it so very skilfully (see page 190). Promotion is a status reward and the need for it can explain why clients will often fight to get a job where the monetary reward is insignificant, but the job title apparently bestows increased status.

Possible differences in status are at work in any coaching conversation. *Is this client more or less senior than me? Can I really challenge a client who is older than I am?* It can work the other way around too: a client may worry that a coach is either too inexperienced or too young (lower status) or too experienced (higher status) than they are.

Certainty: We like certainty. Familiarity is comforting. If we have to weigh up every situation on the basis of ambiguity, we will have to engage the precious resources of the prefrontal areas. This is exhausting so we try to avoid it. In situations of uncertainty we become preoccupied until we can create certainty again. Unfortunately uncertainty is a pervading feature of organizational life: *Will there be a take-over? Will work be outsourced to India? How many job cuts will there be? Is my own future at risk?* This need for certainty may also reinforce the importance of clear goal-setting in every session because the process of setting a goal reduces uncertainty.

Autonomy: Many years of organizational research have shown correlations between physical and mental health and the degree of autonomy people have in their work. This is why an inability to delegate, essentially an exercise in giving others autonomy, can mean that a managerial client gets mediocre results from their team members and why it is worth working with such clients to help them learn how to delegate more effectively.

Autonomy needs to be respected in coaching relationships and is yet another reason why advice-giving is so perilous. Even when giving a client some of the vital information which they need in order to come to a decision, emphasize that you know it is the client who has to make the decision and live with the result. 'Here's the information – but it's up to you how you use it. What do you think?'

Relatedness: We are herd animals and cannot live alone. Survival in our earliest years of existence as a species must have depended critically on knowing instantly who was a stranger and might therefore be a threat to the life of the tribe. *Am I in or am I out?* To be banished is the worst possible punishment for human beings, short of death. It frequently lies behind the tragedy of teenage suicide and also behind the rapid descent into ill health and depression of people who describe themselves as chronically lonely. The need to belong rubs directly against our need for autonomy and the majority of us will barter at least some autonomy for the sake of feeling accepted by others. In coaching, everything we do is about relatedness. If we do not feel a bond with the client we cannot work with them. It is the essence of why coaching works. *Are we alike enough to work together, for instance sharing similar values? Does this client accept and like me? Do I accept and like him or her?* If the answer to any of these questions is *no* on either side, then the coaching will come to a rapid close.

Fairness: Perceived unfairness creates resentment and anger: a threat response. Unfortunately organizational life abounds with obvious unfairnesses. For instance, low morale in an organization can often be traced directly to the enormous gap between the salaries of extremely well-rewarded senior managers and the meagre wages of their workforce. Managers who devise 'values statements' and then demonstrate contempt for them in their own behaviour, a boss who has favourites or who resources one department more favourably than another, a foreign owner who abruptly closes down an entire factory – all of these will generate a similar response.

In practice, all the emotional elements that are triggered by SCARF needs (or threats) may be present at once, something that can explain the extremity of response in clients

Elizabeth

Elizabeth had worked successfully for the same organization for 30 years. She had to compete for a job in a reorganization. The job went to a younger rival with considerably less experience Elizabeth was made redundant on terms that she found ungenerous and disappointing. The decision had been made by a colleague whom she had regarded as a friend, so the betrayal felt overwhelming. She was full of vigour and energy and needed to earn a living, but knew that at 58 it could be difficult to fight age prejudice and to find a new job.

At her first coaching session she was trembling with anger at how she had been treated. She kept returning worriedly to how she was going to pay her mortgage and voiced her shock at what felt like the duplicity of her colleague. Sleepless nights had become the norm. Would she have to sell her house? How would she talk about her departure to people who had been her peers and juniors? Would her marriage survive all the changes? Would her health hold up?

In Elizabeth's case, her sense of herself as a senior and respected person was threatened – she felt she had lost status in her own and others' eyes. She faced an uncertain future in the job market and did not know if she would be able to pay her mortgage and keep her house. The decision infringed her autonomy because it had been made by someone else. Her need for relatedness was compromised – she would no longer be part of the team and she felt the 'betrayal' by the former friend keenly. Finally, the decision felt unfair because a person with significantly less experience had been appointed, leading Elizabeth to conclude that the whole selection process had been a *set-up*. Explaining the SCARF model to Elizabeth was immediately helpful. It turned what had felt like a hurtful and shaming personal experience into something that made sense as a biological as well as a social phenomenon. Her view was that it significantly shortened the adjustment time.

You can also use the SCARF model with clients when it comes to making new decisions. When Elizabeth was playing with ideas of establishing a portfolio career I drew a blank grid on a flip chart, like this:[3]

Categories	Status	Certainty	Autonomy	Relatedness	Fairness
Pluses? (rewards)					
Minuses? (threats)					

As I asked her questions around each, she filled in the boxes. I have found this far better than simply making a freestyle list of pluses and minuses, not least because it acknowledges that it is powerful emotions and the strong needs and drivers that lie beneath them that make up our minds, not lists based on logic.

Imagined experiences are virtually as powerful as the 'real' experience

The power of human imagination is awesome. This can be a plus or a minus. The brain does not seem to make much distinction between a remembered or imagined experience and the actual experience. On the positive side, it is why visualization of a peaceful scene can calm the amygdala down, or why recalling a success can precondition us to repeat it.

One intriguing experiment demonstrates that this is no trivial feat. In his book *The Brian that Changes Itself* (2007), Norman Doidge describes an experiment where mental rehearsal was shown to be virtually as effective as the real thing. Two matched groups of total beginners were taught to play the piano. One group practised with a real keyboard. The other group sat in front of the keyboard and imagined playing the pieces, including hearing the sounds and moving their fingers. Both groups devoted two hours a day to this activity. The group that did the actual practice were slightly – but only slightly – ahead of the other group when both were assessed, but when given one session of actual practice, the mental rehearsal group did just as well. The success of the British cycling team in the Olympics and other international competitions is attributed by them and others to the coaching they had from the medical doctor and sports psychologist, Steve Peters, who describes these and other techniques in his book *The Chimp Paradox* (2012).

Neuroplasticity

It used to be thought that our brains had a fixed number of cells which declined in number over the years, making new learning difficult. This turns out to be misleading. The brain is 'plastic' and is able to make new connections at any time, a concept that is described as neuroplasticity. Focusing energy and intention can change the brain. Its physical shape will evolve in response to how it is used. So, for instance, violinists often have a hugely expanded cortical region in the area of the brain that governs use of the left hand (involved in fingering). A friend who studied for three gruelling years to become a London cab driver would certainly endorse the enormity of the task involved in *The Knowledge*, the exam that London taxi drivers have to pass to be licensed, and would not be surprised to learn that the hippocampi (memory centres) of professional taxi drivers can be enlarged because they have had to work so hard to remember a vast mass of spatial detail. In both these examples *intention* is important: the changes have happened as a result of practice, commitment and hard work.

The best way to change behaviour is not to work on what is 'wrong' but to develop new behaviours, creating new neural pathways which can, over a period of time, become dominant. So, for instance, for people who suffer from obsessive compulsive disorder (OCD), rather than teaching them to confront the behaviours which trouble them, it has proved far more successful to teach them how to interrupt the thought. For more on this see *Brain Lock*, by Jeffrey Schwartz (1996).

Overcoming old habits

Now let's suppose that you want to learn a new way of overcoming an old habit, something that is getting in the way for you. Typical examples might be reaching too readily for that evening glass of wine, worrying about how to deal with a particular colleague at a meeting, being unable to delegate a task, or staying late at the office despite being too tired to work.

Yes, the human brain is plastic: it can go on making new connections indefinitely. But as the reverse side of this strength, the more we reinforce a habit, the harder it is to change. One of the best ways to do this is through mental rehearsal. Constant rehearsal of the imagined better way can make it much easier to change behaviour. Technically what is happening is that you are growing new connections (synpases) between the neurons in your brain, including strengthening the myelin sheaths that reinforce the pathways.

Follow these steps first.

1 **The goal**
    What is it you want to change? This should be stated in the positive and in the present tense – i.e. as if it is already happening – and should be as specific as possible.
    So don't say: *I want to avoid staying at the office late every day* (a vague statement and a negative, so the brain will just remember the words *stay* and *office*, thus reinforcing the very thing you want not to do).
    Do say: *I leave the office every day at 6pm with a light heart.*

2 **Triggers**
    What triggers the problem? Think about how you want to respond differently.

e.g. *I see the last emails coming in and I know I can deal with them tomorrow.*

3 **Thoughts and feelings**
Think about what thoughts and feelings you will have in your mind when faced with the problem-stimulus.
I am calm and accept that it is fine for the emails to wait.

4 **Imagining your actions**
Think about what you will be doing – imagine it in detail.
I get my things together, say goodnight to colleagues and walk out calmly to the car park, looking forward to a pleasant evening.

5 **The benefits**
Think about the benefits doing all of this will bring you.
I am proud of myself, calm and energized, enjoying my feelings of freedom.

Now rehearse all this in your mind making it a smooth sequence. See yourself doing the actions, hear any sounds, experience any feelings.

Now rehearse it again and again. Do at least ten mental rehearsals a day.

Here is the account of how one client got on with this technique:

Vanessa

My problem was my overwhelming sense of duty about my to-do list. It was creating problems with my husband who saw me continually putting my professional and domestic tasks over my relationship with him. I was also constantly tired, harassed and irritable.

I talked it through with my coach first and agreed that my goal was to release at least an hour of relaxation a day just for me. I learnt some mindfulness techniques and then set aside time to do mental rehearsals of the new routine. Of course, this in itself became a 'task' on my to-do list but that was OK. I quickly got to enjoy my rehearsals and realized that just doing them was something I was looking forward to. The remarkable thing was that, within a few days of practising, I found that I was going home at 6 pm instead of 7.30 pm, that I was not switching on my laptop at home, kept Saturday totally free and that somehow I was already doing the very thing I had wanted for such a long time.

In reading this account, you should note that I combined showing Vanessa the mental rehearsal protocol with using the Kegan-Lahey *Immunity to Change* approach (page 178), where we identified her fears about change, which in her case were about associating tasks and duties with being a 'good person', and her 'big assumption' was that neglecting them would show that she was an 'inadequate person'. Practising alternative behaviours was part of her set of experimental tests of the assumption.

Attachment patterns in early life shape the brain

Sixty years of research has shown without doubt that we need love in order to flourish physically. So, for instance, like other primates, if you deprive human infants of being touched and cuddled they fail to thrive. In their book *A General Theory of Love* (2001), Lewis, Amini and Lannon describe the work of the psychoanalyst René Spitz showing that children reared in foundling homes under such regimes invariably became withdrawn, lost weight and often died. Death rates in some such orphanages were routinely 75 per cent – a staggering figure.

Another impressive and well-known study, 'The Infant Strange Situation', is described in Daniel Siegel's readable and influential book *Mindsight* (2010). The babies were faced with an experimental situation where their mother left the room for a short time. The study made direct correlations between the babies' behaviour and the patterns the observers had seen. These children were followed up in adult life.

Securely attached children, 60 per cent of the sample, cried bitterly and greeted the mother with ecstasy and relief when she reappeared. These were the children of mothers who had shown immediate responsiveness to the babies' needs in the earlier observations. As adults, these people were able to build secure relationships and had a good chance of combining confidence with self-awareness. When they appear in the coaching room, these clients are the ones every coach likes to work with: often high-flyers, open to new ideas, eager to learn, prepared to take responsibility for themselves. In neuropsychological terms their attachment circuits are in good order.

Twenty per cent of the babies were what the experimenters described as demonstrating *avoidant attachment*. The children made no fuss when the mother disappeared and showed little interest in her return. These mothers had been indifferent or cold to their babies, often ignoring their cries and minimizing physical contact. In adult life such babies were cool in their relationships and were often seen by others as controlling and difficult to like. All coaches will meet and work with a large number of clients of this sort. Such children learn to live with being ignored and criticized in equal measure. They acquire a prickly independence. They have learnt that emotion is dangerous so it must be suppressed. As clients I notice they often have a striking lack of emotional vocabulary. I remember one such client telling me in all seriousness that he really had no idea what people meant by 'feelings'. Most probably the left prefrontal cortex is overdeveloped in such people. The left prefrontal cortex is literal, likes lists, facts and logic. It is digital in its approach – yes/no, right/wrong, on/off. The right hemisphere mediates social behaviour. It is more holistic and non-verbal, controlling visual and spatial perception, empathy, concern for others and autobiographical memory. It is the part of the brain which enables us to imagine what must be going on in someone else's mind. In people shaped by avoidant attachment, the right hemisphere is likely to be underdeveloped: they are severely rational in their thought processes, are impatient for others to fall in with their ideas and have little awareness of or interest in how others see them, or ability to empathize. They turn up frequently in the coaching room because their careers can progress smoothly until the point where task intelligence is no longer enough and they are expected to interact skilfully with peers through rapport and subtle influencing rather than through chilly power. Even if you do not ask for autobiographical detail from your clients, your assumption should be that when you see extreme rigidity in a client's thinking you could be working with the product of this kind of childhood. It is not at all uncommon for coaches to receive demands from organizations to transform such people: 'Please make him emotionally intelligent.' Be realistic about the chances of this happening because they are small. Emotional intelligence is not a software program that can be installed with a few clicks into the human brain. In his dense and scholarly book *The Master and his Emissary* (2009), Ian McGilchrist argues convincingly that in Western society we have generally glorified the left hemisphere at the expense of the right, resulting in a mechanistic overemphasis on structure, logic and materialism, at great cost to ourselves.

Ten per cent of the babies demonstrated *ambivalent attachment*. Their mothers had been inconsistent. Sometimes they were attentive, sometimes they were dismissive. In the experiment, when the mothers left, the baby had often already shown jumpiness and uncertainty. Their behaviour was clingy and agitated. As adults their typical behaviour was anxious and sometimes over-emotional. We meet these people as coaches when they say they lack 'assertiveness' or ask us to help them with overarching difficulties such as 'confidence'. Usually, 360-degree feedback will reveal that colleagues view them with suspicion because their behaviour is needy, inconsistent and capricious, or you may find that colleagues avoid them because they talk obsessively and abuse the boundaries with other people's time and energy.

Experimenters described the final 10 per cent of the sample as *disorganized*. These were the children of chaotic and troubled households – for instance, where one or both parents was abusing drugs or alcohol. The babies' response was predominantly one of fear, often cringing from the mother, alternately crying and trying to avoid contact. These babies typically grow up unable to attach or relate to others. In effect their ability to create emotional connections with others has collapsed. They have been severely damaged, often responding impulsively and unwisely to others, overly dependent as teenagers on peers who are products of the same type of upbringing.

As a coach, all of this research, and its links with patterns laid down in the brain, demonstrates how important it is in coaching to accept that we have the whole person in the room with us. It also shows that, wherever feasible, we should ask clients for an autobiographical account (page 117) even though we know that the hippocampus, the seat of memory, does not develop properly until we are 7 or 8 years old, so we will have implicit rather than explicit memories of life before that time. Following this path will show us – and the client – not only what happened in the client's early life, but also how the client is interpreting these events. The hopeful feature of all of this is that it is the story you tell yourself that governs how you respond. A client who told me a doleful tale of her life in a succession of foster families was able to reframe this in coaching as surviving the emotional wasteland in which she had grown up. She had been able to make a happy marriage and to form strong attachments with her own children. Another, a gifted paediatrician, had experienced several traumas in childhood. His mother had left the family home when he was six, his father had then married a woman who was hostile to the existing children, and this client had also had successive surgeries for an orthopaedic problem. He said that he had become a paediatrician precisely because he knew how it felt to be lonely and frightened as a child.

Neuroscience is young, and all of its current conclusions must be seen as tentative: hints, beginnings, shadows, suggestions, hypotheses. New material is emerging all the time. Little is known for sure, but it is not a field that we can ignore. The stimulus to engage in coaching is rational: it involves the left prefrontal cortex. In coaching we need to keep this part of the brain engaged for as much as possible of the coaching session while also accepting the supreme importance of emotions. It makes no sense whatsoever to avoid emotion – for instance, by being too embarrassed to ask how a client feels. It is feelings that will get in the way of change and feelings that will liberate the energy for change. Far from dreading the 'dependency' of our clients we need to build an emotional connection with them. It is through dependency on someone dependable that we become centred and whole in childhood, and we can mirror this process in coaching, remembering that empathy is a biological as well as a social phenomenon. Finally, we are as much affected by all of the above as our clients, so our first task is to manage these issues in ourselves.

Notes

1   If the ball costs 10 p, then the total cost would be £1.20 not £1.10.

2   Pomodoros are 25 minute units, named after the Italian tomato-shaped kitchen timer of the technique's inventor. You set the timer and do one task uninterruptedly (www.pomodorotechnique.com), then take a five minute break.

3   I was given this idea by Professor Paul Brown. It appears in its full glory in his book, co-written with Virginia Brown, *Neuropsychology for Coaches* (2012).

5 Simple but not easy: the skilled language of coaching

Asking the right questions, phrasing your comments in just the right way . . . this is a prime coaching skill. When done well, it looks effortless. When not done well, it gets in the way. When you can do it well, you have cracked one of the most challenging barriers to effectiveness as a coach. This chapter looks at some of the common traps for coaches and describes how to get around them.

As with so many other domains in coaching, this skill falls into the category of *simple but not easy*. Successful coaching involves an intense awareness of the language you use, and this does not come naturally to everyone. When coaching well, your language will have a purity and probably also a brevity that your everyday conversation does not normally have or need. Each word will count.

Knowing the traps

At the risk of appearing to emphasize the negative, I'm going to describe some of the most common traps, all of which I have fallen into myself and seen many times in other coaches.

Here is an example, taken from a recording of a real-life piece of coaching:

Client: I need to work shorter hours. My work–life balance is all wrong.
Coach: Have you tried asking your PA for feedback on where your time is going?

In this example, the client has named the issue on which he wants to work. The coach's mind immediately springs to a possible powerful solution: raising the client's awareness of how he currently spends his time by suggesting he asks his PA for feedback. This could be a good idea because PAs tend to see managerial behaviour in the raw.

This is how the conversation continued:

Client: I need to work shorter hours. My work–life balance is all wrong.
Coach: Have you tried asking your PA for feedback on where your time is going? Her perspective would probably be very useful.
Client: No, I haven't.

Coach: That would be really useful – often I find that my clients don't really know where their time is going and the PA is a day-to-day observer. As a starter for change it's really useful.
Client: Well . . .
Coach: It's something you could do between now and the next session.
Client: Well, I don't know . . .
Coach: OK, just a thought . . .

As a coaching conversation, this one is going nowhere. If we speculate about what each side was thinking but not saying in this very typical piece of dialogue, it would probably go like this:

Thinks but doesn't say		Actual dialogue
This is such a huge issue for me. I've been round and round it so many times. I wonder if she can really help me?	**Client**	I need to work shorter hours. My work–life balance is all wrong.
Oh help . . .! This is a biggie. Where on earth should I start? I know! That exercise where you ask the PA for their feedback. That will help him.	**Coach**	Have you tried asking your PA for feedback on where your time is going? Her perspective would probably be very useful.
This sounds like a time-management course. I didn't come here for that.	**Client**	No, I haven't.
He's resisting, so perhaps I'd better push it.	**Coach**	That would be really useful – often I find that my clients don't really know where their time is going and the PA is a day-to-day observer. As a starter for change it's really useful.
There's no way I'm going to do this. Just because her other clients find it useful doesn't mean that I will.	**Client**	Well . . .
Perhaps I'm not being persuasive enough?	**Coach**	It's something you could do between now and the next session.
Absolutely not!	**Client**	Well, I don't know . . .
What on earth do I do now?	**Coach**	OK, just a thought . . .

While the speculations about the client's thoughts are just that – speculation – the coach's thoughts are entirely authentic, because she described them to me in Technicolor when, as her supervisor, we listened to the recording together.

Trap 1: Advice-in-disguise questions

This coach, like so many others, has fallen into the trap of asking advice-in-disguise questions. These questions come from the coach's wish to be helpful through offering his or her own solutions, dressed up as questions. The give-away is the first word:

Have . . . ?	Was . . . ?	Is . . . ?
Haven't . . . ?	Wasn't . . . ?	Isn't . . . ?
Would . . . ?	Has . . . ?	Should . . . ?
Wouldn't . . . ?	Hasn't . . . ?	Shouldn't . . . ?
Do . . . ?	Did . . . ?	Were . . . ?
Don't . . . ?	Didn't . . . ?	Weren't . . . ?
Does . . . ?	Are . . . ?	Can . . . ?
Doesn't . . . ?	Aren't . . . ?	Can't . . . ?

For instance:

> Have you thought of . . . ?
>
> Would it be a good idea if . . . ?
>
> Should you check that out with someone else?

There are about 30 of these constructions in English. These questions invariably come from the coach's agenda, not the client's. A sure sign that you are falling into this trap is to notice that your question can be answered yes or no and that your sentence begins with a verb. The questions suggest that there is a right answer, and of course that is the one in the coach's mind.

Apart from all the other disadvantages created by offering advice described in Chapter 2, there are two other, equally compelling ones for avoiding these questions. First, as in the example above, they can be readily deflected by a client who has two easy options: mindlessly agreeing immediately or abruptly declining to enter further into the debate. The client's energy is going into evasion instead of into thoughtfulness and learning.

Trap 2: The why question

When you ask the question 'Why . . . ?' it seems at first like a benign, open question. In practice it is another trap. The question 'Why . . . ?' invites defensiveness which takes the form of analysing and intellectualizing.

In this example, the client has raised the question of a highly unsatisfactory team meeting. This client already knows she has difficulties in chairing meetings and wants to improve.

Coach: Why did you decide to hold that team meeting when you did?
Client: Well, our policy on meetings is that we never let more than ten days go past without a team meeting and it was already nine days since the last one so I thought it was time . . . (*ramble, ramble, ramble*)

The coach's real questions were about what was in the client's mind before calling the meeting and what she wanted to get out of the meeting. The coach has not had his real questions answered here because by starting with the word 'Why . . . ?' he has triggered a defensive response which gets nowhere near the real issues for this client.

The 'Why . . . ?' question is also unhelpful because it often focuses on the client's motivation. Nine times out of ten when you ask this question you will get the response 'I don't know', or 'It's just how I am.' If the client already knew what her motivation was, she might not be asking for coaching on the issue.

Coach: Why did you lose your temper with X?
Client: I don't know. I just seem to have a short fuse.

Similarly, 'Why . . . ?' can seem like an interrogation or an accusation. For many people it reminds us of the kinds of questions that we were asked as children by our irritated parents:

Why did you get your clothes so muddy?

Why do you fight with your brother?

Why have you lost your bus pass for the third time this year?

When asked like this, it can easily be interpreted by the client as having the underlying meaning, 'Why were you so stupid?' The reply you get is then likely to be either the blank shrug that goes with 'I don't know' or a long-winded and defensive justification. In brain chemistry terms the word 'Why?' alerts the amygdala, the brain's alarm signal (Chapter 4), the client feels attacked and therefore is unlikely to be totally honest with you and cannot think clearly.

Trap 3: Researching the data

This is a more subtle trap, but it is a trap nonetheless. Let's suppose that you have a new client from an organization that you don't know at all. The client begins his account of a problem concerning a poorly performing member of his team. The temptations might be to ask the client for an organization chart or to explain any unfamiliar acronyms he is using; to establish how big the team is and how their roles relate to that of the problem member; to ask how old the team member is and how long they have been in the job.

All of this is unnecessary. The client already has this data so it is pointless to ask them to give it to you. It will be far more important for you to take the client into areas that they have never considered and that means asking a different type of question. The most likely explanation for your behaviour is your own anxiety:

> 'Do I really understand this client's organization?' (Probably not, but you don't need to)

> 'How is this team like other teams I know in different organizations?' (Irrelevant – it may be or may not be)

The pertinent data – pertinent to the client, that is – will emerge when you ask the right questions. Anything else is simply postponing the moment when you get to the heart of the client's issues. When you find yourself searching for data, notice it as a sign that you are at Level 1 listening (see page 38), more concerned about whether you are asking the right questions than in truly listening to the client. Extra facts are a distraction and will take you away from the real issues rather than towards them.

On one of our coach training courses, my colleague and friend Jan Campbell Young was working with Annie, a promising coach who had spent her career up until that point as a distinguished university teacher. Noticing how often Annie spent relentlessly searching for facts in her practice coaching, Jan memorably burst out, 'Annie, you are not doing a PhD thesis on the client's problem!' I remind myself of this with an inner smile of recognition when I am tempted to start the equivalent type of questioning with a client.

Trap 4: Asking about people who are not present

A client presents you with a puzzle. Let's say it is about how to harness the flagging motivation of their PA. The trap here is to ask about the PA's motivation or concerns.

Coach: What does she feel about it?
Client: Who can say?

None of us can ever know for sure what another person's motivation is. Clumsy probing about other people's motivation or feelings may confirm the client's belief that the other person is the problem, rather than looking at their own contribution to it. You may encounter another variation of this temptation. Let's say the client is thinking about a radical change of career. You know something of the client's personal circumstances through other questions you have asked. You now ask, 'What would your mother/wife/husband/partner/boss think about this?' Again, it is a distraction from the client's own responsibility to speculate about what the not-present other person might think. Interestingly, I notice that when we are tempted to ask this kind of question, the third party is often an authority figure. Asking about that person's views might therefore seem to be implying that the absent person has the final power to decide, and may have to be placated or manipulated in order for the client to have their own way. In this way, old myths and excuses could be unwittingly perpetuated.

Trap 5: Long and double questions

As a coach, when you ask long questions you are at risk of turning the spotlight of the coaching onto yourself. Long questions normally come out of uncertainty. Inside, the coach is thinking: 'What shall I ask next? If I go on talking I'll get to something eventually and it will cover up any pauses which might otherwise embarrass me . . .' As a coach, you cannot afford the luxury of doing all your thinking out loud. It will only confuse your client if your questions have long preambles followed by many dependent clauses, garlanded with phrases intended to give yourself time to think: *sort of, you know* and *I mean*. This coach found himself falling into this trap:

> So when you have this *sort of* problem, *you know*, with punctuality, and I know you've described it as baffling, and how it really, *sort of*, annoys your boss when you're late for her meetings, I wonder, *you know*, what the circumstances are – *I mean* whether it's when you're really hassled about everything else that's going on in your life? *Know what I mean?*

Not surprisingly, the client's response was: 'Yes – I mean no . . . I don't know. Could you repeat the question?' The question the coach was really asking was: 'What are the typical triggers for unpunctuality for you?' If he had asked the question this way, the client would have found it much easier to answer, though possibly also more challenging.

Buried inside the long question there are often two or even three subquestions. An example would be:

So tell me how you first came to feel concerned about this. Was it when you first joined the company or did it start later? And has that concern always been as strong as it is now?

This kind of question comes across as a barrage, however gently it is asked. It confuses because, as the client, you don't know on which bit of the barrage to concentrate. I notice that when coaches ask this kind of question, the client's most frequent response is typically 'Err . . . um . . .', or 'You've lost me there.' If you know that this style of questioning is a particular trap for you, take a breath, give yourself a pause, gather your thoughts and only then ask your questions – one at a time.

Tactics that work

All these traps, and the types of question that go with them, have one thing in common. They narrow the search for answers, rather than broadening it out. They confuse and distract. They focus attention on one place rather than persuading the client to extend out to many places, including, often, the places they might at first rather not look. One way and another, they all lead to dead ends.

The coach's freedom

As a coach, you are in a remarkably free situation. You have the luxury of remaining detached from whatever outcome the client achieves. It really doesn't matter. You want the client to get an outcome which will make a positive difference in their life, whether it is greater clarity or a workable solution, but you are not attached to any one path.

You don't need to know the whole story, only the bits of it that matter to the client now.

The past is less important than the present and the future.

You don't need to be right.

You don't need to understand the context in order to be able to coach effectively. I often coach clients whose technical worlds are literally incomprehensible to me. One example included a nuclear engineer who considerately asked me at one point early in our coaching whether it would help me if she briefly outlined the laws of thermodynamics as she was giving a technical presentation to non-technical colleagues and wanted to run it past me. I reassured her that her explanation would be a waste of our time. I might understand the individual words, but it would be unlikely that the whole sentence would mean much.

ˑ client managed a complex overseas operation in a country
cal system is as different from the standard Western democracy
ble to be, with internecine manoeuvrings, widespread corruption
ᴀᴜᴜ a great deal of physical danger. This client was relieved to discover that he did not need to give me potted histories of the various factions involved. Whether or not I knew about them was irrelevant to our success. Similarly, I have coached theologians, lawyers, doctors, actors, IT specialists, interior designers, architects, retailers, pharmacologists and other scientists, finance directors, actuaries, production designers, civil servants, ambassadors, hospital managers, chefs and many others without knowing anything about their professional worlds except perhaps as a consumer.

In fact, it is even more liberating than this. It is a positive help to know nothing about the context or the content. The more you know about the content, the more likely you are to be seduced into the role of expert.

This case has been supremely well made by Timothy Gallwey in his *Inner Game* books, for instance *The Inner Game of Work* (2000). Gallwey worked for a time as a tennis coach and came to realize that the real opponent for a tennis player was not the person on the other side of the net. The real opponent was in the player's own head. A player without bodily self-awareness and further handicapped by lack of self-belief was almost bound to fail. Gallwey began his *Inner Tennis* courses with the explicit aim of coaching participants in the techniques of mental and physical self-awareness rather than in some preordained set of tennis techniques.

The contrast with traditional coaching is instructive. The traditional coach relies on his or her own ideas of what makes, for instance, a good serve: 'Watch me and do it like this', or 'Keep your eye on the ball at this or that point.' This would be followed by feedback from the coach to the player: 'At the crucial minute, you let your arm drop and took your eye off the ball.' In this example, the coach is doing most of the work and the player is robbed of responsibility. The coaching turns into a performance to please the coach rather than the player taking responsibility for their own game.

In the *Inner Game* approach, the roles are reversed. The coach asks open questions aimed at raising the player's consciousness of their physical and mental states with the aim of the player taking the responsibility and doing the feedback on him- or herself:

- What worked then?
- What didn't work?
- What was in your mind at the start?
- What do you need to do now?
- Where was the ball when you connected with it?

The results were startlingly successful – so successful that an *Inner Ski* school was started too, with coaches trained in the same technique. In his book *Coaching for Performance* (1996: 37), Gallwey's then collaborator, John Whitmore, tells a wonderful tale of how the ski coaches were able to coach people in tennis, in spite of knowing literally nothing about the sport:

> Several of our Inner Tennis courses were so overbooked that we ran out of trained Inner Tennis coaches. We brought in two Inner Ski coaches, dressed them in tennis coach's uniform, put a racket under their arms and let them loose with the promise they would not attempt to use the racket under any circumstances.
>
> Not entirely to our surprise, the coaching job they did was largely indistinguishable from that of their tennis-playing colleagues. However, on a couple of notable occasions, they actually did better. On reflection the reason became clear. The tennis coaches were seeing the participants in terms of their technical faults: the ski coaches, who could not recognize such faults, saw the participants in terms of the efficiency with which they used their bodies. Body inefficiency stems from self-doubt and inadequate body-awareness. The ski coaches, having to rely on the participants' own self-diagnosis, were therefore tackling problems at cause, whereas the tennis coaches were only tackling the symptom, the technical fault. This obliged us to do more training with the tennis coaches to enable them to detach themselves more effectively from their expertise.

Effective questions in coaching

The most effective questions in coaching have a number of characteristics in common. They raise the client's self-awareness by provoking thinking and challenge, demanding truthful answers by cutting through obfuscation and waffle. They are short and are likely to begin with the words *what?* or *how?* They go beyond asking for information by asking for discovery and they encourage the client to take responsibility for themselves. Effective questions stick closely to the client's agenda. They lead to learning for the client.

Brevity

The most powerful coaching questions are often extremely short because they cut to the heart of the issue. The ideal question is between 7 and 12 words long. I believe the most powerful question of all is this one: 'What do you want?' Although another strong candidate is: 'What needs to happen to . . . ?'

Ros

Ros is a new chief executive who has inherited a less than ideal team. She expresses lack of confidence about her own ability to cope and also a rising level of concern about her finance director, Isobel. The coach encourages her to let off steam for a few moments.

Ros   . . . and then Isobel made it much worse by once again correcting me in a meeting and telling me that as I'm not a finance specialist, I had no idea what I was talking about and she couldn't really understand what on earth I was going to do about interpreting the accounts – on and on and on. I was so annoyed. And her manner with her team is awful – she's rude and she consistently loses her best people. We really can't have senior people behaving like she does.

Coach: What do you want?

Ros: I want her to go!

Coach: So what needs to happen to make that happen?

Ros: I've got to talk to my chair and get him on side and then find a civilized way for her to leave as soon as possible.

At last – clarity. Once these words 'I want her to go' have been spoken, the question then becomes how it can happen, not whether or not it is a good idea.

Sometimes the most effective question is a single word: 'So . . . ?'; 'And . . . ?'; 'Because . . . ?' Or even a questioning silence.

You could even say that any coaching conversation reduces itself essentially to three ultra-short questions: 'What?' (identifying the issue); 'So what?' (implications); 'What next?' (action).

Some super-useful ('magic') questions

When I was relatively new to coaching, I was fortunate to get sent by my then boss to a course on organizational consulting run by Columbia University. There I encountered a set of questions which were so obviously special in their impact on people that I immediately adapted them to my coaching work. There is an equivalent in therapy – so-called 'magic questions' – from which these questions had probably sprung. This list, much adapted, has proved its worth time and time again as an outline script, not just to me but to the thousands of other coaches I have met on courses and at conferences. It will work in almost any situation, regardless of the setting or the issue. There are se' eral points to note about it. The questions are short and content-free. They do not include the word 'I' and they work elegantly as a natural progression, starting with asking the client to state the problem, going on to restating the problem as a goal, then to naming options and finally to first steps to action.

Here are the questions:

1   *What's the issue?*
    This asks the client to state the problem. It can often usefully cut through a client's lengthy account by asking them to summarize what the problem actually is.

2   *What makes it an issue **now**?*
    Issues that clients bring to coaching have typically been around in the client's life for a long time. But often there is some immediate provocation or development, even if this is in the form of anger or worry. This emotion will provide energy for change and resolution. That is why it is worth naming and surfacing it.

3   *Who owns this issue/problem?*
    If the client does not own it, there is no point in discussing it. You can only coach the problem owner. Some clients come to coaching in order to find out how to change someone else, whereas the basic assumption of coaching is that you can only change yourself. This question puts the onus back onto clients to own whichever bit of the issue is theirs.

4   *How important is it on a 1–10 scale?*
    If the problem is not important, then why are you and the client wasting time discussing it? Importance captures the idea of issues with potential for major impact on a client's life. Anything the client scores at less than 5 should be set aside.

5   *Implications: what are the implications of doing nothing (or of letting things carry on as they are)?*
    This question builds the pain created by contemplating staying stuck. When we are in the client role many of us like to imagine that the default scenario can continue for ever, whereas inside we know perfectly well that it cannot and that we are ignoring the discomfort the problem is creating. Naming out loud the likely consequences of inactivity paradoxically builds energy for change. You might want to follow this question with a further probe: . . . *and what would be the implications if that happened?*

6   *What have you already tried?*
    This question stops you offering pointless advice which the client has already tried or considered and it also lets you in early on the client's thinking. Most coaching problems have already been the focus

of a great deal of energy and thought on the client's part. You need to know what this energy and thought has produced. If the client has not tried anything yet, that will also provoke an interesting discussion.

7   *Imagine this problem has been solved. What would you see, hear and feel?*
Up until now, the client has been deep in the problem. You will typically see this reflected in the way the client has been sitting and talking – often slumped or despairing. By asking this question you tap into their optimism. Clients will sit up straighter, stop frowning and will look generally lighter. Asking the question at this stage prevents you coaching on the symptoms rather than on the underlying causes.

8   *What's standing in the way of that ideal outcome?*
This question broadens out the client's thinking. Expect new insights to occur from this point on.

9   *What's your own responsibility for what's been happening?*
An essential question. The client is always part of the problem as well as part of the solution. This question makes that assumption explicit and encourages clients to see how they have, maybe at an unconscious level, been sustaining the problem through their own behaviour.

10   *Imagine you're at your most resourceful. What do you say to yourself about this issue?*
This question assumes that underneath all our typical confusion, at some level we do know what we should do. Another version of this question: 'If I could give you a pill which contained all the courage and insight you needed, what would you do?' I have yet to find a client who could not find an instant reply to this one.

11   *What are the options for action here?*
Now that the question has been looked at from several angles, the client can begin to consider the options for change.

12   *What criteria will you use to judge the options?*
Options are even more useful when you have criteria against which to judge them. Typical criteria might be: practicality, cost, fit with the client's values, time – and so on.

13   *Which option seems the best one against those criteria?*
At this point you are narrowing down again towards action – including, of course, just pondering.

14   *So what's the next/first step?*
The answer may be to do some more research, to have a conversation, or to make a big life decision.

15   *When will you take it?*
Asking for a commitment to *when* makes it more likely that the client will actually do something different as a result of the coaching.

Frameworks for coaching conversations

If you are new to coaching, you might benefit from one of the many models which offer frameworks for a coaching conversation. One of the best known is **GROW**, an acronym which stands for **G**oal, **R**eality, **O**ptions and **W**hat [will you do?]. The beauty of a framework is that it is easy to remember and is a reminder that a typical coaching conversation has a flow where there is a natural sequence to the questions. This gets around the absolute beginner's typical mistake which is to ask for the goal but then to go straight on to options, as here:

Coach: So we've got a goal!
Client: Yes, it's how to increase the amount of exercise I do.
Coach: OK – so what options do you have?

This may look perfectly fine until you realize that the question is unlikely to take the client any further than they have already got on their own because it does not explore what they have already tried, let alone what else is going on in the situation.

The OSCAR model

At an international coaching conference a few years ago, I was lucky enough to sit in on a session run by Karen Whittleworth and Andrew Gilbert where they were presenting their **OSCAR** model. I liked it immediately and it became the foundation of the book we jointly wrote, *Manager as Coach* (2012). OSCAR has several advantages over GROW, not least that the C in the middle stands for Choices and Consequences, giving the client the opportunity not just to generate options but to weigh them up. The W of GROW is replaced by the more explicit Action and Review.

I now introduce OSCAR to all the coaches I train and find that they like it for its simplicity, practicality and memorability. If you are already an experienced coach, then you can make any model work – and probably don't need a model at all. But if you are a beginner, my guess is that you will find this one useful.

This is how it looks:

OUTCOME
The destination

- What would you like to achieve from today's session? (short-term outcome?)
- What is your long-term outcome?
- What would long-term success look like? What would be different?

This is where you help the client clarify the outcome they want around the issue they have raised.

SITUATION **The starting point**	• What is the current situation? • What's actually happening? • Who is involved? • What makes it an issue now?

This is where you get clarity around where the client is right now. The purpose is to raise the client's awareness and the questioning in this section is for the benefit of the client, not the coach.

CHOICES and **CONSEQUENCES** **The options**	• What have you already tried? • What choices do you have? • What options can you choose from? • What are the consequences of each choice? • Which choices have the best consequences?

This is where you help the client to generate as many alternative courses of actions as possible, increasing their awareness about the consequences (upsides and downsides) of each choice, including the practicality, cost, fit with the client's values, and so on.

ACTIONS **The detailed plan**	• What actions will you take? • What will you do next? • How will you do it? • When will you do it, with whom? • On a scale of 1 to 10, how willing are you to take those actions?

This is where you help the client review the options generated, to clarify the steps forward, and to take responsibility for their own action plan.

REVIEW **Making sure you** **are on track**	• What steps will you take to review your progress? • When are we going to get together to review progress? • What action are you actually taking? • How far might these actions move you towards your outcome?

You should see frameworks like GROW and OSCAR as well as my list of 'Magic' questions as useful guidelines, not rigid instructions. What they do is to help keep you on track with an order and a form of questions that will always give you something you can ask, until the point where you develop your own frameworks and style.

Summarizing

Summarizing is important. It can look at first like a rather mechanical, lumbering and unnecessary interruption to the client's flow. But this is a misapprehension. First, it shows that you are listening because you cannot summarize accurately unless you have been listening. Second, it reassures clients that they have been heard and that you are keeping track of things. This is particularly important where there has been a period of intense and discursive conversation. Equally important, it keeps you in the frame and emphasizes your role. Also, it gives you a check that you really are understanding what the client is saying.

Summarizing provides punctuation. The coach's summary makes it a two-way and not a one-way conversation. When you feel you are getting confused by the twists and turns of a client's story, that is probably a reliable sign that you need to summarize. If so, try saying to clients 'I'm getting a bit lost here – can I try a summary?' Summarizing also helps us to get beyond the panic of Level 1 listening (page 38). If you know you can always summarize, you know you will always have something to say which is respectful to the client and helps you get back on track.

Genuine summarizing has these features:

- It does not contain any judgement of your own.
- It does not interpret.
- It uses the client's language.
- It ends with a question – 'Have I got that right?', or 'Is that a fair summary of where we seem to have got to?'
- It is authentically a summary and therefore brief, rather than a polly-parrot rendering at the same length as the client's own account.

Some useful summarizing phrases are:

I think it would be useful to summarize where we've got to here . . .

There seem to be three or four main views that you have been putting forward . . .

Can I check that I've really understood the points you're making here? What you feel is that . . .

So, to summarize so far . . .

Or even the very brief, 'So you feel angry/sad/happy/confused about this?'

Assuming a positive outcome

The best coaches are naturally skilled at using language which assumes a positive outcome. In effect it is a hidden order. They consciously slip in the constructions which convey that success will be inevitable. This is the linguistic equivalent of the placebo effect in medicine. When a doctor conveys that he or she believes the placebo will work, the patient may get better, in spite of the fact there is nothing but inert ingredients in the pills. Hypnotherapists do the same: *When I count to ten, your arm will feel heavy.*

The unaware coach conveys doubt and may say:

> *If* you *try* to learn how to control your nerves when you give a presentation *I* *think* you'll *probably* find that your problems with volume *may fade away.*

The italicized words convey misgivings. As the client you will pick up this doubt – the coach is not certain that you can succeed, therefore you may not.

The skilled coach will use a different construction:

> *When* you've learnt to control your nerves, *you'll find* that your problems with the volume of your voice will *disappear.*

I heard this exchange on a beginner coach's tape recently:

Client: (sounding very anxious) I don't know how to stop myself getting angry with Sharon. Every time I try to talk to her I get so annoyed because she witters on and on and I've given her hints that I don't like it but I'm afraid I may just have an explosion, then she'll probably carry out her threat to lay a grievance against me for bullying . . .

Coach: Well, if you try to have the conversation in the slightly different way we've discussed before, you might find that it turns out a bit differently.

Client: (dubious) Mmm, I suppose so . . .

Coach: Yes, you ought to try it – you never know, it might work.

When you look at the dialogue you can see clearly that in trying to be encouraging and not too directive, through her convoluted and tentative language, the coach is actually conveying a belief that the suggested tactics will not work. When asked about this in supervision, the coach was amazed – 'But I did believe they would work!'

To counter this tendency, use phrases which assume success, such as:

As you continue to improve . . .
When you've learnt this . . .
Once mastered, this will feel . . .
You will feel better when . . .
When you've practised this skill five or six times you will find
that . . .

Similarly, beware of telling clients that something will be *difficult* or *tricky*.
Essentially your role is to expect success because this way you will convey
it to the client. This increases the chances that this is what will happen. When
you label something *difficult*, you create the expectation of failure. One of
my former dance teachers seemed to me to make life twice as hard for himself
and his learners by announcing that we were going to find some particular
sequence *a stumbling block*. Sure enough, we stumbled. Another teacher with
a class of identical ability says nothing at all about whether it is easy or difficult, but just takes that same section a little more slowly, briskly assuming
that we will master it – which we do.

Naturally you need to temper all of this with realism. It is not appropriate
when you have serious doubts or when it would be unrealistic to raise expectations too high. But on the whole I find that grounded optimism gets much
better results than doleful prediction of obstacles.

Encouraging clients to be specific

When a client is bewildered, angry or concerned about an issue, he or she
may begin by explaining it through extravagant generalizations, assertions
or comparisons. This is a sign that feeling has taken over from logic and
also a signal to you that the issue is important to the client. Encouraging the
client to be specific is often the swiftest way to begin unpacking what is really
at stake.

Here are some examples of how to use the technique:

The client makes a comparison:	This is the worst boss I've ever had.
The coach surfaces the comparison:	Worst in what way? Or, worse than what specifically?
The client makes a generalization:	She's always late.
The coach challenges the generalization:	Always? No exceptions?

The client makes a bald assertion:	I don't like the way this organization is going.
The coach asks for a specific example:	What specifically don't you like about the way the organization is going?
Alternatively, the coach asks for the opposite:	So if everything were going well in the organization, what specifically would be happening for you?
The client states implied rules which indicate firmly held beliefs:	We should know exactly how this recruitment programme is going to be organized.
The coach surfaces the implied rule and asks what the result would be of changing the belief:	What would happen if you didn't know exactly how the recruitment programme was going to be organized?

Look out here for *must* and *should*. For instance, if a client says 'I must have advance warning of changes in plans', the coach might reply, 'What does having advance warning of changes do for you?'

Can'ts may represent particularly strongly held self-limiting beliefs:

The client says:	I can't hope to change the way I work.
The coach replies:	What's stopping you?

Looking out for nominalizations

The study of linguistics has given us the ugly neologism *nominalizations.* Don't let the clumsy label put you off. A nominalization is a noun, adjective or verb which has been turned into an abstract concept. These words are used by politicians, preachers and advertisers all the time, precisely because they are vague. So a politician promises us *modernization* of health services, *excellence* in schools, or *efficiency* in government. A motivational speaker may talk about *values, happiness* or *truth*. To make sense of these words, we have to fill in the blanks ourselves. There is no behaviour specified. In fact many politicians deliver speeches, whole parts of which are also entirely without verbs. Each listener will create their own meaning, lulled into a false sense of shared understanding. So clients may say they are locked into *misery,* or seeking *enlightenment,* or *paralysed by indecision.* If in doubt about whether you are hearing a nominalization or not, ask yourself if you could buy it, carry it away as a physical entity, or see it in actual behaviour. If not, then you are hearing a nominalization.

When you hear nominalizations always ask the client to clarify. Here is an example:

Client: I feel a bit depressed about the state of my organization.
Coach: Depressed: that's an interesting word. What is depressing exactly?
Client: It's the way we as a senior team seem to be detached from what is really going on. We hide in our nice offices as if we're afraid to venture out – and I think we are! We know our people believe we've lost touch with them and I really don't know what to do about it.

Running the conversation like this will stop you assuming that when the client used the initial word *depressed*, he meant sadness, anxiety or clinical depression. What he really meant was something a great deal more particular.

Sticking to the client's language

The effective coach notices and picks up on the client's language. When clients are talking about issues that really touch them, their language changes: it becomes more vivid, sometimes more direct, often more metaphorical. It gives you clues about what really matters to the client, and this is virtually always worth exploring.

Sean

Sean, a BBC executive, constantly used metaphors that were virtually all military. His *troops* were going to *go over the top* in their *battle* with the *enemy*. This *battle* might be an enjoyable *joust* or it might *go nuclear*. When I pointed out this pattern to him, he was amazed and thoughtful. 'Well, yes', he said, 'I see my department as being engaged in a life or death struggle for survival. We're fighting the independent production companies and our BBC bosses for commissions and if we don't win it will be the sack for all my producers.'

Metaphor and its importance

It is impossible to explore any abstract concept without using metaphor. In fact metaphor saturates our conversation, even though we may be quite unaware of how much metaphor we are using. It is possible that as many as 1 in 25 of our words are metaphors. Never underestimate how powerfully the language we use can affect how we think.

This has been repeatedly demonstrated experimentally, most vividly in a series of experiments designed by two researchers at Stanford University, Paul Thibodeau and Lera Boroditsky.[1] Subjects read accounts of crime in a fictional city, including statistics. One set of these reports contained the word *beast*, describing crime as *preying on* the city. The other used the metaphor of a *virus* which was *infecting* the city. These words were used only once. Subjects were then asked to recommend action to solve the problem. The group which had been exposed to the beast metaphor recommended vigorous police action (*hunting down, catching, imprisoning*) while the group exposed to the virus metaphor preferred *diagnosis, looking for root causes, cure* and social action. These results were only marginally affected by political affiliations. Intriguingly, few of the subjects attributed their reasoning to the metaphor. Most believed that they had been influenced by the statistics. This clearly has serious implications for any kind of political and social discourse – for instance, newspapers whose headlines use phrases like *immigrants flooding in* or *swamping*, or which describe well-paid bosses as *fat cats*, most probably have a profound impact on our attitudes. But there are also huge implications here for coaches. Just asking your client to describe the same story using a different metaphor can potentially entirely change how they think and feel about the issue.

So in the example above, the essence of the dialogue went like this (shortened for the sake of brevity here):

JR: So Sean, I notice how many military metaphors you're using: *war, fight, nuclear, joust* . . .

Sean: (looking a bit startled) Yes, yes, I am, because that's how it seems.

JR: What's the evidence that it is actually a *war* or a *fight*?

Sean: (long pause) I suppose it's their behaviour. (he takes a little time to explain some of this)

JR: Well, we haven't got them in the room – just you. How do you think it's influencing your own behaviour to describe it like this?

Sean: (another long pause) Probably a lot. (he describes it)

We then discussed how effective Sean thought these tactics were. Answer: not at all – in fact, totally counterproductive.

JR: Let's just play with some language here. How else might you describe it?

Sean: Maybe a *parley*, a *negotiation*, a *conversation* . . .
JR: And how does it seem when you frame it like that?
Sean: (suddenly energized) Quite different. This is making me think! I need some new approaches here, otherwise I'm going to go down the same old path.

This conversation was a turning point: the beginning of devising a new and successful strategy for the department. This was backed up by coaching in which Sean developed and practised the influencing and negotiating skills he had neglected for so long in his thirst for a fight.

Clean language

The concept of probing language, especially metaphor and simile, has been refined and made more elegant and accessible by *neuro-linguistic programming* (NLP) enthusiasts, notably David Grove, an outstanding therapist who built on work by Milton Erikson, a celebrated mid-twentieth-century hypnotherapist. The ideas are well explained in the book, *Clean Language*, written by Wendy Sullivan and Judy Rees (2008).

Essential propositions

- The coach must notice the client's exact language, including their similes and metaphors.
- Using the client's exact words creates rapport – the essential foundation of any coaching/mentoring. Clients will feel understood at a very deep level.
- The coach uses phrases that are, as far as possible, 'cleansed' of any of his or her own presuppositions, interpretations and assumptions.
- The coach draws attention to any of the non-verbal signals that accompany the client's words – e.g. a raised arm, a hand on heart, a jiggling foot – without making any of the popular interpretations of so-called 'body language' – e.g. that crossed arms means defensiveness.
- The coach directs the client's attention to their own gestures, metaphors and language and asks the client to interpret them through expanding on them.
- Doing this enables the client to understand their own 'perceptual world' – for instance, their own assumptions, blocks and barriers – and to see how these link with behaviour, including the behaviour they would like to change.

Unclean language: an example

Client: I feel trapped in my job
Coach: So how could you find a way out?

In this example, the coach assumes that the client wants to find a way out. The hidden instruction is that this is desirable and that the client should find a way out.

Clean language alternative

Client: I feel trapped in my job.
Coach: And what kind of trapped is trapped?
Client: It's a deep hole and I can't climb out.
Coach: And what happens when you can't climb out of this deep hole?
Client: I turn in on myself, I shut down (client wraps arms around body)
Coach: (copies client's wrapped arms briefly) And when this happens and you turn in on yourself and shut down, what happens next?
Client: I stop asking for help – which I should!
Coach: And if you did ask for help, what would happen?
Client: I'd magically leap out of that hole: in fact I can and should – and I will!

How to do it

You slow down your speech and there is an implied sense of wonder and curiosity in the way you ask the questions. You match the client's idiosyncratic emphases and pronunciation and you are scrupulously careful to use only the client's language, metaphors and similes.

Useful phrases

And what kind of [ ] is that [ ]?

And where does that [ ] come from?

And that's like . . . what?

And what happens next?

And is there anything else about [ ]?

Tell me more about [ ]

What does [ ] mean for you?

If you had [ ] what would be happening?

Occasionally, applying the principles of Clean Language can produce transformative moments for the client:

Fran

Fran was referred by her boss who reported puzzlement about Fran's performance. Recently appointed to a leadership role, her early promise had fizzled out. Fran had lost the confidence of her team, was frequently turning up late for work, and had missed an important off-site meeting with what seemed like an implausible excuse. The boss's attempts to find out what was going on had got nowhere. Coaching was openly described to Fran and to me as a last chance to 'get your leadership style in order' before disciplinary action kicked in.

Fran's first session was intended to be about work issues, but in reality we spent the whole session on her private life where, thanks to that reliable tool, the Life Scan Wheel (page 148), she made an unprompted sudden decision to pour out a tragic story. Fran, of British-Somali background, had married a Nigerian man. Cultural and personal differences began to damage the marriage and, with no warning, her husband took their two children from London to Nigeria and refused to return. She discovered that he was in considerable debt and that their house was on the verge of being repossessed.

At this session we discussed the whole question of telling her boss what was going on in her private life and agreed that disclosure was essential. We also discussed how she could get legal advice about reclaiming her children and dealing with her financial problems.

Some weeks passed. At her second session Fran reported that she had now told her boss and her team about her personal circumstances. Things had improved dramatically at work as a result. She was renting a small flat and was applying to the family court to get access to her children. I asked her to reflect on how she would sum up her feelings about the whole experience.

Client: I feel I've been in a tidal wave
JR: What kind of a tidal wave is that?
Client: Huge, overwhelming, a tsunami. I've been standing on the shore helplessly watching, seeing the sea roll back, knowing it's coming, unable to do anything to protect myself. (silence, several seconds) Feeling powerless, knocked over.
JR: Knocked over . . . powerless . . . and then?

Client: (very loudly) Yes, oh God, yes – that's exactly how it's felt. How amazing! I see myself there.

JR   And then . . .?

Client: And then the tide's rolled in and I'm standing knee-deep in water.

JR: Is there anything else about that water?

Client: (very energized) Dirty, full of wreckage, it's the wreckage of my life. Actually I'm in a house and the water has surged through it, leaving me standing. I'm just watching. When it all happened I couldn't run for the hills where it's safe.

JR: The hills would be safe. (short silence) You say you're still standing and the hills would be safe. Which way are you facing now?

Client: (sounding amazed) Oh God, I'm sideways, I'm sideways . . .

JR: Sideways. Which way would you like to be facing?

Client: Forward, forward . . . I'm going to be heading for the hills. Yes, I can see myself facing forward and away from that sea; even though that tsunami's not going to happen again, but the tide will still keep coming in and I need to get to safety.

JR: If you had that, how would that feel?

Client: (very slowly and quietly) A bit scary but a lot better. A lot, lot better.

JR: So better for you is . . .?

Client: Feeling I'm in control for the first time for nearly a year.

I noticed Fran had a slight sheen of sweat on her forehead. She was sitting upright and forward in her chair and alternating smiling with a look of astonishment. We discussed what had just happened. Her response was: 'Being able to say it all is brilliant, listening to my own metaphors and realizing how powerful they are; being able to tap into my feelings and say all this to someone who's not judging me. Feeling back in control!'

Two years later Fran was divorced, had recovered her children and had reached a reasonably amicable settlement with her former husband. She had moved within the same organization to a similar job in another city. In reviewing our work her comment was, 'Our tsunami conversation was a huge turning point for me – I'll never forget it. Everything improved for me from then on because I no longer felt at the mercy of stuff I couldn't control.'

Exploring feelings

This core coaching skill has the simplicity of the obvious, and, along with that, the risk of it being constantly ignored.

Virtually all clients already know what the 'solutions' are to their problems. Examples might be:

Problem	Solution
I can't manage my time	Prioritize
I don't know what to do about my career	Take logical stock of your career and follow the rational path
My boss is difficult	Give your boss some feedback

The reason clients find it difficult to follow the apparently obvious path is that feelings are getting in the way. Many of us, but particularly people with a strong preference for logic and rationality, act as if we believe that logic will solve the problem. Logical methods of problem-solving are even taught on management development courses, but as the evidence from neuropsychology shows (Chapter 4), feeling precedes logic by a long way in our responses to an event.

The logical solution may be obvious, but remains unimplemented. For the problems above, for instance, why can't the client take their own advice?

I could prioritize	but I am driven by assumptions from my early life about hard work and my identity is bound up in work.
I could follow the logic of career choice	but I am terrified of novelty and change.
I could give my boss feedback	but he frightens me, as all male authority figures do.

This is why, along with looking at issues rationally, it is important to enquire into the feelings. No client issue worth the focus of a coaching session will ever be without a feelings aspect. As coaches, our role is often to help clients articulate feelings that have been there but unrecognized, or to help them say out loud what they have kept inside.

Warning

When you ask a client about feelings, you will often get a thought. The symptoms of thoughts are clients who say, 'I feel that . . . this is exciting/interesting/worrying.' As soon as you hear the word *that*, you are getting a thought.

You are getting a feeling when a client says, 'I feel excited/worried.' Point this difference out to the client and press for the feeling.

There are two natural places to ask for feelings. The first is at the beginning of exploring the issue. The second is at the end when the decision has been made by the client about what to do.

Note: there are only a few questions in this area that the coach needs to ask, and they can be asked constantly:

> How does that feel?
> Tell me about that feeling . . .
> What does that mean for you specifically?
> How does that translate into your behaviour?
> Say more . . . ?

Moving the discussion on

Closed questions have their place in coaching:

> 'Have we exhausted that topic?'

This implies that the answer is yes and will allow you to move on quickly to the next part of the session.

Linking questions or statements are also useful here. Links combine a brief summary of the discussion that has just happened with a look forward to the next section. Here's an example:

> So in this part of the discussion we've looked at how the pressures on the business are affecting it in a number of ways (you then briefly enumerate them) and our plan now is to look in more detail at each of these. Is that OK?

For daily examples of how to do this elegantly, examine any live discussion programme on television or radio. Broadcasters call these links *segues*, meaning a technique of sliding seamlessly from one topic to another by making a link between them.

The simplicity that counts

The kind of language I have described in this chapter goes beyond technique, though technique is important. A coaching-aware client may also be perfectly aware of any 'techniques' that you are using. My client S, with whom I have worked for two years, so we know each other well, had asked me in the course of our coaching how he could develop coaching techniques himself as a way of enhancing the performance of his team, and I had taught him some questioning techniques. In our session recently, where I was pressing him on some issue or other, he suddenly said in mock exasperation, 'Couldn't you just ask me a closed question for once?' In agreeing that my question was entirely appropriate, we were reminding each other that coaching means fresh thinking for the client and that such thinking is hard work.

Language in successful coaching is the disciplined simplicity that comes from trusting clients to tap into their own strengths. It is about paring down to the essence – having the questions, but understanding that you don't need to have the answers.

Note

1   For a full account, go to www.plosone.org – Metaphors We Think With: The Role of Metaphor in Reasoning, 2011.

6 Taking stock: the learning client

Our prime task as coaches is to facilitate self-awareness and learning for the client, and that is impossible unless you and the client have a shared understanding of where the client currently stands. This chapter looks at techniques for making this initial assessment.

Clients bring a whole range of issues to coaching. These may show as urgent dilemmas or as nagging background puzzles. It would be quite usual to find that, in any one client, several major work and life issues present simultaneously.

Clients have many times assured me that they are completely different people at home from how they are at work. This, in itself, should set alarm bells ringing, for both coach and client.

This client, for instance, vividly described himself thus:

Evan

I say goodbye to my wife and son, heartily kissing them both, and set out on the walk to the station. I always feel melancholy leaving them. As I'm doing it, I feel a bit like a cartoon character. In the cartoon, I start as Domestic Man, a nice, mildish, smiley pussycat. Domestic Man is blinking slightly helplessly through his glasses, then he gradually transmogrifies into the dark and frightening Work Person who gets off the train in London. The briefcase, which would look a bit of an affectation for Domestic Man, has become a weapon of mass destruction. The glasses magnify the piercing eyes. The suit, which would look like an Oxfam donation on Domestic Man, suddenly fits in all the right places. Instead of an amiable slouch, Work Person seems about seven feet tall, has a towering stride, and a don't-mess-with-me scowl to match.

Evan ran a Directorate in a large organization where his reputation was for intimidating and demanding leadership. In requesting executive coaching, Evan knew that something was wrong somewhere and saw coaching as a way to find out what it was. Initially he imagined that we would be looking exclusively at his work world. But part of the secret of finding the answers he needed was in looking at the connections – and indeed disconnections – between the two selves he so powerfully described when given the opportunity to talk about his whole life.

Whatever the issues a client brings to the coach, there will be a sequence of necessary stages through which coach and client must pass:

1   Where, who and what am I now – in my life, my work, my relationships, my skills?
2   Where, who and what would I like to be ideally?
3   Given those answers, what goals do I need to set for myself?
4   How can I achieve and sustain those goals?

A feedback-exclusion zone?

Beginning the self-discovery journey starts with a well-rounded scrutiny of where the client is now, and most of us live in a feedback-exclusion zone where the Scottish poet's well-known plea remains an impossible dream:

> Wud that God the gift wud gie us
> To see oursels as others see us.
>
> (Robert Burns)

Few of us really see ourselves as others see us. In the corporate world it is striking how isolated senior people can be and what a high cost both they and the organization can pay for this isolation. In her riveting account of the late 1990s crisis at Marks & Spencer, still one of the most dramatic examples of corporate failure in the last decades, Judi Bevan lays it out with stark clarity. She compares Sir Richard Greenbury, the chief executive who led Marks & Spencer to the brink of complete collapse, with Margaret Thatcher, who did the same for the Conservative Party:

> Like Margaret Thatcher, Greenbury was an example of the classic leader who hung on too long. Surrounded by weak people who pretended at all times to agree with him, he was eventually pushed out by those he believed were his loyal lieutenants. The parallels with him and Thatcher were clear. Both possessed of towering egos, they had rallied the troops in times of crisis and then allowed themselves to be diverted, seduced by the perfume of power. They both failed to nurture a worthy successor, or to bring in new blood. Their increasingly irrational behaviour was tolerated by their acolytes, who found them inspiring on the way up, as long as the formula produced success. For Thatcher, the catalyst for her removal was the poll tax, for Greenbury

it was the profits collapse and the attempted coup by Keith Oates. Both were great leaders whose tragedy was that *they failed entirely to appreciate the impact of their personalities on those around them.* They both tended to shoot messengers bearing bad news and so the bad news ceased to reach them – until it was too late.

(Bevan 2002, my emphasis)

This reminds me of being a young participant on a BBC management development course when the then reigning Director General was invited to come and hear our possibly somewhat naïve proposals about how to solve the BBC's organizational problems. Most of the time he remained affable and politely interested. However, he suddenly flipped into glacial overdrive at the notion that there was anything wrong with the morale of the BBC's staff, then generally accepted as a major problem, snapping pettishly, 'Don't tell me staff morale has never been lower. Morale has *always never been lower.* Let's get on to the positive, shall we?' Needless to say, with self-preservation sensibly to the fore, our suggestions were made in a noticeably more timid way after that.

In general, the people around us don't tell us the truth. Leaders don't get told the truth by those around them. They don't get told the truth by their bosses and are even less likely to get told the truth by those they manage. They don't get told the truth about the organization and they don't get told the truth about their own leadership styles. There is no mystery about why.

First is the shoot-the-messenger tendency where colleagues who feel, rightly or wrongly, that their futures depend on the patronage of the leader, hesitate to challenge. It is easier to buy time and to whimper in corridors with fellow sufferers than to confront.

The fear of ejection is very real. We can see what happens to the majority of whistleblowers, large or small: they find it difficult initially to get taken seriously and, when they do, many seem to end up leaving the organization, often because they have been forced out. Giving feedback is a high-level art, and in spite of the fact that it is a skill taught on more or less any management development course in the Western world, it is still more often talked about than done. Giving honest feedback will name the pluses as much as it identifies the minuses, but it can still feel like making criticisms, and to do that face-to-face is uncomfortable. It can feel like attacking the person, and therefore we dread that it might be hurtful to the recipient.

One large study of US managers showed that only half of the sample had ever asked for feedback (Jackman and Strober 2003). Among the many reasons cited were a number of familiar avoidance patterns. These included:

Reawakened childish dependence: being given feedback potentially awakens the feelings of being a child upbraided by more powerful parents. The feedback receiver dreads being chided for behaviour that falls short of the parental ideal.

Procrastination: the subject of the feedback knows something is wrong but cannot bear the idea of exploring it.

Denial: it might get better if just ignored.

Brooding: the person has a morbid preoccupation with the negative and an overwhelming sense of foreboding. Dread of what they might discover becomes magnified.

Jealousy in relation to others: the potential feedback subject fantasizes that others will emerge more positively from the exercise and hates the idea of being benchmarked in case this turns out to be true.

Self-sabotage: the subject looks for ways to make the expected negatives real.

Breaking through the feedback-exclusion zone

You could describe almost the whole process of coaching as being about breaking through the feedback-exclusion zone because an essential preliminary of any successful coaching is increased self-awareness. There are some particular tactics and approaches that coaches can use to help the client with the very first stages of the coaching process. You will have your favourites. These ideas are meant as a menu of options – you will never have time to use them all.

The core questions at this stage are:

> Who are you as you see yourself now?
> How much do you know about your impact on others?
> What are the pressing issues for you?

Autobiography: how did you get from there to here?

I have always regretted it when I have not asked clients for a brief account of their lives so far. If you are going to do it, the first session is your best chance. It builds intimacy and rapport and also establishes that you are interested in the whole person, not just the work person. The whole person has evolved from life experience, so hearing a client tell their life story is one way you begin to understand the client's world.

There are a number of other compelling reasons for doing it. For all of us our feelings about authority evolved from our relationships with our parents and authority figures such as teachers. Our relationships with peers will have ffected by how we got on with siblings and early friends. These influences on relationships at work will have important effects on approaches to leadership, to being a colleague and to being a follower. Patterns of emotional response are laid down in childhood and have biological as well as psychological impact (see also Chapter 4). It is worth looking for the common patterns as a way of understanding the client's issues. What clients emphasize and what they leave out is always relevant to their view of themselves. Few clients will ever have told a complete life story to anyone previously and most enjoy the experience.

A framework for asking about the client's life story

Tell the client that you expect this part of the session to take about 30 minutes, but note that this is a 30 minutes that you will need to manage tightly. I have heard many recordings of first sessions where the coach seemed to have disappeared from the conversation just making sympathetic noises in the background while the client talked on – and on – with the story of their life. This is not desirable. (See Annex 1 for ideas about managing the first session.)

You will not need to ask all these questions. Pick what appeals and develop your own versions of them, as you see fit:

- What effect has birth order had on you – e.g. the experience of being an only child/the youngest of four?
- Who did you admire when you were growing up?
- Which parent were you closer to?
- What shaped your values as you were growing up?
- If you had to point to one experience in your childhood that had a major impact on you, what would that be?
- What's your happiest memory?
- What effects have marriage/partner/parenting relationships had on your life?
- How have you got through the tough times in your life?
- In what positive ways would you say you have grown and developed?
- How did you make your career choices?
- What skills and abilities have you discovered that you have?
- What themes and patterns do you see emerging in the story as you have told it?
- What are the links to the coaching we will be doing?

Doubts and hesitations

Of all the tools and techniques taught to coaches, asking for a life story is the one that raises the most questions. Some coaches quail at the very prospect of doing it. Here are the most frequently asked questions:

Where organizations are paying for the coaching and expect the focus to be on performance, won't they object if they hear I did something that sounds like psychotherapy?

Not if you have made it clear before you start the coaching that you take a whole person approach. 'Whole person' includes how that person has developed and grown, so a brief look at the past is essential. This is nothing like psychotherapy where looking at the past could take many hours of talking.

What if the client objects, on the same grounds?

If you present it apologetically with no justification for why you are introducing it, yes, the client might object, especially if the way you phrase it sounds like prurience on your part. Described confidently and with a convincing explanation, few if any clients will refuse. If a client did refuse, ask them respectfully what their reasons are and leave it at that: maybe privately add to your data about this client that they could have a stronger than usual need to defend their privacy. It is more challenging to work with such people.

Couldn't I leave it till later in the coaching programme when the client and I know each other better?

Yes, you could: it's up to you. But a strong reason for doing it in the first session is to build rapport and the foundation for future sessions.

What if the client tells me a horror story about bereavement, abuse or neglect?

Yes, they may. It is striking how many senior leaders have had grim childhoods. See it as a great compliment. The client has chosen to confide in you with this sensitive data. It is very unlikely that you are the first person to hear the story and you should never assume that there is anything you need to 'do' (see Chapter 11). Just respond with empathy and ask them what their feelings are now about whatever they have described, then how it has shaped who they are. Count on the understanding that clients choose what they tell you; you cannot *force* them to disclose. Never expect to hear all the most important events and data during this discussion: more – often much more – will probably emerge later when trust has grown between you, but this is a beginning.

Very, very occasionally you may hear a story where it is clear that a past trauma has not been well managed. In these cases ask the client how to proceed – for instance, 'This feels like something very serious and upsetting for you. What do you feel we should do about it in this session?' Be guided by the client's answer.

When I tried it, the client talked and talked and I felt helpless; it took up the whole session

This happens when, as the coach, you make a vague general statement such as: *'Tell me about your life'* and then sit back submissively while the client begins at birth, rattles on merrily and still has not got to their third decade by the end of the session. Instead, you have to manage the discussion firmly. Clients may not know where to start, so unless you guide them they may begin with 'At 18 I left home . . .' You are in charge of the question framework, so give the client prompts, summarizing and interrupting politely if necessary.

Are there ways of containing the time it takes?

Yes. The easiest is just ruthless time management and awareness of how long the answer to each question is taking.

The Lifeline exercise is an alternative, sent to the client in advance so that they have already done some sieving and editing of their story before they tell it to you.

Lifeline

Fill in this sheet so that it represents the story of your life so far, identifying low points and high spots.

Age/date	Lows	Highs	Comment

Annette

Annette was chief executive of a consultancy, a firm of which she was a founding director. She described herself as having had a lonely childhood with little overt affection. She was the daughter of two famous theatrical people, both of whom married several times before and after being married to each other. At the last count, she told me, she had three living step-parents, many step- and half-siblings, but no full siblings. Early recollections were of being *prinked up*, as she put it, *to appear as a fashion accessory at glamorous parties*, followed by many bleak moments, including being sent to boarding school at a very young age. Her own marriage and children were important to her, but she had chosen to work in London during the week while her husband worked on his own business from home, 40 miles away.

What patterns emerged for her in telling this story? She said that for the first time she understood how pervasive had been her lifelong feeling of being alone in a crowd. It had toughened her up and she felt she could deal with any challenges in her professional life, including dealing with troublesome client organizations. She felt that in telling her life story she had had a moment of insight into the performance aspect of her job: 'I enjoy making pitches for work. I enjoy preparing, I enjoy dressing well for it and I do it well. I've suddenly thought this might be something I've inherited from my parents, though I hate to say it! In fact even the rackety nature of my job could be a bit like theirs.'

And the links with the coaching on which we were just embarking? 'The main reason I'm here', she said, 'is that I need to understand more about my style with my staff.' The firm was beginning to struggle in its ultra-competitive market place and Annette had had hints from her team that part of the reason was that, as the founder, Annette hugged too much work to herself and was a charming but remote presence. 'They tell me they don't know what I feel about them', she said. 'Mmm . . . I wonder why I've never realized this before, that it's got a lot to do with protecting that little girl I used to be in those early days . . .?'

Understanding the pattern also creates a moment of potential choice for the future. *This is how I've been up until now. That was then, this is now. I can choose to be different.*

Just occasionally it can feel as if the telling of the story is almost all that needs to happen. The most dramatic example I have ever encountered was this one:

Michael

Michael came to his first session with one burning issue. His boss, Felix, had decided to expand his team from four to eight. Michael was deeply uncomfortable about this change, feeling that it was a strategic mistake and that it would make decision-making far more complex than it needed to be. Felix and Michael had a close relationship – in fact they had worked together for ten years and Felix had brought Michael into their present company. Michael's role in effect was to be special advisor to Felix and had helped him do what he described as 'keeping the stupidities of the organization at bay'. They socialized outside work and their families got on well.

In describing his early life, Michael painted an unusual picture. He was one of eight children in a tightly knit fundamentalist Christian household which held severe and inflexible views about mixing outside the exclusive society created within the minuscule church community. He was one of a pair of fraternal twins right in the middle of the family. He and his brother – at first subtly and then overtly – rebelled against what they saw as the strictures of the family's way of life, its religiosity, its harsh rules and its stifling lack of privacy. They even developed a special twins' language which their parents could not understand. As adults they had broken away, completely rejecting their faith. This had included 'marrying out' and being cut off from the family as a consequence.

As he was telling me this, Michael suddenly broke off, stared at me wildly, smote his forehead melodramatically and said, 'Oh my God, I've just realized . . .'

'You've realized . . .?'

'Eight children . . . eight as the size of the new team! Felix is not my brother is he! The team is not my family!'

Michael's realization that he had unconsciously brought a deeply shaping childhood experience into his work was a profound and liberating moment for him. He realized that he had been making false assumptions about the changes ahead and was then able to think completely differently about the work situation.

Alternative approaches to autobiography: A Life in the Day

When the *Sunday Times* newspaper began its colour supplement in the early 1970s, its then editor, Hunter Davies, devised a brilliantly simple but endlessly fascinating back page feature called *A Life in the Day*, often mistakenly described as *A Day in the Life*. The person who was the focus of the article was asked to describe a typical apparently humdrum day: what time they get up, what they eat and drink throughout the day, how they get to and from work – all the way through until bedtime. Asking clients to give you *a life in the day* is a wonderfully revealing and mutually useful exercise, especially where you know you have the luxury of working with clients over a longer period, so there is less time pressure.

The activity can reveal fascinating data. For instance:

> *Clive* feels so pressured by his job as a finance director that he unwinds by staying up every night long after his family have gone to bed. He surfs the internet for hours. Only then can he relax. His sexual life is suffering as a result and so is his energy, as he still has to get up at 7 am, regardless of whatever time he has gone to sleep.

> *Man Weh* feels the pressure of being the only son of first-generation immigrants from Hong Kong. His elderly parents speak little or no English and he visits them every day. He also feels obliged to devote a good deal of volunteer time to various support groups working for the London Chinese community.

> *Diane* has six cats, four dogs, a guinea pig and two rabbits whose comfort she puts before her own. Her anthropomorphized relationships with them are probably preventing her putting energy into the more demanding area of human relationships.

> *Colin* loves the rough and tumble of the undemanding male company that he finds in his local pub. This is refreshingly different from the competitive relationships he has at work. Pub life also leads him to drink more beer than is good for his liver or his waistline. Divulging this allows him to speak out loud a worry that he might have an alcohol problem.

360-degree feedback

Mostly in coaching we are dependent on *storytelling* from the client as the main source of data. When you commission a 360-degree process you are bringing the *observation* of others into play – hence its value.

360-degree feedback is a planned process of soliciting comment from a selection of people in a range of relationships all around the client (hence the label 360-degree). These people will typically come from whatever significant constituencies there are in the client's work life – for instance, peers, boss or other seniors, customers/clients, and people who are direct reports. Occasionally clients will suggest adding their partner or adult children to the exercise and there seems no good reason to refuse such requests.

Where you are doing executive coaching, it is vital to make the compelling business case to the client for the self-awareness that 360-degree feedback can bring. 360-degree feedback is not just another nice-to-have – it can also be critical to the success of the business. In his book *The New Leaders* (Goleman *et al.* 2002), Daniel Goleman quotes research into what distinguished the leadership of a number of highly successful US healthcare companies from the least successful ones. Positive performance was measured by return on equity, share price and so on over a ten-year period. He says:

> Tellingly, the CEOs from the poorest performing companies gave themselves the highest ratings on seven of the ten leadership abilities. But the pattern reversed when it came to how their subordinates rated them: they gave these CEOs low ratings on the very same abilities. On the other hand, subordinates saw the CEOs of the best performing companies as demonstrating all ten of these leadership abilities most often.

> (Goleman *et al.* 2002: 95)

Self-delusion was associated with poor company performance and a high level of self-awareness with company success. In one of Goleman's own parallel studies he also found that the more senior the managers, the more they were likely to inflate their own ratings. 'Those at the highest levels had the least accurate view of how they acted with others.'

There are a number of different ways that 360-degree feedback can be done.

By the client

This is the simplest and most direct method. Ask the client to pick eight people and to contract with them for some private time face-to-face and for honest answers to the following questions:

> In what ways do you think I am already effective?
> In what ways do you think I am less effective?

What could I do to improve my relationship with you?

What would be the one piece of advice you would give me about how to improve my effectiveness?

Prime the client on how to encourage honest responses, pressing for examples and further clarity, and writing down everything their feedback givers say without editing. This method has the tremendous advantage of people owning their opinions directly to the client and the client hearing them without any intermediary. However, it does depend on clients being able to stay in non-defensive mode when they hear things they don't like, and it also depends on the ability and willingness of the feedback givers to be straightforward.

Questionnaires

I devised many 360-degree questionnaires in my earlier days as a coach, some for large leadership development programmes. But I gradually became disenchanted with what my own and rival questionnaires actually delivered. This is not to say that all such questionnaires are poor because some are excellent, but having seen many dozens over the last few years the good ones seem to be a small minority.

Many are not devised by psychometricians and contain poorly worded items. There is no guarantee that respondents are interpreting the items in the same way. So, for instance, the same behaviour may be given a score of 4 by one colleague and a score of 5 by another on a 5 point scale. In an attempt to be comprehensive some questionnaires have hundreds of items, taking substantial amounts of time to fill in. Most respondents don't want to be mean so there is a bias to the positive, making results hard to interpret – and luring devisers of the questionnaires into alleging that differences of half a point are significant. Misunderstandings abound – so, for instance, if the item does not have a 'don't know' box, some respondents may click 3 on a 5 point scale, believing it to be 'neutral', whereas this would normally count as a negative response. Where people have many such questionnaires to complete for a number of colleagues they may get so fed up with the process that they just click on any old box in order to get the wretched process over as quickly as possible. The true value is in the narrative comments, but these are commonly just a single sentence in each category, headline-only assertions rather than helpful evidence on behaviour. Some such comments are just bafflingly opaque, frequently misspelt and carelessly punctuated.

You could say that any feedback is better than none, but I find that when my clients have been subjected to this process they are more likely than not to have ignored it, even when it contains messages to which they should in fact have paid attention.

Bespoke 360-degree feedback through interviews

This is the superior version of 360-degree feedback and it is the process I now prefer. As with the questionnaire version, the client nominates and prepares the respondents. You call them under conditions of non-attributable confidentiality, conducting the same structured interview with each, exploring areas such as creating direction, leadership style, performance management, influencing style, communication, and so on. You then write a report for your client based on what you have heard. My reports typically run to seven or eight pages. The advantage of this method is that you can probe for examples and for clarification. You can also explore any interesting inconsistencies – for instance, that the client's impact on more junior people is different from their impact on seniors. The disadvantage of this method is that it depends critically on your ability to ask good questions, to stay objective, to avoid convergent thinking at the same time as not missing the important themes, and to write the report in a way that your client can hear. For added objectivity you might want to commission a colleague who has never met the client to undertake this process for you or to partner you in it.

Debriefing

With all forms of 360-degree feedback, the debrief is the place where the learning begins. Your role here is to help the client look unblinkingly at the messages, positive, negative and middling and to steady and reassure clients who only see the negative. Remind clients that feedback is not an instruction to change: they can choose what they take notice of and what they ignore. You can help them make links to how they see themselves and to other feedback they have received over the years and to make links with their own perceptions of their learning agenda.

The impact of 360-degree feedback is usually considerable.

Annette, continued

Annette decided that there was an information gap for her – she simply did not know what people really thought and felt about her, so she decided to commission some feedback from me.

Annette's feedback confirmed many of her own insights into how others saw her, but it also surprised her. People in her team saw her as calm, composed, stylish and aloof. Her team saw that her ability to make shrewd judgements about the future market and its trends was an important contribution to the firm's success.

Her composure even in a crisis, which both she and others saw as one of her greatest assets, was also perceived to be a weakness. 'Does she actually have feelings?' asked one person exasperatedly. Similarly, her drive, another considerable plus, also had the power to alienate. 'I think she just sees us as invoicing machines' was how one person put it. Many people spotted her failure to grow a successor, pointing out that this was putting the firm at risk.

Similarly, they spelt out in painful detail how undermining they found her difficulty in delegating. The extent of their annoyance and frustration came as a shock to Annette. But perhaps the biggest shock of all was that when asked about what they perceived her values to be, the majority of the people filling in the questionnaire said they did not know. Others assumed that Annette's core motivation was creating personal wealth, a big turn-off for the majority of her staff.

Getting 360-degree feedback was supremely useful for Annette. It allowed her to test her own ideas about what she needed to develop against what other people saw. Like many other clients, the majority of the criticism was about the overuse of her strengths. The process allowed her to make informed decisions about which parts of the feedback to pay attention to and which she could downplay.

Annette was a mature, focused client, already halfway there in terms of self-awareness. Sometimes you will coach people for whom this is not true.

Here the 360-degree process has the potential for enormous shock because how the client sees him- or herself is so much at odds with the perceptions of others. Your role here is to stay steady, calm and compassionate. There is an ever-present danger of colluding. This could include some or all of the following:

It's not true.
It's their fault that they don't see your virtues.
It was a bad day for them when they filled it in.
These must be someone else's results.
The methodology is flawed.
It's only the view of a few people, if more had been asked it would look different.
You used to be like that but of course you've changed
. . . and so on.

Malcolm

Malcolm was poised to leap to the most senior tier in his organization and initially asked for help in dealing with the promotion process. In discussing his agenda, it emerged that he had a number of pressing problems with his current job and we agreed to extend the remit of the coaching to include them. It was clear that 360-degree feedback would help. The dismally negative messages in the report alerted me to the need for extra care in the debrief. People saw Malcolm as an angry bully, impatient, prone to inexplicable rages, impossible to please and unable to develop any but the most able of his team. His saving graces were grudgingly seen as his intelligence and his expert knowledge.

For someone others saw as a bully, Malcolm looked white-faced, shaky and shockingly upset when we met for our session. He was soon in tears. I asked what the tears were about. 'Shame', he said. 'I've had an insight into what it must be like to be managed by me. I'd hate to be managed by me. They don't even like me do they? How could I have got to this?'

Most of that session was spent in constructing exactly what behaviour Malcolm's colleagues saw and why it had the impact it did. We got down to micro-behaviours: the way he sometimes darted forward in his chair; his piercing stare when puzzled; the jabbing finger when explaining his point of view; the way he raised his voice when confronted.

We also looked hard at the fear of failure that lay beneath all of this and how this fear drowned out perspective. In looping back to his autobiographical account, Malcolm made the clearest possible links to a childhood with a bullying and alcoholic father. 'I learnt to fight back then, but what I've got to learn now is that I'm not fighting him – he's been dead many years in any case. I despised him but I'm doing the same kind of behaviour. It's urgent for me to get to like myself and then to start liking others, rather than fearing how they might damage me unless I get in first!'

Several years later, I met Malcolm in another context. He told me that he had never been so frightened in his life as he had been at the moment of receiving that report and that the jolting shock had been the painful but necessary beginning of a new life.

Other useful data for the first session

Ask clients to bring along anything that they think might help give a rounded picture of who they are. This might include their latest appraisal, a staff survey involving their department or organization, and their CV/résumé.

The CV, for instance, may look like a bland, factual document, but actually it tells unerringly how that client sees themselves – or presents themselves to the world, not least what it leaves out. Where clients have already done psychometrics relatively recently, ask them to bring the results with them.

Psychometrics

As part of the 'know thyself' theme for clients, it is useful to be able to offer them a suite of psychometric questionnaires. Psychometrics means, literally, measuring the human mind and as a science it has been around for many decades. What is measured and how you measure it and which method is best will continue to be the focus of fierce debate. There are thousands of questionnaires available, many of dubious merit. You may prefer to rely on the few tried and tested instruments which are backed by convincing research, are easy to understand and have proved genuinely enlightening to clients time and time again.

The case for psychometrics

Many of us assume that the way we approach the world is, plus or minus a few unimportant details, just like the way others approach it. Psychometrics offer a way to demonstrate in just what ways we are like and unlike others. Psychometrics give a short cut through what might otherwise take many hours of further discussion and the language of psychometrics can become a useful shared vocabulary not just between coach and client but between client and other clients.

Using two or three such instruments gives several different methods of approach because the starting point of each will be contrasting but valuable. Here are some popular choices for coaches. You can buy the starred items without being licensed:

> *The Myers-Briggs Type Indicator*™ (MBTI), first developed by Isabel Myers and her mother Katharine Briggs in the middle years of the twentieth century and constantly updated ever since. The underlying framework is Jungian. Clients emerge as having a preference for one of 16 different personality types. The Indicator highlights preferred thinking style and offers hypotheses about the behaviour likely to be associated with each style.

> *The FIRO-B*™ (Fundamental Interpersonal Relationships Orientation – Behaviour), first developed by the US psychologist Will Schutz for the US Navy during the Korean War. The questionnaire produces scores against six dimensions of need and style in terms of how we typically

ve with others and may help explain why we do not always get
; we want from others.

16 PF (Sixteen Personality Factors) was first developed by the
ish psychologist Ray Catell. *The OPQ* (Occupational Personality
Questionnaire) is recognizably in the same genre as the 16 PF.

The Belbin Team Roles Questionnaire. This well-known questionnaire identifies which of nine possible informal roles in a team the
client will typically prefer to play.

*Career Anchors: Edgar Schein's approach to uncovering career
motivators. The basic proposition is that in every life there is one
driving motivator. The questionnaire and booklet (2006) suggest a
format for uncovering what this is. Especially useful for clients where
career is the focus.

The Hogan Personality Inventory is another comprehensive personality assessment emphasizing the 'bright side' of personality and
is usually partnered by the *Hogan Development Inventory*, which
explores the 'dark side' of personality – the qualities most of us have
and which, in certain circumstances, could derail our careers.

*The Thomas-Kilmann Conflict Mode Instrument, first developed
in the 1970s. Five typical conflict-management styles are identified,
giving clients the opportunity to see which they tend to prefer and
which they tend to avoid.

The Enneagram has until recently been an orally taught approach
to personality, said to be based on Sufi thinking and incorporating
a spiritual dimension. There are now questionnaires available which
help identify which of the nine personality types represents your typical style. For a useful briefing on the general approach, read Palmer
and Brown's book, *The Enneagram Advantage* (1998).

Using psychometrics skilfully

The most important question to ask is why you are using a psychometric questionnaire at all. I sometimes observe undue interest from coaches
in questionnaires such as the MBTI. We can all be attracted to these and
other tools and techniques out of anxiety. The thinking goes something like
this:

> If I have a questionnaire to administer and interpret, at least I will be
> on safe ground. I won't have to worry so much about what question
> to ask next. I'll have a structure to help me.

When this is your motive, recognize it for what it is: a way of exerting control over the client and over your own fear of incompetence. Using a questionnaire or any other coaching tool for this reason only postpones the moment of coming face-to-face with the fear and, paradoxically, ensures that you will stay at Level 1 listening (page 37). You could also be tempted to use questionnaires indiscriminately, blind to whether or not the client really needs them. As the old joke has it, 'Give a boy a hammer and he'll discover that everything needs hammering.' Work on your listening skills and questioning technique first.

Don't meddle in this area without training. Licensing training is usually necessary: you can't buy the questionnaires unless you are a registered user. Training prevents disrespectful use of such instruments, on the basis that they could come to seem like an interesting but essentially trivial exercise of about as much importance as a magazine quiz. Training may seem like an expensive and time-intrusive exercise, but where you are planning to use high-quality and well-researched instruments it repays the investment you have made, many times over.

The best time to use psychometrics is at or near the beginning of a coaching programme. Some coaches plan a half-day meeting for the second session where they debrief a number of instruments together or send them to the client in advance of the first session after a conversation about whether or not they might be useful. If you have the qualifications and experience, this is probably the ideal way to do it.

However wonderful a psychometric questionnaire is, and many are wonderful, it is never the whole truth about a person. All questionnaires have weaknesses depending on their underlying theoretical base and how skilfully they have been designed. They are also self-report instruments, so they are always potentially open to being filled in as we would hope to be seen rather than as we really are. High-quality questionnaires have safeguards against this tendency, but none is completely foolproof, so all questionnaires depend to some extent on the subject's willingness to take the risk of being candid. Results can also be affected by mood or by particular periods of stress or crisis.

Carl Jung, on whose thinking the MBTI is based, described his typology as 'compass points in the wilderness of human personality'. Those are wise words.

The feedback discussion is at the heart of the process. It involves allowing enough time for a full exploration and asking how the client felt answering the questions as well as reassuring them that you will be keeping their results confidential. Acknowledge any scepticism or irritation as healthy while briefly explaining the underlying theory behind the questionnaire. Explore how far the results match self-perception and any other sources of feedback, and ask the client for examples of behaviour which match reported results as well as seeking examples of behaviour which do *not* match. Finally, spend a little time looking at strengths and development areas and agreeing how to take these forward.

In using psychometric questionnaires you are potentially disturbing the balance of power in the client–coach relationship. In the normal run of a coaching conversation, the client has the information and you have the questions – in pursuit of a shared understanding. With psychometrics, you have expert information about the questionnaire. This could disadvantage the client and probably explains why many clients will express nervousness about completing a questionnaire when unfamiliar with its purpose:

> Will it tell you something about me that could be uncomfortably revealing?

Poor use of debriefing techniques can include what one of my colleagues dubs *psychological rape*: telling the client that they are something devastatingly unpleasant from the lofty pinnacle of your expertise:

> The questionnaire tells me that you are undemocratic in the way you run your team.

> You are at risk of imploding if you don't manage your stress better.

> You don't delegate very well do you?

This is why the principles of creating trust through respect must prevail here as elsewhere in coaching. If the client does not want to take a 'test', even after you have given them your best shot at reassurance, then don't press it. Taking any psychometric questionnaire should be voluntary. Watch out for any tendency in yourself to make arbitrary assertions about what a client can or can't do (jobs, skills, relationships) on the basis of the results of the questionnaire. None of them has sufficient predictive validity to do this, but in any case such an assertion would be an abuse. Equally importantly, it's essential to resist the temptation to over-interpret. Your role is to explain. The questionnaire results are hypotheses only. Any interpretation should be left to the client. Be alert to your own results on the same instruments, sharing them with clients in the interests of equality and keeping constantly aware of the biases and blind spots which might influence how you work with your client on these same issues.

It can be tempting to assume that questionnaire results represent some kind of final judgement on a person, regardless of that person's own view of themselves. One of the most important questions in the debriefing discussion is, 'How does this seem to you?', or 'How does this tally with how you see yourself?' The client's answer here has to be the best and last word on the topic.

For executive clients, it will be essential to include a steady look at what the organization needs from the coaching as well as what goals the client has from a scan of their personal lives. This is the subject of the next chapter.

7 Choosing the future: creating goals for coaching

If excellent questioning is one pillar of coaching technique, another must surely be setting robust goals. This chapter sets out why it matters to set goals and how to do it, including how to involve a sponsor where there is one and how to include goals for personal life.

Findings from research

Goal-setting as an aspect of motivation has been one of the most minutely examined areas of management and has been the focus of many hundreds of studies. It has also been the centre of many research projects in sports science – for instance, what part does goal-setting play in improving the performance of athletes? The outcome of these studies gives a remarkably consistent picture.

We are right to be concerned about goal-setting because the research shows – without a doubt – that the very process of setting a goal directs attention and therefore affects behaviour and can improve performance. Waffly, vague goals don't do it: the more explicit and measurable a goal is, the more effective it is likely to be as a way of changing behaviour. It is better to have a stretching goal which has intermediate, measurable steps, than to have an overarching easy goal. Goal-setting is at its most effective when it builds on strengths – so it is more motivating to ask *How can I be even better at something I'm already good at?* than *How can I tackle a weakness?* Developing strategies for coping with the inevitable difficulties en route can make the difference between success and failure.

The research shows that it matters who sets the goal: a negotiated goal in which you participate in an unforced way is likely to have the biggest impact. There is a difference between *performance* goals, which are about avoiding appearing incompetent, and *learning* goals, which are about mastery. Learning goals are far more effective in enhancing self-esteem and in their long-term impact.

There is a firm match in these findings[1] with what we know works with goal-setting in coaching. Goal-setting matters. It matters to the client because getting clarity on goals begins the whole process of change. It matters to the coach because without this clarity you will not be able to work well with the client or measure the success of your coaching.

Where and how goal-setting goes wrong

When you are aware that a session has had an uneasily unsatisfactory feel to it, assume until proved otherwise that poor goal-setting was the cause. Here is some of what can go wrong and how it happens.

The coach assumes they know what the goal for the session is, but never clarifies it – and the real goal is something different

This phenomenon is well expressed in the reflective diary that Suzie submitted as part of her Diploma portfolio. This was her second session with János, a 45-year-old former librarian who had been unemployed for a year, and had said he was looking for a job. But Suzie had established that János still yearned to recapture the modest success in the music industry he had enjoyed as a young man:

Suzie

I really struggled in this session. It seemed to start OK, but as it went on I felt more and more worried. He was very polite and so was I, but the time went *sooo* slowly! When I asked him for feedback, he said he wasn't sure that coaching was right for him and that maybe two sessions were enough. I felt so hurt! I was giving him my time for free! I also felt angry though tried not to show it, but inside I was thinking, *Well why don't you get off your backside and look for a job, for heaven's sake, do you really want a job or are you content to sit around feeling sorry for yourself for another year . . .!*

However, when I played the recording back, it all became so very clear what had happened. I had assumed that the goal was how to find another library job. But I had never asked the question that would have established whether this was the goal for the session or not. The real goal lurking there somewhere was whether he should have one last go at establishing himself again as a musician. I know literally nothing about the freelance music world. I had assumed that he would want another job like the one he had held previously. Whereas, for János, none of this turned out to be correct. I just didn't pick up his reluctance to pursue the 'proper job' option because I never questioned my own assumptions.

Suzie's experience is salutary and is also common. It is so easy to assume that you know what the client's goal is. This can happen even with experienced coaches. In fact it may even be more tempting for those experienced coaches who have heard so many of the same issues before – or believe they have. *Oh yes*, you think, *this is my old friend better time management*, or, *It's that good old work–life balance issue again.* Whereas actually, it may be nothing of the sort.

The coach confuses the client's responsibility to set the agenda with the coach's responsibility to clarify and frame the goal

As Suzie's experience also shows, while it is the client's job to create the agenda, it is the coach's job to frame the agenda items into the goals on which coach and client can work. It is a mistake to assume that clients will arrive at their sessions with perfectly formed goals. Much more frequently, client and coach use the first part of each chunk in a coaching session to get clear exactly what that goal is. It is normal for clients to be at least a little vague or confused about the goal and for the real goal to emerge through skilful questioning on the part of the coach. In fact, if the client was already totally clear about the goal, they might not need the coaching at all. This is because clarity about the goal may already be generating the motivation that will sweep the client towards achieving it.

The coach allows the client to chatter on about what has happened since the last session without intervening to agree goals

All coaching sessions will rightly start with a catch-up. *What has happened since we last met? How did you get on in that important meeting we discussed?* But some clients can let this account run on seamlessly into the body of the session. The goals might be implied in this chatter, but because they are never made explicit, confusion is the usual result.

Getting stuck on 'problems'

Typically what happens is this. The client presents his or her issue as a problem:

> I can't manage my time.
> My business is failing – we've got terrible results this quarter.
> I feel stressed all the time.

The coach's sympathy is aroused – she wants to help. She then dives into the many dimensions of the problem: how much, how many, how awful . . . quickly feeling as hopeless as the client. Where you have the benefit of a video recording or actual observation you can see both client and coach literally sinking deeper into their chairs with the misery of it all. Sympathetic chat, yes, but coaching, no.

Being asked to change someone who is not present

Here the client presents another variant of the problem-scenario. The client says:

> My boss is awful – I can't bear her.
> I've got this poor performer in my team.
> I'm working with someone who's cheating the company.

The trap here is to ask a lot of questions about the non-present person: How old are they? What is their role? What is the behaviour they do which is so upsetting? Soon, unless you manage it carefully, this leads into the realms of speculation: Why do you think they behave like this? What are they thinking when they do this? How do you feel they might respond if you did this or that thing?

When you go down this track you are potentially colluding with the client, tacitly agreeing that the problem is *out there*, rather than *in here*. The only person you have in the room is the client, and they are one half of the relationship. You can't coach someone who is not present. Nor can you coach a client on a problem which they do not own – only on the part which is theirs. So, for the client who suspects that a colleague is cheating the company, the goal cannot be, as hinted by the client, to stop him cheating. But the goal might be, after discussion with the client, to assess the evidence that cheating is indeed taking place and then to tackle the dilemma of what to do about it.

The goal is enormous: far too big to work on in any one session

When clients have stored a high degree of misery and uncertainty inside themselves for some time, the relief of having a sympathetic and non-judgemental person to discuss it with can be overwhelming. When asked about their goals for coaching, they may say something like:

> I want to know what to do with the rest of my life.
> I want to be happier.
> I need to develop a better leadership style.
> I want to know why I'm still single at 40.

While these are important underlying themes they are far too big to manage in one session and must be broken down into sub-goals where you can work one chunk at a time. Also, the bigger the overall goal, the more likely it is that the mental blocks and barriers are substantial, will only dissolve slowly, and that consequently the 'answers' will emerge gradually. It is most unlikely that the client will suddenly have a eureka moment where an easy solution to a major and long-standing problem just plops into place, though to read some accounts of coaching you could imagine, as a naïve coach, that this is an everyday occurrence.

The client doesn't actually have any goals

This may seem odd. Surely every client has a goal – isn't that why they've come for coaching? But now that coaching has become a popular intervention in organizations, coaching is being widely offered to whole cohorts of staff – for instance, as follow-up to a management development programme. Here there may be explicit pressure to attend a given number of coaching sessions. This can lead to serious discomfort for the coach:

Jade

After I completed my coaching qualification I was desperate for clients and felt delighted to be asked to be one of the coaching faculty for a big telecoms company where there was a leadership development programme that was more or less mandatory for a particular level of staff. The first session was fine because it had a set structure that every coach was obliged to follow: to debrief some psychometrics and then review the client's 360-degree feedback. After that it was up to the client. I had many people in this programme who cancelled their sessions at the last moment or who arrived looking blank about their goals. When I asked what they wanted to get out of the session they would look down, shake their heads, or sometimes scowl. 'I don't know' was a frequent reply. I soon realized that they felt it was impossible to say they didn't want or need the coaching and that they were displaying their resentment at what they felt was a waste of time. The impact on me was to feel utterly useless: I felt it was my fault. The difference when I left that faculty and began to find my own clients – people who really did want to be there and did know what they wanted to work on – was just amazing.

A coaching conversation is unlike other kinds of friendly discussion in many ways, not least in the emphasis it puts on change. Even anger is better than apathy. The awareness of dissatisfaction is what creates our energy for transformation and improvement. Where a client believes that nothing needs to change, there can be no coaching:

Jonathan

Jonathan was a newly-appointed ambassador and had just been through a five-day leadership programme at the UK's Foreign & Commonwealth Office. Coaching was on offer to all participants as a follow-up. When I asked him what challenges his new role would involve this was how the conversation went, in shortened form:

Jonathan: Well, this posting is the apex of my career. It's a very important country strategically for the UK and I'm looking forward to going there. It's going to be great. My wife and I . . .

JR: (Interrupting) Sorry to interrupt you, but coaching is really about working with you on the challenges that the new role will bring. What do you think those will be?

Jonathan: Well, I think I can take them all in my stride really. You see this is the apex of my career, and . . . (and on round the same loop several times).

While it was perfectly possible that Jonathan could have benefited from coaching, he did not really believe he needed it because he seemed to have no immediate or longer-term goals that coaching could satisfy. Privately I mused that it was not the role of the coach to be audience to the client's theatre. This was a charming and able man, but I was willing to forecast that any coaching would quickly peter out and I was not prepared to live with the disappointment and frustration that this would involve.

There is a more benign version of the problem presented by the client who seems not to have any goals. For instance, when you are working with an experienced client – that is, someone who has worked successfully with you or another coach previously over a longish period of time – they may well tell you that what they value about the sessions is the chance to reflect in a free-flowing way on whatever has happened since you last saw them. They may use the metaphor of the sessions as a 'sounding board'. When this happens, stay alert to your own awareness that you do not have a classically framed goal, prompting the client to explore whatever seems to be emerging from the topics that are on their mind. Useful questions here will combine brief summarizing with a tentative suggestion about the agenda for the session:

> So it seems from what you're saying that your relationship with [name of boss] is changing. I'm wondering if we should explore that today?

> I notice that you seem preoccupied with the issue of how those team meetings are going. Is that important enough to put on our agenda for this session?

When to say no to taking on a client

It's a tough old world out there for coaches. At workshops on how to develop a coaching business, the number one question for everyone in the room is 'How do I get new clients?' A neglected question is when to turn a prospective client away. I will rarely take on a new client without a so-called *look-see* or *chemistry* conversation whose aim is to assess the viability of the relationship from both sides. Lack of goals is one of the main reasons that I will tell a client not only that I am not the right coach for them but also, sometimes, that I doubt they need a coach at all. The million dollar question here is, 'If we could wave a magic wand, look into the future and say that this coaching has been successful, what would have changed for you?' Where what people need and what you offer is clearly a poor match, suggest other sources of help. Some people are not coachable, especially if their levels of self-awareness and capacity to take responsibility for themselves are low.

Here are some common situations when it would be sensible to say no:

> The would-be client is a young graduate who is unemployed and has returned home to parents who, much as they love him, really don't want him there. Desperate to get this giant cuckoo out of the nest, the parents decide that coaching is the solution. You agree to a look-see conversation with the potential client, but when this happens, you find that this young person seems to be prepared to indulge their parents by agreeing to the coaching, but has very little motivation of their own. Without motivation, no coaching can be successful.

> The prospective client is referred by their HR professional. On enquiry you find that there are serious performance problems where the person's technical ability is being questioned. The client him or herself is keen for the coaching to happen, but how much difference

can it really make to the likely outcome? Probably very little. You are a coach not a mentor. This organization may want to be seen to be doing the right thing – before an inevitable parting takes place.

The client tells you that they are 'curious about what coaching is' and wonders 'if it might be fun'. Or says that because the organization has made it available, they may as well give it a try. Or, it's free, so why not? None of these is a strong foundation for future work.

During the conversation to assess mutual fit, the client displays unusual, extreme or odd behaviour which could indicate mental health issues. If you feel, after due consideration, that this is what might be going on, then keep away – this is not your field.

The prospective client talks a lot about the failings of others and how if only they would change, everything would be fine. This tells you that their ability to accept responsibility for themselves is low – an essential precondition for coaching. It's possible that you could work with this person, but be aware that progress could be slow.

A good friend asks you to coach them, for instance on preparation for a job interview. You can never be as candid with a friend as you can with a client. Coaching is a blend of high support and high challenge. If you value the friendship, say no and suggest a trusted colleague instead.

Never be afraid to refuse the assignment if you can see that the client's level of coachability is low. Where this is the case, it is unlikely that the coaching can be successful.

The price of failing to set real goals

There is a high price to pay for failing to tackle these familiar problems. The coaching goes nowhere. If there is a sponsor who is paying, this person is likely to be annoyed and disappointed. Reputation is everything in coaching and your reputation will suffer. As the coach you feel incompetent, and lose confidence.

What happens inside the session is that it begins to acquire a going-round-in-circles air. This is because it is going round in circles. No goal has been set so the coach cannot ask powerful questions and gets stuck on what to say next. The client's real goal has not been identified so both parties are likely to endorse the polite fiction that they are engaged in coaching. But inside, both will have the feeling that something is wrong. Both may be blaming themselves – the coach for not knowing what to do to retrieve the situation, the client for failing in the role of client. Alternatively, both parties may be blaming the other. The coach finds herself disliking the client for his vagueness and the client finds himself criticizing the coach for not bringing a solution any closer.

At this point the coach will experience the energy swiftly leaching away from the session because the client will be stalling and blocking. The coach gradually begins to do more and more of the work, stepping up interventions in frequency and length, while the client seems to disappear from the conversation.

Solutions

- The first part of the solution is to notice what is happening: you do not yet have a goal you can work on. Next, remind yourself constantly that it is your job to provide *the process framework of the session*, meaning its mechanics such as goal-setting and timekeeping. Never leave this to the client or assume that, if you did, the client could or would want to do it.
- If you notice that the first five or ten minutes have passed and that you have not agreed goals, stick at it with the client until you do have a set of proper goals for the session. Don't let the client wriggle out of it. Interrupt if necessary (see page 188). Be prepared to express your unease.
- Where clients present their issues as negatives, aim to flip the negative to a positive. You cannot work on a negative. For instance, it cannot be a goal to say that you would like to avoid losing at tennis. It is a goal to say that you would like to win your matches. So, for instance, if the client says, 'I can't talk to my sister without there being a row,' you respond, 'So you'd like to be able to learn how to talk to your sister with calm on both sides?'
- Make sure the goal includes the phrase *how to*.
- If the issue is a dilemma, the goal may be how to get clarity on what the issues are rather than necessarily finding a solution on the spot, or it may be to weigh up all the alternatives and make the actual decision. So the client says, 'I don't know whether to stay in my present job or look for a managerial role.' You respond, 'So you'd like to use this session to get clarity about whether to stay put or look for a managerial role?'
- Where the client still resists, again express your unease and say, 'I'm still not sure that we have a real goal here.' Other useful phrases are:

> Assuming our coaching today is successful, what would have changed for you as a result?
>
> What's our goal for this session?

What would an ideal solution here be?

What help do you need from me on this?

- Distinguish the goal *for the session* from the goal around the *issue*. So the overall goal might be that the client wants to prepare for a job selection process, but the goal for the session might be to get feedback on how he or she is answering typical job interview questions.

Getting the knack

When put like this the whole goal-setting process possibly sounds tedious and long-winded. It is actually a knack, and need take no more than a few moments, but like so much else in coaching, the knack is acquired through a high level of self-awareness, plus training, practice and feedback from a more experienced coach or supervisor. Goal-setting need not be humourless and mechanical. It should not feel like a *technique* that you are practising on the client, rather something that emerges naturally from a conversation characterized by empathy and goodwill.

Note that experienced clients do realize the importance of proper goals and will begin to frame them in a way that means you and they can start work straight away. A short while ago, a client with whom I have worked off and on for some years, through several different jobs, leapt into the room and scarcely had his coat off before saying, 'I know you're going to ask me what my goals for the session are and I know you won't let me get away with anything fluffy. So here are my three goals for the session in priority order and I suggest we spend the first 45 minutes on that one and then see how we go.' Naturally, I agreed to all this with meekness, grace and good humour.

Transactional (performance) and transformational (learning) goals

In coaching we are working with two different kinds of goals, often simultaneously. *Transactional* or *performance* goals are specific tasks that a client wants to achieve. These are often externally imposed and have an emphasis on short-term performance. Sometimes they have the flavour of dodging failure or of avoiding looking incompetent. Examples would be:

- Enrol for the gym and go twice a week.
- Run my departmental meeting to time.
- Get through a job interview successfully.

- Recruit a new marketing manager.
- Deliver an effective presentation to the Board next week.
- Carry out appraisals with all of my staff by the end of February.

There is nothing wrong with such goals: I work on goals like them with clients all the time.

However, *transformational* – or *learning* – goals have much more power. These are the goals that are about intrinsic satisfaction. They are internally focused and are about increasing capacity to deal with similar situations and dilemmas whenever they arise, rather than with achieving a short-term task. It really only needs a moment or two of reframing to help the client see the difference:

Transactional goal	A transformational equivalent
Enrol for the gym and go twice a week.	Discover what I enjoy and can sustain to improve my physical fitness and then commit to it.
Deliver an effective presentation to the Board next week.	Increase my awareness of what constitutes effectiveness in presentations and apply it effortlessly whenever I have to give one.
Carry out appraisals with all of my staff by the end of February.	Develop my understanding of how to manage performance well; develop the skills to do it every time.
Get through a job interview.	Present myself with impact and integrity in any situation where I am the focus of attention or competing with others.

Business and organizational goals

When you are working as an executive coach, the whole process of goal-setting becomes at once more complicated and easier. It is more complicated because there is more to consider and easier because, if you do it the right way, you will have a far better grasp of the real issues in the client's life. Executive coaching is fundamentally a business proposition where client and coach work together for the benefit of a third party – the organization. It is not enough to say to the organization, in effect, *Trust me to work with this client – it will bring value to the organization – honest!* If you do this, coaching becomes a mysterious process – a secret between coach and client. And since the organization has no input into the purposes of the coaching it may become suspicious about its focus, let alone having any way of assessing return on its investment.

When the coach is uneasy with business processes and maybe does not have a strong personal background as a senior manager, coaching can become more like life-coaching where the emphasis is exclusively on personal relationships and personal goals. This is unlikely to be what the organization needs from the process.

The organizational context provides yet another source of significant demand for change. The organization is part of its environment where there will be pressures from customers or users, competitors, regulators, or from technological advance. So, yet another important conversation that you need to have with the client is to establish just what these pressures are. It is improbable that any individual can be successful acting alone, so the behaviour and attitudes of the client's team are also an important part of the picture. All of these will then have an impact on the performance of the organization.

One way of representing this approach to goal-setting for executive clients is to see it diagrammatically, as in Figure 7.1.

Executive coaching is far more likely to fail when it concentrates exclusively on the circle labelled Leader's behaviour. The more you and your client can include the whole system, the more effective the coaching is likely to be.

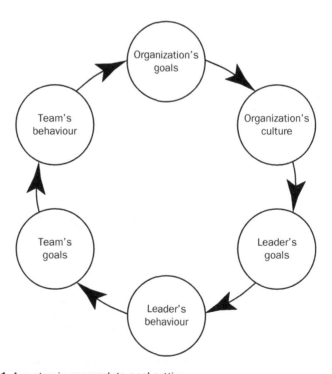

Figure 7.1 A systemic approach to goal-setting

Three- or four-cornered contracting

Make it standard procedure, wherever possible, to ask for a three-cornered meeting or conference call with the client's boss. Where you have a keen HR professional involved, it might become a four-cornered meeting. The purpose is to get the organization's perspective on what they want the coaching to achieve for the client. The conversation will also give you invaluable insight into the culture of the organization and will prevent you getting too fixed on the client's version of events. This is how to do it.

Before the meeting

Ask for the client's consent. Explain the benefits and ask him or her to approach the boss or sponsor. Set up the meeting or call, explaining that it will take two hours altogether, and email everyone to confirm the purpose and timings. Your role is to facilitate the discussion. You are not doing coaching, even though you should expect this to be a meeting for which the client will be paying the full fee. Your aim is to clarify the organization's needs.

Stage 1: meet the boss

Spend the first 30 minutes alone with the boss. Encourage frankness. If your potential client is a problem performer, the boss will often be far more candid with you than they have been up until now with the potential client, but establish whether this is the case by asking, 'So how frank have you been about these issues with X?' True candour is remarkably rare. Useful questions to ask the boss have strong echoes of the goal-setting technique you will be doing with the client in due course:

> So ideally, what will have changed for you if this coaching is successful?
> What's at stake for the organization here?
> How will we evaluate the success of this coaching programme?

Stage 2: boss, client and coach

Ask the client to join you and spend the next 40 minutes facilitating the same discussion. Encourage the boss to be as straightforward about the organization's needs as they were with you when alone. Gain the agreement of the boss to be involved in the 'homework' between sessions, if appropriate – for instance, giving feedback on changed behaviour. The more open the client can be about what is happening in the coaching sessions, the better the outcome because the goals become transparent and public, thus increasing the chances that they will be met.

This meeting also offers the chance for gathering valuable data about the client. You will see at first hand how he or she typically behaves. I have observed a wide range of behaviour here from a client who was visibly trembling with anxiety throughout every minute of our discussion with his boss to one who noisily disputed every point her boss made. When it emerges, as it sometimes does, that the boss–client relationship itself seems to be the problem, I will offer a facilitated meeting for the pair as an alternative or adjunct to coaching.

Be prepared to challenge unrealistic expectations and to agree alternatives.

Stage 3: client and coach

Ask for 40 minutes alone with potential clients to discuss whether they are up for coaching or not. This is especially important if it is the first time you have actually met. You cannot work with a reluctant client, so say something like:

> How do you feel about what you have just heard? (Expect that some clients may be shocked and angry.)
> Your organization has made this time and budget available, but it's up to you whether you take advantage of it or not. How do you feel about going ahead?
> What concerns do you have about this process?
> How will you report on progress to your sponsor?

Stage 4: review at the end of the coaching

When the coaching is finished, negotiate a review meeting or conference call with boss or sponsor and client. The purpose is to enable the client to point out to the funder what has changed, what has been learnt, and how he or she proposes to embed the learning into everyday practice. This is often a crucial part of the process. Bosses can have fixed ideas about the client, sometimes secretly believing that they cannot or will not change. This can be profoundly dismaying to a client who has made heroic efforts to change, but has seen that these changes have not been registered by the funder. Don't comment on the content or process of the sessions, but do help clients articulate what they believe has changed and encourage funders to do the same.

Note that some very senior clients initiate their own coaching programme, paying for the coaching entirely out of budgets over which they have total control. This process may be highly unattractive. It may look pointless and intrusive, in which case you should not press it.

Identifying personal goals

My philosophy of coaching has an explicitly whole-person perspective. So it follows that the goal-setting process must encompass the personal as well as the professional. Coaching will then have a powerful double focus.

Alastair

Alastair is running a hospital, taking over after the previous chief executive was dismissed. He has inherited a large deficit and a demoralized staff, mortified that their hospital has been in the headlines for such negative reasons. However, Alastair also knows from his initial few weeks in the hospital that it has an inward-looking culture with doctors who are hostile to the managers they see, rightly or wrongly, as their 'enemies'. Alastair's organizational goals, agreed in a three-way meeting with his chair and coach, are to:

- reduce deficit to zero within 18 months;
- rebuild the confidence and competence of the executive team;
- reorganize the clinical structures through 're-engineering' based on 'patient journeys' rather than on the old functional structures; this project to be led by senior doctors;
- meet all the government-imposed targets;
- achieve the highest possible ratings by government auditors.

This is a formidable list. After working with Alastair in his first session there were also a number of personal goals. These included:

- finding a permanently sustainable way to reduce his weight;
- increasing his physical fitness and his energy;
- improving his ability to influence his peers so that he obtains commitment, not the compliance which had been a feature of the previous regime;
- delegating more effectively;
- establishing strong relationships of trust with his chair, commissioners and the Department of Health.

The personal and the organizational goals were tightly intertwined for Alastair. He knew he was not, and never could be, the *rescuer* of his hospital. The three-cornered conversation with his coach and boss

demonstrated clearly that quietly inspirational leadership was fundamental to the organization's recovery and the first session alone with his
coach concentrated on the issue of staying physically fit and energetic
as a vital foundation to all the other work.

He could only deliver on the organizational agenda through
addressing his personal needs: developing his team through skilled performance management, including delegating appropriately and learning how to coach them, using positive influencing techniques to nurture
the upward relationships, as well as building strong relationships with
the doctors in the hospital.

It is true that organizations commissioning coaching are by and large only
interested in the behaviour and capability of their staff. Their suspicion that
executive coaching is really just therapy-lite, or life-coaching in disguise, is
often somewhere just below the surface. Senior clients, especially where they
are in extremely exposed and public roles, can experience a sense of distress
and dislocation. They will report a feeling of meaninglessness in their lives.
Some are classic overachievers who want to step away from long hours and
their obsession with competence, but don't know how to do it. For this reason,
coaching is always more powerful if coach and client can work on the area of
private life as well as on the mechanics of behaviour in a work context. There
are many hundreds of possible tools and techniques you can use to access
this material and you will have your own favourites. I have picked several to
describe here that I have found consistently useful.

The Life Scan Wheel

This simple, powerful and well-known exercise is rightly a favourite for
coaches. Sometimes known as the Balance Wheel, or the Fulfilment Wheel,
it asks you to assess your satisfaction with your life as it is now, comparing
it with how you would like it to be. The centre of the Wheel represents zero
fulfilment or satisfaction and the outer edge of each wedge represents total
fulfilment (see Figure 7.2).

The case for using this tool is that it encourages clients to see their lives
as a whole – often for the first time. It conveys the expectation that, as a
coach, you are as interested in the personal aspects of their lives as in the
work aspects. Also, it is another way for clients to tell you about what is currently going on in their lives.

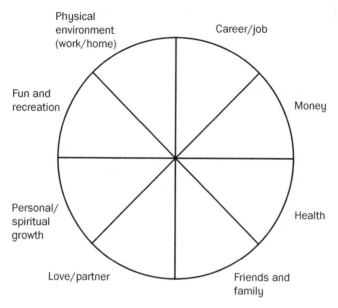

Figure 7.2 Life Scan exercise

Directions: This exercise asks you to assess your satisfaction with your life as it is now. The centre represents zero satisfaction. The outer edge represents 10: total satisfaction. Rate each wedge on this 0–10 scale, then draw a line connecting each one. What kind of wheel emerges?

For many clients this is a relatively painless way to pass on important information to you. Here is one example:

Richard

Richard: I'm really proud of my relationship with my partner, Bernardo. We've been together for 15 years. I'm keen to be seen as a good example of an 'out' gay man in a powerful position, but this also poses me a problem.

Coach: How is this a problem?

Richard: Because my company wants to move me to a country where Bernardo would not be able to get a visa and we refuse to be separated!

Using this tool allowed Richard to declare an important issue, his sexuality, in a swift and legitimate way, rather than having to find some other means of giving the coach such vital data.

How to use the Wheel

Send it to clients in advance of the first session, explaining how to fill it in and asking them to bring it with them, then at the session, ask clients to talk you through the thinking behind the way they have scored each wedge. This should take ten minutes or so. You are using it to establish an agenda for coaching not as the prompt for coaching in this session (see also Annex 1 for help on running the first session). Don't press clients who either say directly or indicate indirectly that they do not want to talk about any particular area, but log it privately for possible future exploration. Ask clients what links they see between the way they have scored the different wedges. An example might be that a client who has scored his satisfaction with work at 8 or 9 has also scored his partner relationship at 1 or 2. Sometimes when a client wheel looks like this, the client has poured everything into work at the expense of a marriage. It has become a negatively fulfilling cycle: work is enjoyable and rewarding so the client puts love and energy into it; the marriage is unfulfilling and unrewarding so the client dodges putting love and energy into it, thus ensuring that it becomes even less fulfilling and rewarding. This may seem like a simple and stunningly obvious connection, but it is often a point that the client has avoided seeing until that moment.

Ask about how much energy the client has for change in any areas that show low satisfaction. Don't assume that a low score means a willingness to change, or even that your role should be to challenge reluctance to change a low score. Then, finally, ask how the areas of satisfaction and dissatisfaction link to the client's initial ideas on goals for the coaching.

Alternatives to the Wheel

There are many alternative approaches which you might prefer. For instance, you can invite the client to name and develop the categories. For this you need a large sheet of paper – a flip chart page is ideal. Hand the client a set of pens and ask them to draw a pie chart in the centre of the page, leaving plenty of space to add further rings. This inner circle should represent how the client spends their time now. Now add a second circle outside the first, allocating different proportions representing how the client would ideally like to spend their time, listing the benefits this would bring. Add a third circle, writing in each category what will need to change in order to bring these changes about.

Kevin

Kevin was a 53-year-old senior manager in an oil company. He was a 'lifer' – someone who had spent his entire working life in one organization. He had lost his zest for work. Kevin was frustrated by his inability to devote time to the Third World charity which reflected his strong religious beliefs. In his inner circle he drew a number of wedges for work, indicating 'organizational politicking', managing his team, visiting chemical plants, going to conferences and travel.

Kevin's job involved at least 80 days a year of international travel, and he had increasing distaste for the stresses this created. His marriage was a longstanding, loving relationship and his wife had recently retired. A generous salary was matched by a generous company pension scheme, so money was not an issue.

His second circle showed a dramatic contrast: work reduced to a small proportion of the whole and the leisure pursuits much enlarged. Benefits included better health, increased time for relaxation, learning Spanish and enjoying his marriage. In the third circle, Kevin described what needed to happen to bring about the ideal. Essentially this meant talking to his employer about voluntary redundancy and moving to a consultancy role, refining his consultancy skills, learning Spanish 'properly' and concentrating on the work he really enjoyed.

Two years later, all of this had happened. Kevin freelances for his old company and several others, and also gives free consultancy to his favourite charity, where his hard-won worldly wisdom is much valued.

Drawing your life

Many clients have endlessly analysed their situations. They can articulate exactly what is wrong, yet somehow things still stay the same. For these clients, it can produce a much better response when they move away from the comfort of words and analysis to using the playful, creative parts of their brains. Here is one way to do it. Hand the client a large piece of paper and a clutch of juicy felt-tip pens in a range of colours, or use a drawing app on a tablet computer if you or they have one. Ask them to draw two pictures. The first: how your life is now. The second: how you would like your life to be. Reassure the client that no artistic ability is required and let them loose to draw, then talk through the results, asking the client what needs to happen to move from the present to the desired future.

An ideal day

Invite clients to tell you the story of their ideal day from the time they get up in the morning to the time they go to bed. What would be happening? What, specifically, would they be doing? Ask clients to use the present tense, describing the day as if it is actually happening. An alternative, which is especially useful for clients with work–life balance issues, is to hand the client a blank diary representing a complete week. Say: 'Imagine you have given up your present job. Fill in this diary with an ideal week of activities which do not include paid work.' Most clients find this an absorbing exercise – I usually ask them to complete it between sessions. The follow-up discussion will include topics such as:

> How difficult was it to fill all the time? (Usually it is impossible)
> What would it be like to live this life?
> What would it be like to live your life with this as the yardstick rather than fitting your private life around your work?

Identifying life purpose

Sooner or later in any substantial piece of coaching, one big question appears: 'What's my life purpose?' Underneath this question is the one virtually all of us must ask ourselves at some point: *What meaning does life have anyway?* A sense of pointlessness is often behind the initial request for coaching. All of this is immeasurably bolstered by the myths and fantasies with which we surround ourselves. The most popular include:

I'll be able to slow down tomorrow.	Reality: unlikely. Working with manic energy becomes a habit.
Working long hours now will clear time for me later.	Reality: the longer the hours you work, the more you train others to expect those hours as your norm and they will obligingly fill up your in-tray for you.
Buying my children nice things will make up for the time I can't spend with them.	Reality: nice things can never replace parental time.
I am my job – they couldn't manage without me.	Reality: they forget you more or less as soon as you have left.

Asking about core life purpose cuts through all of this, and often comes as a shock. It is why, even in the real and apparent trauma of sudden redundancy or sacking, clients can feel energized and optimistic. Once you are clear about life purpose, major decisions are much easier. Any turning point can be held up against the life-purpose benchmark. Don't equivocate or apologise to clients about life purpose. It sounds a bit of a portentous phrase – and perhaps it is. But introduce it confidently.

Some approaches to identifying life purpose

The simplest is to ask a series of straightforward questions. Where you have already done an autobiography session with a client, these questions may usefully build on to the answers the client gave you then.

What do other people constantly say that they value about you?
If money was not an issue, what would you do?
What do you enjoy most about your current job?
What skill or task do you perform so easily that you don't need to think about it?
What do you enjoy most about your non-work life?
What unrealized goals are there for you?
What themes or threads run through your life?
What do you want to leave behind you as a legacy?
Who are you when you are at your most generous, most loving and showing the most integrity?

A postcard from the future

This is a simple but powerful exercise. Give the client a postcard. Say, 'Imagine it's some time in the future: choose your own time frame. Now write yourself a postcard from that time, reminding yourself what you are now doing, saying what you love about it and describing what you did to get there.' What this activity does is to make the ideal feel within their grasp, and seeing it written down makes it tangible. Some coaches use a variant where the time frame is six months. The client writes the card, the coach keeps it and posts it to the client six months later.

Giving, not taking

Most clients quickly realize that true life purpose is more about what they want to give than about what they want to take. It is the giving that bestows significance, not the taking. When you are focused on taking, you can never have enough of whatever it is you want to take, whether it is money, fame, power, glamorous possessions, houses, the thrills of chasing sex or of outwitting competitors. When taking is the concern you have to be constantly on your guard because others might steal or damage what you have, whether these are cheeky younger colleagues after your job, a rival for your love, or feckless burglars after your possessions.

This is why working with clients on their life purpose is not the same as indulging fantasies about running away to find your true self, or to recover your lost inner child, wandering about India, wafting incense, wearing loose robes and sandals, or any of the other faux-spiritual quests seemingly encouraged by certain writers and self-described gurus.

Sometimes a simple reframing is all that needs to happen. The client is already in the right arena, doing the right sort of job and leading the right sort of life. What is missing is seeing the significance of the choices he or she has made. People's choices of partner, of job, of work sector, are rarely accidental. Part of our work as coaches is to make explicit what has always been present but partially hidden.

Mark

Mark was running a voluntary sector organization with a successful trading arm. There was a split in the organization between people who saw themselves as tough, commercially focused professionals and the people who believed in its original campaigning mission and purpose. The commercially focused people saw the campaigners as 'fluffy' and the campaigners saw the marketers and finance specialists as cynical opportunists.

Mark straddled the two uneasily. He had grown up in a big Catholic family in West Belfast and as a boy had naïvely joined in riots and fighting 'because it was fun and exciting'. It had given him insights into what it was like to feel beleaguered and disadvantaged. Early on in life, Mark had discovered that he had a gift for advocacy. He had used it in a student debating society and it took him seamlessly into a series of what he called 'sub-political' roles – for instance, working for an English member of parliament as a researcher.

It was easy for Mark to answer questions about his life purpose. 'Righting wrongs' summed up his answers. He was never happier than when fearlessly acting as David against the Goliath of an apparently more powerful adversary. The stress for him was that his role increasingly seemed to be constraining him from drawing on his strengths.

The choices seemed simple: change jobs or refocus the job he had. He chose to refocus the job he had, feeling that the core purpose of his organization was indeed close to his heart and that he could easily reposition the role by concentrating on the external, ambassadorial role while also directly heading up the campaigning function inside the organization and appointing a new director to head up the commercial operation.

Now the commercial activities of the organization were aimed at supporting campaigning, rather than the other way around. Mark described himself as 'springing out of bed each morning, knowing I'm doing what I was born to do!'

Identifying values and drivers

Asking about life purpose takes you into the territory of the being self rather than the doing self. It is saying to the client, 'What really matters to you?' You may get answers to this question through exploring life purpose, or you may prefer to look at it through activities explicitly designed to identify the client's values and drivers. This approach is especially useful with clients facing career dilemmas because they start by identifying answers to the questions 'What do you really want?', 'What's important to you?', rather than where so many clients believe they have to start, which is with 'Who will hire me?' Knowing what your values are is also a powerful way of reinforcing goals.

Being 'in the zone'

Sports people describe moments of maximum performance as being 'in the zone': a time when you just know that you are going to win, play or perform well, doing as well or better than you ever have before. And the wonderful thing is, it feels effortless. The same phenomenon has been called 'being in flow'. It has been described many times over the centuries, often linked with spiritual awareness, but today the phrase is most associated with one of the founding fathers of the modern positive psychology movement, Mihaly Csikszentmihalyi (2003).

These moments are characterized by time passing quickly – your sense of time is distorted along with a feeling of exhilaration – mind and body seamlessly joined and a sense of conscious happiness, playfulness and energy. You have clear goals that are tightly linked to strongly-held personal values and a focused sense of attention to the task in hand, along with confidence: lf-consciousness or embarrassment. Usually there will be a high level of immediate feedback enabling you to adjust your performance without difficulty and a feeling that the activity is *intrinsically rewarding*, so there is an effortlessness in it. You have a sense that you are achieving something stretching enough to be challenging, but not so challenging that it becomes overwhelming; there is a feeling of being in control – you can do it, anything is possible.

Introduce the idea of 'being in flow' to the client and ask them to identify up to four such moments in their life – more if you have the time and inclination. Encourage them to think about moments from their personal as well as professional lives and also moments that cover different phases or decades. By asking for several such 'peak moments' you will be creating a richer picture. Scribble down all the key words as they talk: don't edit what you hear. You could use a flip chart for this: it makes the themes easier for clients to see later. Most clients talk fluently about these moments. Prompt them with further questions such as:

- What made this moment or time special?
- Who else was present or involved? What were they doing?
- What was it that you specifically did that made it so important?
- What were your feelings then?
- What was achieved, done or learnt?
- How did you feel about that achievement or learning?
- What values and beliefs were you calling on?
- What need was it serving?

When clients have finished, hand them the pages and a highlighter, asking them to mark the words that jump out for them and then to synthesize them into a list. Suggest possible links and themes, if they are struggling – sometimes such links may be easier for you to see than for them – then list the values and drivers that emerge. Now invite them to ponder the implications. Some possible questions here might be:

- Having listed these values and drivers, how do they seem to you?
- What is so important about them for you?
- What surprises are there for you in what is *not* on your list?
- How far are you satisfying them in your life currently?
- What is it like for you when you are honouring these values?
- What is it like for you when you are not honouring them?
- What needs to happen to make these values real drivers in your life now?
- How prepared are you to make those changes?

This exercise focuses only on the positive and virtually always tells clients more than they first realize. For instance, a participant on a coach-training course identified one peak moment as getting the opportunity to sing the part of the Angel in Edward Elgar's popular oratorio *The Dream of Gerontius* in her local cathedral. The Angel guides Gerontius from this world to the next. Singing this role encapsulated her talent for singing, her need for performance and limelight, and also the need as a coach to do something for others that had profound meaning for them.

This exercise has multiple uses, especially where the focus is career. For instance, you can ask the client to assess how their current job or life stacks up against the criteria the exercise has revealed. Often there is a poor match and this can accelerate the client's determination to do something different. Or if the client is offered a new job but has doubts about whether to accept, it is always worth revisiting this list. And in any knotty dilemma that the client brings to you, you may want to say, 'Let's see how any decision would measure up against that list.' This can significantly shorten the period of vacillation.

While goals are important to client and to coach, there is also a toxic trap awaiting those who take them as the be-all and end-all. Eckhart Tolle makes the case potently in his book *The Power of Now* (2001). Commenting that our whole lives can be about waiting for the future, the book celebrates the liberating energy of living in the present. Tolle contrasts 'small-scale waiting' (in bus queues, in a traffic jam) with 'large-scale waiting' – for a better job or more prosperity. Large-scale waiting, especially without any of the action that will make the goal real, reduces the quality of your life now. The goals he associates with such pointless waiting he calls 'outer goals', all of which eventually end in failure. This is because outer goal achievements are subject to the impermanence of all things. He warns against waiting as a state of mind because it could mean that you only want the future while rejecting the present. Setting goals is important, but not at the expense of feeling alive now. In terms of the model of coaching I put forward in this book, he is warning against the doing self taking over from the being self:

> Your life's journey has an outer purpose and an inner purpose. The outer purpose is to arrive at your goal or destination, to accomplish what you set out to do, to achieve this or that, which, of course, implies future. But if your destination, or the steps you are going to take in the future, take up so much of your attention that they become more important to you than the step you are taking now, then you completely miss the journey's inner purpose, which has nothing to do with where you are going, or what you are doing, but everything to do with how.

(Tolle 2001: 71)

And just in case we get too carried away with the seriousness of it all, I cannot resist adding the Woody Allen joke sent to me by Derek Adams, a thoughtful reader of the first edition of this book:

Q: How do you make God laugh?
A: Tell him your plans.

Note

1   For two helpful views in this area, see Bandura (1997) and Locke and Latham (1990).

8   Coaching clients through change

*All changes, even the most longed for, have their melancholy; for
what we leave behind us is part of ourselves; we must die to one life
before we can enter another.*

Anatole France

This chapter describes several useful frameworks for understanding and
working with clients through change. All have their place; they offer a mix of
theoretical and practical strategies: think of them as a menu of options. Some
of them overlap, some are better known than others or more useful with some
clients than with others.

When clients come for coaching, they do it because they want their lives to
change. But the desire for transformation is not the same as making it happen
and there are few coaching clients who have not already tried all the obvious
routes. Change is complex because even when we freely choose it, there will
be some loss. When I left my room at the BBC's undoubtedly grim buildings at
Elstree just outside London for the last time, ready to start working full-time as
a coach and running my own business, I looked at the trees, the only ones on the
site, and felt a wrench, knowing I would never see them again. At the farewell
party given me by colleagues that night, I realized that this was probably the last
contact I would have with many of the people there. I had eagerly sought this
change, knew I had made it for the best of reasons and that the decision could
not be revoked, but I still remember the poignant mixture of sadness and joy.

How much more difficult then it is to deal with what is imposed: redundancy, being obliged to take a less satisfactory role or to move house in order to
keep your job, being left by a partner, facing a health crisis, getting dismissed,
failing an exam, bereavement, the disappointment of not getting a job you badly
wanted. These are the changes that you often could not predict or prevent, did
not cause, can't control and can't avoid. Potentially they can lead to feelings of
powerlessness and anger. You meet them again and again in the coaching room.

The Kübler-Ross framework

Elisabeth Kübler-Ross was a Swiss psychiatrist and teacher whose pio-
neering book *On Death and Dying* (1997), first published in the mid-1960s,

came well known because it revolutionized the way we look at death by challenging its taboos and embarrassments. Often described as a study of bereavement, in fact her first interest was in how people receive news they perceive to be catastrophic. The focus was on patients with terminal illnesses but her framework quickly came to be seen as equally useful for people coping with any kind of loss or change. Although her ideas have been attacked as simplistic, I find that they stand the test of time as both profound and simple. They are useful in two ways: as a constant reminder of the psychology of change and loss with which we and so many of our clients struggle, and also as a framework to teach to clients so that they understand their own processes better.

Her work identifies six typical stages of grief, represented as the change cycle in Figure 8.1.

Anticipatory grief

You know that something has changed for ever, but it is not yet over and may not be for some time to come. You feel overwhelming and most probably silent sorrow for what you know will be lost, yet you feel guilty and possibly self-indulgent about the intensity of your emotion. Typically you bottle it up. It feels wrong to express it.

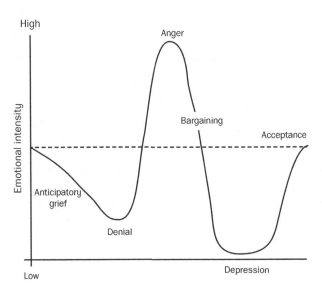

Figure 8.1 The change cycle

Francis

Francis was a charismatic performing arts specialist working with me on making the change from a professional to a managerial role. He knew he had to give up many of his previous shocking habits – gossiping, manipulating, having favourites – if he was to move from amusing, talented maverick to respected leader. He was an eager learner, confessing readily to his faults, amazed and delighted that there were actually well-tried methods of motivating people that did not depend on coercion. When we did the Life Scan exercise (page 148), he told me, his entire demeanour changing, that his wife, Mia, had endometrial cancer. At our third session he told me that Mia's cancer had spread to her liver. Her condition had deteriorated rapidly and she now needed a wheelchair.

'I've been able to cope up till now', he said, 'but the wheelchair is a symbol of what is to come. I know she can't recover but I don't know how long she can live. I have already lost her. I feel desperate but I can't show it to her or anyone else and especially not to the children.' His melancholy dignity was moving and the rest of our session was spent working out some better tactics for coping than simply turning his grief inwards.

Denial

At the denial stage we are numb. We know, intellectually, that the change has happened: the company will be taken over, we will lose that job, a partner has left, that an adored parent has died, but emotionally we cannot yet take it in. To outsiders it may look as if we are adopting head-in-sand tactics:

Eira

Eira ran a small organization which had merged with a competitor and she had just been told that she was not a candidate for the chief executive role in the new company. In her coaching sessions, where the planned focus was on how to get a new job, Eira described with bafflement that she was continuing to run her organization as if nothing had happened. 'I'm still doing my weekly meetings, I'm still going through my usual routines. I can't feel anything though I think I should. It's as if I'm outside it all. I'm actually still working on a business plan for next year. How bizarre is that?'

Of course it was not bizarre at all, merely the normal protective mechanism of the human response to change kicking in.

Anger

At the anger stage we look for someone to blame. This horrible event must be someone's fault so this person should be punished or at least say they are sorry. We will tend to divide people into goodies and baddies – there are no in-betweens. Often enough, the anger may be well justified – some corporate behaviour is beyond belief in its callousness and cowardice. Or we may cast ourselves as one of the baddies, assuming inappropriate personal responsibility for what has happened – 'if only I'd ...' Sometimes there is indeed some culpability in the client's past behaviour. If so, encourage them to express their guilt at the same time as helping them put it into perspective. Remind them that most probably they did the best they could on the data available at the time, that mistakes are inevitable because we are only human and it is unlikely that any blame will be theirs alone. Asking clients what they have learnt that they can apply to similar situations another time is also a powerful way of coming to terms with the painful responsibility for a failure.

Very occasionally, clients, in the temporary madness of their anger, may propose dangerous remedies – for instance, taking their organization to court in a case they could not win, or stalking their boss. Where you can see, because you are outside it, that this course of action would be catastrophic – or against the law – it may be time for plain speaking. Offering some perspective through a coaching conversation may be the client's best hope of avoiding a personal disaster.

In the early days of therapy it was assumed that anger should be expressed as a way of getting it said and done with. Hence, clients were encouraged to beat cushions, shout and rage. However, it seems dubious now that this is helpful. Rather it seems more likely to fix the enraged person into anger as their default mode. Anger can be addictive; we can enjoy the righteousness of our rage. In reality it increases the likelihood of making the false logic of black and white thinking more permanent. Clients can take refuge in claims that they are only seeking 'fairness' or 'justice' when it may be nearer the truth to say that most anger is about what *I need* versus what *others need*. People who are in a high state of emotional arousal are not calm enough to be coached. The more primitive the emotional state, and anger is a primitive state, the less likelihood there is of learning and of the prefrontal cortex, the seat of logical thinking, being brought into play. You may find it more helpful to calm an angry client and then to work with them on how to manage their anger than to encourage them to vent their rage in the session.

Mostly, when a client is recognizably at this point in the change process, it works simply to acknowledge the anger and to explain that it is a normal part of the adjustment to change. Ask:

> Who are you angry with?
> If they were here, what would you like to say to them?
> What would it take for you to move on from this anger?

Accepting some personal responsibility

When the black and white thinking of the anger phase is passing, it is often useful to help clients distinguish between shame, blame, guilt and personal responsibility. We will usually have contributed something to the change and, in the interests of learning and moving on, it can be therapeutic to consider calmly what that might have been.

Hilary

Hilary had worked for a hotel chain for 12 years as their learning and development specialist, getting positive feedback on her own training courses and believing that she was playing a valued role in the company. When the news came that her post was redundant she experienced it as a wounding personal rejection. Her feelings of anger were still strong four months later. In her second coaching session we looked at what responsibility she had for what had happened to her career. The answer was that she had stayed in the same post well past her real interest in it because it had allowed her to be home in time to collect her children from school. She had not kept her bosses informed about the strategic value of her work. Instead, her tactics had been to get on with her work quietly, believing that its merit would speak for itself. Understanding the nature of this private bargain with herself was the key to moving on, including accepting that no one but the individual concerned can ever manage their career.

Bargaining

Bargaining is a good sign, although it may not seem so at the time. It means that we have accepted, at least in part, that the change will happen. In the original work with dying patients, it was described as bargaining with God: 'If I pray really hard, and promise to live a pure life, then maybe I'll survive.' In coaching work we are more likely to see it in the kinds of desperate compromises that clients suggest. For instance, one client, whose wife had left him for another man, offered to move house if she would come back.

A client who had been sacked by his company instigated a grievance procedure in an attempt to stave off the formal letter ending his contract. Another client, sorely disappointed by her failure to win the job she wanted, proposed a new role as deputy to her successful rival. It is unlikely that any sustainable solution can be produced by bargaining because it is most probably a forlorn bid to deny the inevitability of the change. As coaches, our role may be to offer reality-testing by asking questions like:

> How far would this solve the underlying problems here?
> What would be the balance of upsides and downsides?
> Imagine yourself a year from now living inside this solution. How do you think it would feel?
> What would need to happen to make this solution work for you?

Depression

We feel paralysed. We are indecisive. The anger has gone but has left behind a sense of powerlessness. This is a difficult stage for the coach as well as for the client. Clients may cancel their sessions and have too little energy to tell you why, even if they know. It may look as if they have lost interest in coaching. Contact them if you suspect this is happening and express your willingness to continue. Be prepared to follow up with more emails or phone calls if there is no response. I sent one such client, someone I knew well, an email with a tick box that he could return with minimal effort and with five choices:

> I am fine and don't need any more coaching, but thank you for what I have had.
> I am fine for now, but might need some coaching in future.
> I am feeling too miserable to contact you right now.
> I am miserable, but could be persuaded to have another session – though not yet.
> I am miserable, but a session would help – and if Angie [*my patient PA*] would arrange it and contact me, it would be useful.

His later comment on this possibly over-cheeky email was:

> It was so wonderful to get that. It broke the frozen skin of my sadness. I thought, why am I sitting here so wrapped up in ME? And someone does care. I got on the phone to Angie straight away and booked my session.

The underlying cause at this stage in the change process is that we have fully realized what has been permanently lost, and with it goes a withering of belief that anything we do can have a positive impact. We doubt that we can be happy again. This is particularly true for clients whose identity has been tightly bound up in their work and who have lost their jobs, or for a bereaved client who feels as if the centre of their lives has been squeezed out by the death of someone they loved dearly. Where the client does appear for his or her sessions, the event may have a lifeless air. When you see this happening, name it. Work at the feelings level first and avoid intellectualizing. Ask the client what would help, both in terms of how you run the actual sessions and on practicalities. The answer is often to design the small steps which work towards healing and renewal. When you recognize that you are in the presence of a serious mental health problem rather than just sadness, your coaching must be aimed at encouraging the client to find medical help (Chapter 11).

Acceptance

Acceptance and adjustment are close partners. The change has happened or will happen. We begin to experiment with new behaviours. Cheerfulness creeps in occasionally and cautiously. We begin to believe that we can live with what has happened and that life will go on. Confidence trickles back. The coaching springs to life again.

Beware of believing that this change cycle is a rigid process. We may pass through its stages in any order or miss some out altogether. Typically it is literally a cycle: so a client who has apparently reached the acceptance stage may return many times more to anger, bargaining or depression. These labels are simply useful tools to gain understanding about what is happening.

As a coach you should also look out for clients who get stuck at one point in the cycle, most often at denial or anger, returning again and again to *what-ifs* and *if-onlys*.

Dealing with transition: William Bridges' model

The writer William Bridges has another useful framework for making sense of change. He describes it in his book *Managing Transitions* (1991) where the focus is on change in organizations. It maps well on to the Kübler-Ross change cycle. He suggests that the formal process of the change and the psychological adjustment to it are two different phenomena. This is because although the formal change has been made, the psychological adjustments have yet to happen. So, for instance, you may notice that clients who have been forced to leave their jobs will frequently speak about 'we' and 'our', unconsciously talking as if they are still at their old workplaces.

Bridges describes three phases of change, suggesting that their boundaries are messy and overlapping and that this is what causes the delay in adjustment (see Figure 8.2).

Phase 1: Endings

A change has to take place, but before this can happen at the psychological level, not just at the legal or physical level, the old has to be let go. That is what we find hard. It is no good stressing what benefits the new regime will bring if what has been lost is not acknowledged. Something will always be lost, whether it is the comfort of our old familiar ways of doing things, our status, our previous good health, our beliefs or our expectations. The immediate focus is on ourselves: How will this affect me? Questions linked to this are:

> Who now has the power?
> How are decisions being made?
> Which of the old rules still apply – and what are the new ones?

Working with clients at the Endings phase
There are many strategies that can help clients adjust to the new reality. First, ask what will change and what will stay the same: suggest that clients

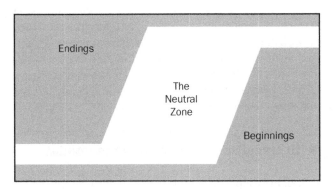

Figure 8.2 The three phases of transition

distinguish between the two. The more you stay outside the change, the more it feels like something being done to you so getting involved is usually better: ask clients how they could increase their involvement in the change. Encourage mourning by naming what has ended: for instance, ask 'What will you miss most?' It also helps to celebrate the ending. Just as a funeral helps the survivors realize that the loved person really has died, so will parties and rituals in other circumstances where something is irrevocably over. Where people will be leaving an organization – or a relationship for that matter – some celebratory marker will help.

Rose is one example of a client who managed this phase with textbook expertise:

Rose

Rose had narrowly missed promotion to a senior job in a pharmaceutical company. In our sessions Rose allowed herself some private rage, anticipating the synthetic sympathy of senior male colleagues who might be secretly pleased that an overtly ambitious woman had not got the job.

With Bridges' helpful framework in mind, I asked Rose, 'What has really ended here?'

'My career in this organization' she promptly replied, 'I really have to move on.' We discussed how she could contact headhunters and reinvigorate her network of professional contacts. Within a few months Rose had been offered an impressive new job and had decided to take it. Now her questions were about how to leave. Her instinct was, as it so often is, to slink off. I asked Rose what she thought might be helpful at this Endings phase.

'Well, I have to have the big party, even if I don't really want it – you know how I hate all that tired speechifying and ritual? But I have to have it for others as well as for me.'

'Yes, I think you do'.

'And I have to treat it as an important event'.

I gladly accepted the invitation to a magnificent formal party and watched from the sidelines as Rose delivered the speech she had rehearsed with me: a generous acknowledgement of the strengths of the organization and a confident look towards her own future.

Some clients cannot manage the Endings phase with this degree of graciousness. They are tempted to indulge their desire for revenge and to express their disappointment in violent terms to whoever will listen. At one farewell party the leaver had created a 'graffiti wall' out of flip chart paper, inviting his guests to fill in the 'bricks' with harsh messages for the managers who had dispensed with his services. The embarrassment of his guests was palpable. It is sometimes hard for clients to see that recklessly expressing their anger at what they see as betrayal will have instant backwash on the person who gives vent to it so publicly. When clients do describe such a wish, I will typically ask, 'When you've been on the receiving end of this kind of unloading, how has it felt?' The answer, invariably, is some mix of the following: awkwardness, pity, dislike. This is usually enough to deter a client from pursuing such an unwise path.

Phase 2: The Neutral Zone

This phase has something in common with the depression phase of the Kübler-Ross framework. Bridges describes it as feeling as if we are in continuous whitewater. Energy disappears. We withdraw and become self-preoccupied. We are more prone to illness and accident. We are unsure what has ended and even more unsure about whether the new beginning has actually started. Old weaknesses resurface. The essence of the Neutral Zone is ambiguity. However, maybe for this very reason, the Neutral Zone is also potentially a time for rethinking and creativity because at this stage we have an overt longing for answers. It is often the point where client and coach make first contact.

Kees

Kees had made London his home when his Dutch company had acquired a UK competitor. But now, yet another acquisition had made his own director job redundant. Underneath this familiar explanation of why a job move was necessary there lay the less palatable truth that Kees, though popular and likeable, was a problematical colleague. His insistence on doing everything himself created decision bottlenecks for his staff. His obsession with detail meant that he often focused on the smaller picture at the expense of wider strategic need. With 25 years in one company, it would have been understandable for Kees to have felt aggrieved at his fate or frightened at the prospect of having to start again. But this was not so. Coming for coaching at the point where his formal notice to leave had just been issued, Kees loved the concept of the Neutral Zone. He embraced the tough messages of his 360-deg. feedback with courage.

'I see this as a time when I can learn all over again', he beamed. 'I'd got stale, been in one place too long. I know I can tackle all this stuff that's driven people nuts and I can't tell you how ready I am to learn how to do it better! I am a very lucky man to have this opportunity.'

Kees and I worked on what he described as a *triple track*. Track One was an assessment of his whole life and led to a realization that he needed to pay more attention to his family and friends. Track Two was job search, and it started by identifying his strengths, many of which, for instance his fluency in five European languages, had been underused. This linked tightly with strongly-held values about the importance for him of being 'A Citizen of Europe'. Track Three was relearning how to be a leader, revisiting past dilemmas, avidly reading articles and books and, at his insistence, arranging meetings with other clients from whom I anticipated he could learn. Every one of my many emails from Kees ended with a smiley face symbol. When he sent me the email to tell me that his bid for a job in Zurich had been successful, there were three smiley emoticons attached – 'One for each Track!'

Working with clients in the Neutral Zone

Explain the value of the Neutral Zone to clients, reframing its inevitable discomforts as a positive opportunity to learn. Encourage the thought that the common complaint about 'having nothing to do', or even, in dying organizations, 'too much to do', is rarely true. Business-as-usual may have ceased, but the task now is to concentrate on preparing for the future – for instance, through training or job search.

Encourage clients to create a Neutral Zone for themselves – for instance, if they are tempted to go straight from an Ending to a Beginning. Taking even a few days' holiday can create a valuable mini Neutral Zone. Many clients can also benefit from a reminder to pay attention to the importance of networking and of keeping their social connections alive to offset the ever-present danger of Neutral Zone isolation.

Phase 3: Beginnings

The formal start and the psychological beginning are two different processes. Even though the beginning may be eagerly sought, it can feel daunting. There may be doubts about whether the Beginning is 'real' or not. There was comfort in the meandering pace and low stress of the Neutral Zone. It was pleasant to get up late, please yourself and to feel free of day-to-day pressures. The decision to take a new step may still feel provisional, even though all the formal procedures, such as contracts, have been completed. The new is unknown – what will it take to succeed? It is normal to feel doubts about competence and capability at this stage. It is also normal for there to be a dip in confidence a few weeks in when the reality of the new situation begins to become clear.

Working with clients on Beginnings

Encourage planning – gathering information, imagining, visualizing, thinking, preparing – they all help with coming to terms with whatever is about to start. Ask clients to imagine a typical successful day under the new regime: What would be happening? Ask clients what new skills they anticipate the beginning will need. How many of these skills do they have? How could they acquire any that are missing? How could they boost and develop the skills they do have?

Encourage the idea that in the first few weeks the task is to learn what the task is, rather than to do it.

As with every other aspect of managing change, getting involved counters feelings of lack of control. Ask clients: *How could you be wholly involved with every aspect of this new life?* Explain the value of early quick wins – these not only emphasize that the beginning is happening but create useful opportunities to underline what has changed and what is now starting.

Self-limiting beliefs

Change can be daunting. Part of the client wants the status quo because, even if things are uncomfortable, there is comfort in the familiarity of the discomfort. This is why we all cling to self-limiting beliefs, even while we are proclaiming our wish to transform ourselves.

Self-limiting belief has been given many different names. Timothy Gallwey (2000, page 82) calls it Self 1 to distinguish it from Self 2: the confident human being full of potential and capacity. Self 1 is the know-it-all who doesn't trust Self 2. Self 1's voice is always ready with self-condemnation, predictions of failure and gloomy comparisons of self with others. When Self 2 can silence Self 1, potential can turn into achievement and growth. Richard Carson (1987) coined the term 'Gremlin' for the same phenomenon: a nagging critical inner voice always ready to sabotage success.

We all have these voices; they are part of growing up and they cannot be coached because they are not rational. They cannot be dismissed or killed off because they are inalienably a part of who we are. The challenge is to unmask, name and manage them, particularly with humour. This way they become less powerful.

Self-sabotaging statements

Here are some sample self-sabotaging statements:

> I'm only (able to do a little . . .)
> I'm no good at . . . other people are cleverer . . .
> Don't stick your head above the parapet . . .
> A person like me could never . . .
> I'll wait until the time is right before I . . .
> I should be . . . (better, stronger, nicer . . .)
> I shouldn't be so . . . (silly, needy . . .)
> I mustn't because (I might be successful; people might laugh; that's for other people, not for people like me . . .)

Listen for these phrases. Usually they have originated in childhood and you will have probed for them when asking clients for their autobiographical accounts (Chapter 6). I remind clients that, as children, their parents or carers probably meant well enough in the limiting beliefs they passed on. Mostly such nostrums were designed, however simplistically, to keep us safe, or on track. As children they may even have done so, but as adults they more often get in the way.

Michael

I grew up in a working-class environment where fear of authority was very real. My parents had learnt to be docile with teachers, the council, the police, and so on. It was important to 'keep out of trouble'. I was told all the time to *keep your head down, be seen and not heard, people like us don't show off*. I internalized these messages to a high degree and I suppose they did help because I did keep my head down and I did work hard and I got to a good university. One of the main benefits of coaching to me was learning that what may have helped as a kid was damaging as an adult. Through the coaching I learnt to see that failing to speak up was leading to colleagues believing that I had nothing to say or else was 'aloof', and that not challenging senior people was letting them think that I was a bit of a pushover. Through coaching, I had to learn all the skills associated with doing this stuff well, because I had never learnt them as a young man.

Spotting other flawed thinking patterns

Many of our clients have already identified some typically unhelpful behaviour patterns. Far fewer are adept at recognizing their typical *thinking patterns*. Often these are flawed. They represent distortions of reality and this is what causes the misery or ineffective behaviour. Listen carefully for these patterns. Note that when under stress from change, a typical small distortion in thinking can become magnified. Here are some of the most common:

The pessimist: Terrible events can and will happen and human beings have no say in whether they happen or not. I hear of some risk or potential danger and immediately assume it will happen to me or my family: terrorist attack, nuclear war . . . once I know it's possible, I believe it is likely. Anything good that happens is temporary whereas bad things are permanent.

It's all my fault: If something goes wrong, it's all down to me. Others did not contribute, nor did the system. I am responsible for the health and happiness of everyone around me.

Other people can make me happy or sad: I hold others accountable for the horrible things that have happened to me or for their failure to make me happy. If only they would see the misery they have caused, but somehow they don't.

My past defines me: If there was some sadness, tragedy or uncomfortable event in my life, I will never overcome it. It will always be with me because it was and is overwhelming. I become a person defined by the event: abused child, widowed young mother, mugging victim.

Super-competent-me: I have to be super-competent at every single thing I attempt, whether in my work or personal life. Not to be competent is a disaster. Failure is unthinkable. I am my role. If you want a job done well, do it yourself. It is appalling to admit to a mistake because people might discover that there is nothing behind the mask.

No-such-thing-as-grey: Things are either perfect or a disaster, black or white, right or wrong. As a person I am either great or awful, and so is everyone else.

It's not fair: I expected everything to be fair, but it's not. Other people get away with things that they shouldn't get away with. They should be severely punished, but often they're not. Someone should always take the blame.

I can change people: I believe it's possible to reform or rescue people. I try everything I can to make them see the error of their ways so that they will do what I want and take my needs more seriously. I give them advice and it's exasperating that they won't follow it.

The disciplined perfectionist: My language is peppered with *musts*, *shoulds* and *oughts*. I work from a series of rigid rules about what has to be done. Where there are actual rules in my organization I believe they should be adhered to, even if everyone else ignores them. If only everyone (myself included) were disciplined about life, all its problems would be solved. I judge harshly when there is any falling-short.

The self-sacrificer/compulsive carer: I believe that you must always be virtuous by putting others first. Life should be about service. My reward will be that others offer service back. Disappointment and anger must be denied when this doesn't happen.

Everything should be peaceful and harmonious: Conflict is scary and always destructive. I must do everything I can to keep the peace. If you expose conflict, nothing will ever be tranquil again. It's better to ignore the danger signs because if you do nothing, it might all go away.

You have to be tough: Life is hard. I have to be tough and look out for myself because if you're not, other people will take advantage so it's better to strike first. Competition in human life is inevitable and healthy. Showing any vulnerability and tenderness means showing weakness, and this is fatal.

The narcissist: The world exists to service my needs. I am the centre, I am special and have a sense of entitlement to attention, success and admiration. I'm not really that interested in others' feelings. Underneath, my ego is fragile, but this is concealed in the super-confident way I feel I must present to the world.

ιches, the most helpful things we can do are to spot the pattern and then, every other transaction with the client, commit to dealing respectfully with what you observe. Then name or ask for the pattern:

> I notice that several times in our conversation today you seem to have reduced your choices to either/or (you then describe what you have heard and noticed).

Or:

> What 'rule' are you applying here? (usually one about cause and effect: 'If I do *this*, then *that* will follow . . .').

Ask the client if they recognize the pattern:

> I'm wondering whether this is a common pattern for you? Can you think of other examples?

Challenge the generalization that lies beneath the pattern:

> Let's think about what alternatives there might be for instance to resolve (whatever problem the client has raised).

Ed

Ed is working with me on his relationship with his boss. He is rehearsing how he will raise the subject of a salary increase. I have already noticed that Ed precedes almost every statement about what he wants with a self-effacing qualifier, such as, 'I know I'm already well paid but now that I'm doing more responsible work I feel I should be getting at least 10 per cent more.'

In discussion, it emerges that Ed's underlying 'rule' is that you are more likely to get what you want if you imply modesty. His self-sabotaging voice, learnt in childhood from a crushingly critical father, is that people will punish and mock if you praise yourself. As a child, Ed's 'rule' has appeared to keep him safe from the perils of boastfulness, and indeed it is true that he presents himself with a charming modesty. The flawed thinking pattern is that it is *always* better to keep the peace than to risk conflict. A further belief is that you cannot mix modesty with speaking up – the two are mutually exclusive. The combined impact of these mental habits conveys the impression that he is not serious about his requests or could easily be outmanoeuvred.

I point out to Ed what I have observed. We discuss the likely impact on the other person of hearing a statement which is communicating such a double message: apologizing for being well paid and at the same time asking for more money. We loop back to our discussion in Session 1 about his childhood, revisiting the likely value of some of these beliefs.

Every time I hear Ed make a statement like this (frequently), I doggedly point it out, or ask him to give himself feedback on the same pattern. Ed begins to realize that this clarifies much that has baffled him in his leadership role – for instance, it could well explain why when he asks people to undertake a piece of work they frequently don't deliver on it.

All of this may sound easy, but it is not. First, the coach needs the courage to challenge. Secondly, the client needs to be able to see that far from being the rational truth they believed it to be, this aspect of their thinking is irrational. Ask clients other questions such as:

Are you sure that's *always* true? *Always?*
What is the evidence?
What do you notice that contradicts this assumption?
What other explanations could there be?
What would it be like to believe the opposite?
What belief would you rather have?

Be alert also to the danger of initiating a side-tracking debate about competing world views. Your own thinking could be as unsound as the client's and you might like to look at the list above to see if you can spot your own actual or potential weaknesses.

Resisting change through 'discounting'

The idea of *discounting* comes from Transactional Analysis. It elegantly codifies the many ways in which we can deny reality and resist change. We may *discount* any evidence which threatens our beliefs about ourselves, the people around us, or the environment in which we live and work. Discounting represents distorted perception and it happens outside conscious awareness. The amount of fierceness with which we cling to a discount is directly related to the intensity of the perceived threat. In this way we protect ourselves from the disturbance and fear that acknowledging the reality might create. Discounting may happen at four levels.

Level 1: Discounting the *existence* of a problem

A smoker may continue to believe that smoking is not harmful. Here the facts established by 80 years of research are denied because to admit the validity of the facts would create enormous anxiety.

When coaching clients discount at this level, they may, for instance, deny that their job is under threat in spite of clear evidence that it is. They may deny strong evidence that there is a problem with their performance or that a central relationship in their lives is at risk. A client with a dishevelled appearance may not know how people view him and the unflattering inferences they draw. A married gay client may discount his true sexual preferences, dismissing his flings with men as trivial deviations from an essentially heterosexual existence. Signs that clients are discounting at this level might be a continuation of old behaviour in the face of obvious threat. Good coaching questions here might be:

What are the known facts?
What evidence is there that this is a problem? How often, how much, how intense?
How reliable is the evidence?
Who might confirm or deny it?
If there are information gaps, how might you fill them?

Level 2: Discounting the significance of a problem

The smoker may admit that smoking is harmful, but may believe that his own genetic inheritance will somehow protect him. He will support this belief by quoting some legendary person who lived to extreme old age and smoked 60 cigarettes a day.

Clients may have had uncomfortable 360-degree feedback but be inclined to blame others or the methodology. Or they may brush it aside by telling you that the people who gave the feedback don't really matter because they have no power to affect the client's future. A brand manager may discount declining sales figures by attributing them to predictable ebbs and flows in the market. At this level, discounting continues until the underlying feelings of fear, disappointment, loss, anger and insecurity have been expressed. We hide under the shelter of rationality because we are afraid of the intensity of our feelings. Useful questions here could be:

> If this were true, what impact would it have?
> How did you feel when you first heard this?
> Where does it fit or not fit with other messages/evidence?
> How could you check out how much this will matter?

Level 3: Discounting the *solvability* of the problem

> The smoker acknowledges that smoking may severely damage his health, but believes that all the usual remedies – nicotine patches, going cold turkey, hypnotherapy – will not work in his particular case.

Coaching clients may express views suggesting that the situation is out of their control – they are helpless. They may retreat into the apparent safety of being victims. Look out for black/white either/or thinking and phrases like 'I can't' or generalizations such as 'I always . . .' Helpful questions here could be:

> When you've encountered this sort of situation before, what did you do that worked?
> When you've seen other people deal well with this situation, what seemed to work for them?
> Who might be ready to offer useful help?
> What skills do you have that you can bring into play here?
> What criteria might you use for finding a solution?
> What could you live with here, even if it's only a partial solution?

Level 4: Discounting the *ability* to change

> The smoker knows that all the usual remedies would work on him, but doubts his capacity to live without cigarettes.

Here the client has accepted the facts, understands their significance and knows that there are solutions, but discounts his or her personal ability to react differently or to live with the consequences. Executive coaching clients may say things like, 'This is who I am – I can't be different', or 'It's all very well for other people, they're younger' (or more adaptable or more employable).

Effective coaching tactics at this level are usually about re-establishing the importance of the goal (see Chapter 7) and its accompanying vision. What will work here are techniques such as drawing, visioning, imagining a day spent in a positive future and re-establishing attention onto positive outcomes, rather than wallowing in problems. Good questions might be:

> What's your overall strategy here?
> What will the benefits be of achieving it?
> Who might help you?
> What first small steps towards the goal might you make?
> Imagine you can cope: what would be happening?
> When learning something new in the past, what did you find were the best methods?

Identifying the pay-off for staying stuck

One of the reasons that we can stay fixed in a problem is that there is some pay-off from doing so. It is worth exploring what this might be.

However miserable clients are about feeling stuck, there is always a benefit. The prison of misery may be horrible, but at least it is familiar. Asking the client to identify how the pay-off works can often be a moment of enlightenment. Ask, 'What is it doing for you to stay stuck here?' Typical pay-offs may include controlling and manipulating others by engendering guilt; creating some personal space and 'reward' for yourself or a moment of 'high' and pure enjoyment. Sometimes it may feel as if, by giving away your power, you excuse yourself from failure because you can always say that if you'd tried you could have succeeded. As that well-known sage Homer Simpson comments: 'You tried your best, and you failed miserably. The lesson is, never try.' Other pay-offs include forcing others to take responsibility for you, which means that you never have to blame yourself if something goes wrong. What all these pay-offs have in common is that they involve avoiding facing up to actual weaknesses.

The Immunity to Change approach

Everything in coaching is about change. Our clients want to change and we want to work with them on the changes they say they want to make. And yet, if you're honest, how many times as a coach have you wondered if you are really just working transactionally with clients? Do you have a private suspicion that what you're doing is tinkering, working at the behavioural level, but not getting to the heart of it? For instance:

> Client A vows to delegate, and yet he still seems to be doing his team's work for them.

> Client B is ashamed of her weight and knows she has to shed three stone, yet she's still fat.

> Client C's life is all work and no private life. His marriage is at risk, but he still puts in 12 hours at the office.

Things may have improved – a bit – thanks to your coaching, but the main problem may remain untouched.

1 Commitment: improvement goal: phrased in the positive	2 What do I do/not do instead? (Actual behaviours)	3 What are my hidden competing commitments? When I think about doing the opposite of what is in Column 2, what fears do I have?	4 What Big Assumptions am I making? e.g. what might a person who listed whatever is in their Column 3 be making about their world and themselves?
I want. . .	What I actually do to prevent my commitment being fully realized. . .	I worry I will. . .	I assume. . .
What commitments does your improvement goal imply?	What I don't do. . .	By engaging in the undermining behaviour, what worrisome outcome are you committed to preventing?	

he way of tackling this has been suggested in the book *Immunity to Change* (2009) by Robert Kegan and Lisa Lahey. Kegan and Lahey propose that we skilfully create our own 'immune system' to change, invariably sabotaging ourselves.

Immunity to Change proposes a four-stage grid as a way to the solution. Try it on yourself first.

Filling in the columns

Column 1: Commitment to improvement

This is essentially about your growth as a person. Look for ONE BIG THING that would have power to transform your life. It must be important to you, have impact for radical improvement in your life and should matter to others who are important to you. The area for improvement is yourself. It should not be something technical like a skill, and should not involve a total personality change – stay with the person you are at core. The goal should be stated in the positive – in other words, not be phrased as something you want to give up, or stop doing.

Column 2: What you are doing or not doing instead of achieving your goal

Write these as actual behaviours, not as attitudes or beliefs and states of mind – and be honest. Enter everything you do that is working against achieving your goal and don't worry about why you do this behaviour or about plans to stop doing it. Go for the behaviours in all their embarrassing glory.

Column 3: Revealing the hidden or competing commitments

This is the worry area. It shows the hidden dynamic, the immunity to change, a set of competing commitments. To fill in this column, take each of your Column 2 entries one by one and ask yourself: *If I imagine trying to do the opposite of this behaviour, what is the most worrying, scary or uncomfortable thought that comes to me?* This thought should have the power of Yuk! Experience the power of this feeling. If you don't experience it you are not there yet. You should feel at risk in some way. People frequently identify an early negative feeling – e.g. 'boredom' or 'twitchiness', 'impatience'. This is not the answer – dig below that: What is the awful feeling that lies beneath? What is the risk?

Typical fears include being incompetent, humiliated, helpless, unloved or of hurting someone we care about.

Our Column 2 behaviour is a way of keeping anxiety at bay and of protecting us. This is what keeps us stuck and prevents us making any progress on our goal.

At the top of the 'I worry I will . . ' box,

Write down the fears: 'I worry I will . . .'

Underneath write: 'So I am committed to . . .' (e.g. not being humiliated, not feeling out of control).

Column 4: the big assumptions

You don't disrupt the behaviours in Column 2 by just 'trying' not to do them. You do disrupt them by identifying the big assumptions. To do this, look at your Column 3 entries. Now brainstorm all the assumptions a person who had such commitments might be making. Ask yourself how far you are making them generalizations – things that are ALWAYS true regardless of circumstances – and ask yourself how strong the hold that they have on you is. Where did this assumption come from? What's its history? What were the critical turning points? Write them down under 'I assume . . .'

Designing tests of the big assumptions

Kegan and Lahey emphasize that such enormous assumptions are never dissolved overnight. Most of us hug our most profoundly self-limiting assumptions – we believe them to represent an absolute truth. We also believe that they are protecting us, which is why we cling to them. They are best dismantled step by step through cautious experiment. The way to do this it to ask: What behaviour change would make for good information about the accuracy of your big assumption? What data might you collect to test it?

Now you create a safe, modest test – an experiment designed to test the assumption. This should be something you can do immediately, not in the far future. Remember, it's an experiment – a test – and does not commit you to anything.

Some options might be:

- Alter a behaviour from Column 2
- Perform an action which runs counter to Column 3 commitments
- Challenge directly a Column 4 assumption

Assessing the different behaviour

- What did you do?
- What happened? How did others respond?
- How might this challenge your big assumption?

Using this approach with clients

You can show clients the grid and work through it with them if you wish. Or you can simply learn it yourself and use it to talk them through the process.

It helps to explain the essential concept of 'immunity' and the apparently baffling way we can sabotage ourselves. Designing different behaviour fits well with the action/accountability part of the coaching process and also assumes that we will be working with a client over a long enough period of time to be able to make a steady difference.

Sandra

Sandra came to me for help with giving presentations. She was in a senior role in a food company. The HR sponsor told me that Sandra seemed 'uptight and nervous' whenever he had seen her perform, and that this skill was intrinsic to her work. An expensive presentation skills course had made no discernible difference. The behavioural approach to coaching would be to deliver what is in effect one-to-one training, perhaps using a video camera for practice and feedback. Instead, we looked at the paradox of how she desperately needed and wanted to be better at giving presentations, already knew exactly what it was she had to do, yet through skilled self-sabotage was making it impossible to achieve.

Using the Immunity to Change approach, we identified clearly what behaviour she wanted to change: this involved developing a confident, racy style of presentation unique to her. Column 2 discussions revealed a skilled pattern of avoidance: refusing invitations to speak, then when it was impossible to avoid them, resorting to mumbling, to last-minute preparation or none, preparing elaborate PowerPoint slides and staring at them throughout the presentation and keeping the whole thing as short as possible. In Column 3, the hidden competing commitments emerged. We explored her belief that the remnants of a West Country burr made people conclude that she was stupid. Then there was the deeper belief that she had nothing to say that others would wish to hear, starting in childhood where, as the youngest of six and the only girl, she was routinely referred to as 'Fat Piggy' and at any family gathering ordered to 'Shut up because who'd be interested in what you've got to say?' She had been literally silenced. In Column 4, her deepest fear was of exposing herself to the possibility of finding out that those childhood taunts represented the truth about herself, that despite her outstanding academic achievements and professional success, she was stupid and incompetent. Together we designed a series of safe experiments to test these destructive assumptions, and slowly, over the next few sessions, began to assemble a different 'reality': people did not care a jot about her accent; she did have in-depth expertise in her subject; she did not need to be cleverer than her colleagues, only clever *enough*; she was already an expert storyteller and could and did bring this talent with profit into her presentation work.

The Prochaska and DiClemente model of change

When I was new to coaching I assumed that when a client told me that there was something they wanted to change in their lives, this meant that they were ready to change it immediately. A hard look at my own life might have shown me straight away that this is not how it happens. We can have every intention of changing, knowing for instance that some personal habit (sloth, procrastination, lack of exercise, drinking too much) is a bad idea, yet put off the moment when we start doing something different.

James Prochaska and his colleague Carlo DiClemente (2007) developed a model (see Figure 8.3) that arose originally out of work with people who had problems with alcohol. It acknowledges the reality that change can take time and that it is normal to relapse, but that when we do it is rare to go right back to the point where we denied that a change is needed. The model describes six stages which start with Pre-contemplation where we are unaware and totally unready for change, to Termination where the problematical behaviour is no longer an issue.

The Prochaska and DiClemente model is a reminder that there is a natural rhythm and timescale to the change process and that the comments and questions from a coach that will work at one stage will not be appropriate at another. Many coaches assume, wrongly, that a client stating an interest in, for instance, introducing more exercise into their life, is at the Action phase, whereas in reality they may still be at what Prochaska and DiClemente call Contemplation. Depending on the circumstances, it can be valuable to show the client the model and to ask, 'So where are you on this spectrum now this minute?'

Fear

Ultimately, we are held back from change by fear. The fear is about loss of control and of being unable to cope with the unknown. Fear is the real

	Stage	Typical client comments	Where coaches can help
1	**Pre-contemplation:** time period, years.	Nothing to do with me, it's not a problem, I ignore it, why won't people shut up about it?	Acknowledge the client's right to this choice. Challenge, but skilfully. Raise awareness that the client themselves has said that there could be benefits to changing.
2	**Contemplation:** time period, six months.	I'm thinking about it. I'll do something, but not yet.	Validate the client's thinking, offer encouragement – I'm here when you're ready.
3	**Preparation:** time period, one month.	It's becoming an issue; I'll explore my options.	Encourage; offer support, spell out the practical help available; discuss small steps that could become the start of the change.
4	**Action:** time period, weeks/days.	I'm committed, I'll do it.	Validate the client's choice without seeming over-eager; ask the client to spell out the benefits of staying on course; discuss substitute activities that ask about supporters.
5	**Maintenance:** time period, six months.	It got to seem so easy, but unfortunately I've had a few relapses.	Acknowledge that relapses are all part of making the change; discuss how to avoid situations and people associated with temptation. Re-discuss the benefits.
6	**Termination**	It's not a problem any more – I don't even think about it.	Acknowledge the effort and skill involved without seeming to patronize.

Figure 8.3 The Prochaska and DiClemente Stages of Change Model

opponent in coaching. Fear ruthlessly targets the most fragile spot, starting as faint doubt and, in the right conditions, growing quickly to terrifying proportions. As neuropsychology now proves, logic is often no help because fear crowds it out, reducing it to a parody of rationality, becoming in quick order anxiety and panic.

In coaching, what we are doing, with the client's full assent, is peeling back the surface of apparent logic to expose the vulnerable core protected, as it so often is, by irrational defences. Naming the fear, looking its underpinning assumptions in the eye, challenging and supporting, offering alternatives, building new skills, working in small steps, being alert to the psychology of human change, showing that you believe the client's life could be what they want it to be: this is what will make the difference. To be successful as a coach you need to be open, warm, curious and honest. These qualities are never more necessary than when working with clients on change. You also need to be unafraid – the subject of the next chapter.

9 Being nice is not enough: adding challenge to support

People who choose a career as a coach tend to see themselves as tolerant, trusting – and curious about human behaviour. We are drawn to coaching because we have a positive view of humanity. We are strongly motivated to help others. Even before we get training, we can probably create pretty good rapport already. When we are beginners we may not always be able to sustain it perfectly or see why it sometimes goes askew, but we grasp the principles. What is much, much harder is to know how and when to challenge. That is the territory for this chapter: why being *nice* is not enough, and how to add challenge to support without destroying the relationship.

One of the reasons that coaching is an unusual kind of discussion is that it includes the possibility of high levels of support and high levels of challenge in the same conversation, all within a framework of respect and rapport and delivered without judgement (see Figure 9.1). This is a rare experience. When you discuss a problem with a close friend, the chances are that the friend will loyally support you. If you are in an uncomfortable dispute, the friend may well reassure you that of course you are right and the other person in the dispute is wrong. Alternatively, you may get into a different kind of debate, one where perhaps a personal relationship has soured or where a boss seems to have taken against you. Here you may experience challenge, but as hostility, spite or rudeness.

Where the client needs and wants to make major changes in their life, it is inevitable that you will have to combine support with challenge. The key word here is *combine*. If all you do is challenge, even when it is done with kindly intent, you will fall into the category of being one more of those people who attack and undermine, and most of us already have at least some of those in our lives. Clients will rarely continue with coaching when this is the case. As a coaching client myself, I had one such coach. He was a perfectly pleasant man, but he always had some little model or theory to give me and somehow it felt as if I should already have known what these were. When he wasn't doing that he was raising what he called *tough questions* about the performance of my department, even though he had actually never been a senior executive himself. I felt constantly reproached and ended the relationship early.

Challenge	High	**High challenge, low support**	**High challenge, high support**	
		Client is undermined, indignant and defensive; coaching likely to end prematurely.	Client trusts and likes coach; can learn even when uncomfortable. Relationship capable of being long and productive.	
		Low challenge, low support	**High support, low challenge**	
		Low impact coaching, just a nice chat; coaching likely to peter out.	Coach colludes with client; client misses opportunities to learn. Longer term, coaching unlikely to be sustainable.	
Support	Low			High

Figure 9.1 Combining challenge with support

If there is neither support nor challenge, then the coaching will lack impact – it will be another meaningless chat that the client could just as well have with an acquaintance.

As a coach, if most of what you do is agree with the client, nodding wisely, head cocked on one side to show how sincerely you are listening as they pour out their story, then several highly undesirable results can follow. You may be encouraging them to adopt the victim-thinking frame of mind in which everyone else is at fault, but they are the acme of purity. Whatever the provocation, most of us have had at least some hand in our own problems; so when others agree that we are victims, this is rightly labelled *collusion* and it does not help the client one little bit. Agreeing that they are victims reinforces the powerlessness that they already feel: *yes, client, you have been wronged and there is nothing you can do!* Where the client has performance problems, your role is to help them see what these are, or might be, and then to work with them on doing better. If all you do is agree that the client is always right, then when you have been hired by the organization, always a third party in executive coaching, your sponsor is likely to be upset and disappointed that coaching has not delivered changed behaviour.

Clients may also be disappointed. In asking in their initial session how people want to be coached, one of the most common replies is to say, 'I want to be challenged'. Most clients do know at some level that one of the most valuable functions of coaching is to expand their thinking, to shake up pre-conceptions, and to add a different perspective. This is unlikely to happen if all the coach does is to agree with the client.

The only viable option is to combine high levels of support with high levels of challenge. In my own experience as a client with a number of different coaches, the best sessions have been those where I was never quite sure what would happen. I knew I had to stay alert and at the same time I knew I would never be humiliated, however much vulnerability I displayed.

Getting to the crux

Getting to the crux describes the skill of forcing a client to name what is ultimately at stake in whatever the issue is. The relief of being able to talk to another person who listens non-judgementally is such that clients will often begin to ramble. Signs of this are that the client tells you the same thing in several different ways, and you begin to feel bored because you have already heard what the issue is. Your instinct may be that the long story is a way of avoiding the main issues. Notice it when the client starts way back in the distant past history of whatever they are describing and gets lost in all the detail: 'Where was I – I'm losing my thread here!'

As a coach, it is not a good use of the coaching session to let the client roam about in all the detail of a story. Getting to the crux is about pinning down what the real issue is – for you and the client. An example might be a client who has spent a long time describing her anger at what she feels was manipulative behaviour on the part of a team member. The client has ended up feeling stupid in front of others. This is not the first time this team member has done this. The conversation between you and the client has begun to take on a circular flavour. As the coach you intervene to say: 'So the crux of it is that you're angry and fed up with this behaviour and want to do something about it?' Naming the real issue allows clients to address the nub and decide what to do about it.

Interrupting

Interrupting people is generally thought rude in our society. As children, we learn that you never or rarely interrupt – it is part of being socialized. Hence, for instance, the mixture of horror, awe and amusement that the tougher journalist-presenters evoke: they break the taboo.

In coaching we also have to break the taboo. The client is paying us to get to the heart of things and coaching time is limited. Also, clients have already probably gone round and round the loop several times with friends. For many clients, there will be a well-rehearsed drone to the story.

Interrupting needs to be done with discretion. There are always caveats to consider. The client may need to get into the detail in order to get the story straight in their heads. They may need the catharsis of talking at length; there may be detail which you need to hear. However, clients often go on too long as a way of avoiding getting to the real point. Talking at length may be a conscious or unconscious tactic – a way of keeping the coach at bay. These clients may tempt you with distractions they know you will find alluring. This is nearly always because you are on the track of some nodal point for change. One British politician owned up to using this tactic with his personal trainer:

> When I am under the cosh being pushed to my personal limit I might suddenly reveal a fascinating piece of low-level gossip to distract him or show intense interest in his life and welfare.

Sometimes, the same clients who play on your politeness may be the first to say later that the coaching was just a lot of pointless talking. Other clients may not know how long is *too long* for talking about an issue and will need your help in establishing it. Some people talk a lot when they are nervous. Interrupting them will reassure them. Clients who are compulsive talkers may know well enough that they are going on too long, but may still have got into the habit of doing it.

You do not need to know all the detail in order to be able to coach effectively – in fact, often you need to know remarkably little – but clients may assume that you need to know a lot of the background. If they go on too long as a matter of routine, both they and you will potentially become dissatisfied. Interrupting in coaching is different from the annoying interruptions we experience in a social conversation because it has a different purpose. In social events people interrupt out of boredom or because they are queuing to speak and get fed up with waiting. Some interrupting is overtly crass and rude: it conveys, *'Now let's get back to the really interesting subject: ME!'* Coaches interrupt in the interests of the client and the coaching relationship.

How to interrupt

- Trust your intuition that it is time to do it.
- Set aside your worries about whether the client will dislike you for doing it – the chances are that they will respect you more. Coaching is definitely not like a polite conversation with a friend.
- Ask permission – 'May I interrupt you here?'
- Use body language to help – e.g. a hand held palm up (traffic-cop style) to the client.
- Follow the interruption with an immediate explanation about your reason for doing it: for instance, 'I'm getting lost here', or 'I'm wondering if I really need to know all the detail?', or 'I'm going to pause

you there because you used a really interesting word just then . . . and I'd like us to explore it'.

Data in the moment

The real catalyst for change is in the coaching relationship itself. What the client does with you, he or she will most likely be doing everywhere else. The most important data you have about that client is how he or she is in the moment with you. This is the data that many coaches pretend to ignore, and it may also be known, but constantly avoided, by most others around the client. Does this client create feelings of fear in you? That is what she will be doing at work. Does this client lose you in his rambling descriptions of what is happening with his team? Ten to one he will be a poor communicator with others. Is the client over-deferential with you? Does a client try to exert inappropriate control in the conversation with you? That is probably what others will experience too.

This data is every bit as important as what the client tells you about events and people outside the room. It is pricelessly valuable. Ignore it at your peril. It is far more significant than either you or the client speculating about inner motivation, intellectualizing or analysing. *How are they affecting you now this minute?*

Giving feedback

To use this data you have to become an expert in the art of giving feedback. This is probably the single most striking way in which a coaching conversation differs from any other conversation our clients are likely to have. Unlike the client's line manager, we have no power to hire and fire. Unlike the client's partner, we have no wish to create or destroy love. Unlike the client's friends, we need not feel we could be putting the friendship at risk if we speak candidly. Coaching is one of the few occasions where anyone is permitted, even encouraged, to comment on the immediate behaviour and impact of the other person. You may sometimes be the client's best hope of being told something of which they seem unaware, something that is holding them back, that everyone around them knows, but that no one is willing to raise. Such things are often about intensely personal aspects of self-care and might include having an unpleasant body odour or bad breath, or that their clothing looks inappropriate in some way: ill fitting, not contemporary, too revealing, dishevelled or grubby. Being able to offer feedback with the honest intent to help the other person learn, and with no wish for self-aggrandisement, endows the process with enormous power, but you have to be willing to move past your own and the client's potential embarrassment.

Anthony

Anthony was a gifted IT specialist who was desperate to move from his current role but was finding it difficult to get past the shortlisting stage. I noticed immediately that he never smiled and frequently covered his mouth with his hand. Despite this I could see, as no doubt everyone else could, that Anthony's teeth were extremely discoloured and seemed to be crumbling.

'Anthony, is it OK to give you some feedback, even if it might be something difficult to hear?' Anthony looked apprehensive. 'Mmm, yes . . . OK.' 'I notice that you're covering your mouth with your hand and it looks as if you've got some serious problems with your teeth.'

After a moment of hesitation, Anthony's reply rushed out. He had a severe dental phobia, had not seen a dentist for more than 30 years and had constant discomfort with his mouth. Shame about his mouth had led him to avoid intimate relationships and he was chronically lonely. His belief was that never smiling – or hiding his mouth behind a hand – hid the problem. He was unaware that a mouthful of dental decay and periodontal disease could pose a serious threat to his general health. My feedback told him that his problem was perfectly visible to others and that it also raised the possibility that he was someone who neglected his health and might therefore have other issues with self-management. Such was his fear of the whole topic that Anthony did not know that there are skilled dentists who specialize in this type of patient and who can use hypnosis or sedation to promise pain-free treatment. Together we did an internet search and devoted two sessions to the topic. When we met again several months later I have rarely seen such a dramatic transformation, physically and psychologically, in a client, and within a short time Anthony had begun dating, had found a new job, and had almost doubled his salary.

Just to be clear, *feedback* is not a synonym for *criticism*.

Being on the receiving end of criticism can be devastating:

> Made me feel like a naughty child . . .
> Felt really frightened – wondered whether my career was on the line . . .

> It was so unfair! I was obsessed by the unfairness – couldn't hear what lay behind it . . .
> Even as he was speaking I was plotting revenge: how dared he talk about me like that!

Criticism attacks the person by making generalized judgements. Criticism is an opinion: *you are* [usually something unpleasant]. This brings out all the defensive and aggressive reactions described above because it contains hurtful generalizations: 'You are a poor communicator'; 'You are sloppy'; 'Everyone thinks . . .' Criticism is tough on the person and is most unlikely to be heard or acted upon because it alerts the amygdala in the brain (see page 69) so thinking processes close down. By contrast, feedback may be positive or negative. When it is negative it is tough on the issues and is given, as all true feedback is, for one reason only: to help the person learn, and at a point where the feedback-giver judges the other person can hear it. Feedback is also about the things that we can change. It would be pointless, for instance, to give someone feedback about their height, their racial origins or their gait. Criticism looks to hurt and is usually a way for the criticizer to unload their anger.

Positive feedback is not the same as *appreciation*: vague, oversimplified compliments which are generally meaningless – for instance, *You are so clever*, or *You handled that meeting well*.

In giving feedback:

- Ask permission every time: 'May I offer you some feedback here?'
- Stick to factual descriptions of what you have seen, using phrases like 'I noticed . . .', 'I saw . . .', 'I observed . . .', 'I heard . . .'

  I noticed that when you were talking about X, you seemed really alive and animated.

  You leant forward and thumped your papers.

  I heard you giving X a really straightforward explanation of what she needed to do – and I noticed how her face relaxed immediately.

- Don't interpret. Describe what you have seen without attributing a motive. So avoid saying something like:

  So I knew you were angry with X . . .

  I saw that you wanted to leave the room straight away.

  Instead, ask a question, using phrases like 'I'm curious about . . .' This asks the client for his or her motivation, rather than you making a guess at it. So say something like: 'I wondered what was going on for you at that moment?'

- Describe the impact on you:

  > When you leant forward like that I felt alarmed just for a second. I wondered if you were angry with me!

  > You started your presentation with a story and I was completely absorbed in it – I wanted to know what happened next.

  > You touched your face a lot while you were talking and that had the effect on me of wondering whether you were really confident about what you were saying.

- Link it to the client's goal by using a phrase like 'I'm wondering how this links with . . .'
- Ask for the client's view of what you have said.
- Agree how you will work on the material that this incident generates.
- Look for opportunities to offer more positive than negative feedback, especially where a client can show you how vastly improved some skill or behaviour has become.
- Choose your words carefully. It is better to say something like 'I ended up feeling a bit alarmed about what you might do next', rather than 'You were intimidating'. There is a fine line between feeding back how the client has had an impact on you and seeming to have taken it personally. The whole point about your feedback is that you are not taking it personally, even while you are describing the personal impact of the client on you.

Here is an example:

Candice

Candice was proud of her track record in production management, had an MBA, and was pleased to have won her job against stiff competition. But soon her boss was regretting the appointment, complaining that Candice was unable to speak or write without recourse to jargon. Candice was annoyed and hurt by this accusation, believing that the fault lay with others for not being clever enough to understand her.

Both Candice and her coach understood that Candice's job was on the line. When Candice began to use convoluted sentences with her coach, the coach found himself as baffled as her colleagues. Instead of glossing it over and pretending to understand, the coach stopped her every time.

'Candice, can I stop you here? I notice how many very long words and sentences you are using. Just now you described *production flexibility analysis* and *Kanaban* with *JIT systems* and *Economic Value Added*, and a lot of other stuff that followed, and I had no idea what you meant. Then I began to feel stupid and that I somehow should be understanding you and it was my fault for not being able to. I wonder if this is an example of the effect you have on colleagues?'

After several more examples along the same lines, Candice began to realize that her coach was no different from her non-specialist colleagues, and that stepping back to ask, 'What does a non-specialist really need to understand here in very simple terms?' would significantly change her impact on colleagues. Because no one else had felt able to take this intrusively detailed and high-risk approach, Candice had resorted to the all-too-human defence of denial. To Candice, being an expert mattered to her above all else, and this is what had led to her exaggerated reliance on technical jargon. The overinvestment she had made in being an expert also became rich territory for the coaching.

To use this approach you have to intend to look at everything: how clients greet you, how they come into the room, what they say in the first few moments, how they treat you, the language they use, the feelings they arouse in you throughout the session. You also need to recognize the data when you experience it and know the difference between how much of this data is generated by you and how much is being created by the client.

Knowing when NOT to give feedback is every bit as important as knowing when you must. I still wonder about a woman client who had startled me on first meeting by being dressed from top to toe as a man, creating immediate puzzlement: Was she actually a transgendered person? Or biologically a woman but presenting herself in male clothing? Or a gay woman who was merely rejecting conventional female attire? The reason it mattered was that this client was constantly getting on shortlists for jobs and failing at the interview. My guess was that interviewers who were meeting her for the first time would feel exactly as I did, and that the distraction this created ensured that she never got the job. At the time I felt that such an extreme choice of appearance was too closely linked to core identity to be challenged with feedback, but now I think it was just failure of nerve on my part.

Who else would have entered this territory without the wish to be hurtful? The key questions here are:

Is this something the client can do something about?

How prepared might they be to tackle it?

If the answers to both these questions are no, then the issue is best ignored. If the answers are yes, then you have a *duty of care* to the client, a concept from the practice of medicine that I find it useful to remember in such circumstances.

Provocation and humour

I am utterly against the idea of the coaching room being some kind of place of worship where a holy hush prevails. In the early years of Person-Centred Therapy, for instance, it always seems to me that clients were encouraged to ramble on for hours while the therapist stifled boredom, anger, pity, irritation, laughter, incredulity and all the other responses which the rest of the world might offer. (I am aware that this might not be a totally fair description of what actually happened.)

When I first started using humour and provocation in my coaching, I thought I was probably a bit eccentric. Other coaches might disapprove, and maybe I needed to keep quiet about it. When I read Farrelly and Brandsma's book, *Provocative Therapy* (1974), I realized that what I was doing was relatively mild by comparison, but seemed to work for similar reasons. Farrelly offers funny, teasing, intrusive, sexually provocative and impertinent comments to the client, often using street language; takes the client's fears and exaggerates them to the point where the client, often spluttering with laughter, has to defend him or herself; offers surreal, outrageous and whacky 'interpretations' of the client's behaviour, but does all of this with care and warmth for the client as the cornerstone and with remarkably positive results. As Graham Dawes comments on the Provocative Therapy website (provocativetherapy. com):

> The shibboleths of psychotherapy shatter. Farrelly's mouth opens (often before he's even given the client a chance to explain the problem) and what comes out is everything you've been told never to say to a client. He even encourages the client in their craziness, throwing out all sorts of advantages their crazy behaviour will bring to the client (albeit the advantages are crazier than the client's behaviour), providing the client with a wealth of justifications for their behaviour

(albeit the justifications are more spurious than any the client has come up with), exhorting them to continue with the behaviours they say they want to stop (albeit cheerfully confirming that the consequences of continuing will be those the client is most anxious to avoid).

I don't go this far. But I do sometimes use approaches that are recognizably in the same genre. The two underpinning hypotheses are these: First, if you provoke the client, *using their own internal frame of reference*, with humour and perceptiveness, the client will tend to move in the opposite direction. In fact, this is the typical response to advice-giving twisted and turned back to the coach's and client's advantage. Second, if you urge the client to continue doing their evidently self-defeating behaviour, the client will tend to move towards a healthier alternative. The overt tone is teasing, joyfulness, lightness, bounce, chutzpah and challenge.

Example 1

A gloomy chief executive client, sinking ever lower in chair, avers that a slight blip in performance could mean the end of his career. I have worked with him for some years, and I know the internal dialogue he will be creating:

Coach: Hmm, yes I agree [copying and grossly exaggerating the client's slump] your life is over. I can see it now, Kim [wife] is getting up at 5 to go and scrub floors in that beer-stinking local pub. Your kids are standing at the door crying and saying that they hate their bog-standard comprehensive school, and you're lurking upstairs feeling like crap because it's all your fault.

Client: [sitting up in chair, trying not to laugh]. That is SO cheeky. Of course it wouldn't be as bad as that. [now actually laughing] At the very least Kim could be getting up at 7 and making me a cup of tea while I loll in bed before she goes off to scrub floors at an office!

Result: exaggeration has forced the client to self-correct. Gloom has vanished and never reappears in the session.

Example 2

A senior diplomat fears delegating and doesn't know how to do it. This has resulted in a life clotted by 16-hour days, bottlenecks for his frustrated staff, and a wife furious because she sees him so little. The client has offered all the familiar excuses to me about why delegation is 'impossible', thus revealing his inner frame of reference.

Coach: [Exaggerated righteousness] Absolutely. These staff are hopeless. Whoever appointed them? [Jabbing finger at client] You could lose control here. It's correct that you should do all their work as well as your own. [Loudly] You're a saint for sacrificing yourself like this! To risk your health and marriage is so noble! Only you can do all this work to your own high standards. The organization will thank you – in fact you'll probably get a knighthood in the next Birthday Honours . . . or maybe even the Royal Victorian Order as well, the Queen will personally . . .

Client: [Interrupting, looking confused and startled but beginning to smile] I think you're going a bit barmy here – are you serious?

Coach: [Over-solemn face] Of course I'm serious. I think the Foreign Secretary will single you out for your exceptional devotion. And why stop at that? The Prime Minister will personally thank you.

Client: [Snorting with laughter, in spite of himself] OK, OK, I get the picture. They never will thank me. I won't get the knighthood. And if I did my wife may have divorced me by then. I assume you think there's hope for me. If so, please tell me what I should be doing and stop sending me up!

Result: prolonged laughter. Coaching resumes with focus on how delegation could happen without losing sight of quality standards. Client comments later that he hadn't known that coaching would involve 'surrealistic comedy with myself as the straight-man'.

It is even possible that Sigmund Freud himself was an exponent of provocative therapy. It is clear that he considered himself exempt from the strictly-no-reactions rule he suggested for others. Dr Roy Grinker, an analysand of Freud in 1932, is reported as describing the great man's practice of allowing his Chow dog, Yofi, to stay in the room. When the dog scratched to go out, Freud said, 'You see, even the damned dog is bored with you.' When the dog scratched again to return, Freud said, 'Well Yofi has decided to give you a second chance so maybe I should too.'

Tough speaking and confrontation

There are several types of situation where tough, frank speaking might be useful. First, there might be discrepancies between what the client says they value and what the client actually does. An example might be a client who says she believes in equal opportunities but recruits and selects people on the basis of stereotype or old boy/girl networks. Then there are those times where the client agrees that a change needs to take place, but postpones the moment when it will happen. For instance, the client may say they are fed up with their current role and want to leave, but makes no actual attempt to seek another job. There may also be times where you have serious doubts about whether the client's proposed course of action is wise or desirable. For instance, the client may be overwhelmed with anger about a boss's behaviour and be prepared to storm into the boss's office the next day. You feel certain that this will not get him the outcome he says he wants.

When you feel you should confront the client, introduce the subject straightforwardly and make the link to the stated results that the client wants, alerting him or her to the possibility that you are going to say something which could be difficult to hear but stressing how much you value and want to support the client. Base what you say on data; keep it descriptive and non-judgemental; talk about 'what is', not 'what should be', then ask how the client sees it. Ask what will happen if the situation does not change, and discuss solutions. Make it clear that it is the client's choice whether or not to make the changes.

For confrontation to be successful your own motivation has to be a sincere wish to help. If there is even a smidgen of feeling that you want to get at the client, or teach them a lesson, don't do it.

When clients make mistakes

Senior executives carry weighty responsibilities. Since they are merely human, the chances are that, at some point in their careers, they make mistakes which can have serious consequences – whether such mistakes are massive gambles on a strategy which turns out to be a bad misjudgement, or errors of management involving individuals. In these circumstances it takes a very mature person to accept accountability without simultaneously feeling crushed by guilt. These clients may turn to you for help:

> Fenton had not listened carefully enough to a whistleblower who had drawn attention to a fraud. When the whistleblower turned out to be right, Fenton had lied about his own part in the cover-up.

> Emma had been part of an executive team which had signed off a massively expensive IT project despite her own strong private doubts about the supplier and the viability of the project at the point where the contract was let. She had not spoken up. The project ran wildly out of control with the whole team receiving severe criticism from the National Audit Office.

A coach walks a fine line in these circumstances. There are so many ways of seeming to help which are not in fact helpful. Trite clichés about everyone making mistakes will not comfort the client. Nor is it probable that the client will truly and privately go along with it if you convey that you believe your client is innocent – it was everyone else who got it wrong.

Even less are you likely to know enough about the case to act as judge and jury on your client's behaviour. But agreeing that a client did something wrong is sometimes as important as reassuring them that they did something right. So a client whose vulnerability was concealed behind a façade of loud sarcasm finally found the courage to ask, 'Do you think I'm a bully?' Since I never saw him at work there was no way of knowing the answer, but my reply was that the behaviour he willingly recounted would certainly have been enough to intimidate me had he been my boss. Another client asked, tremulously, 'Do you think my time in this organization is over?' She had described being systematically excluded from meetings and emails and had just received a highly critical performance review. There was no way I could read her boss's mind or know the answer to her question, but nor could I give her false reassurance, knowing how often it was the case that such events were usually the precursor to a forced exit, and that it was certainly my duty to convey this to her.

The Christian tradition of confession to a priest who will keep your secrets may also alert us about how to work with clients who have made serious mistakes. A confession is a voluntary act and is intensely private. Christianity distinguishes between the sin and the sinner. When it is clear that a client wishes to tell you about something which the rest of their world would condemn, you are doing the client no favours to brush it aside, nor to go to the other extreme by expressing pompous disapproval. As a client there can, paradoxically, be a relief in having someone you know on your side and who then agrees that, yes, you have betrayed self-set standards, and no, this does not define you as a moral failure for the rest of your life. Trust the client to know what he or she needs from you, and ask this question explicitly:

> *What help do you need from me on this?*

Depending on the answer, I have found that the coaching often becomes a discussion about how to forgive yourself and recover moral equanimity, including making amends where this is possible.

When it's always someone else's fault

There are some clients who can seem fixed in the role of victim. You will find this client extremely difficult to work with; the victim position is so very attractive because if others have to change before you do, then you can wait ever. To have a client determined to blame others for their own disappointments invariably takes me to the boundaries of my skills. Suggesting therapy is always a possible alternative, but many clients are not so obviously extreme in their distress as to warrant this tactic.

Carys

At the time we worked together, Carys was a disappointed woman. As a senior accountant she had expected to get the finance director job in her organization. It had gone instead to a colleague she liked but who she also judged to be less competent than herself. Our work initially focused on getting another job as Carys felt she could not stay in the original organization – it would have felt too humiliating.

I encouraged Carys to contact headhunters and to alert her networks to her wish to move. Soon there were two potential offers on the horizon, both of which paid much the same as the job she had failed to get. Carys took one of these jobs, but as our coaching went on into her new job, it was clear that a sense that 'it was unfair' still pervaded her life. She complained about the new job; it was lonely, the office was stiflingly hot, the chief executive did not appreciate her. In every session it seemed that we would inevitably come back to the unfairness of not getting the FD job in her old organization, even a year later.

What can be done for clients like Carys?

Some possible approaches

First you must notice the pattern. The giveaways are that the client comes to coaching looking for a way of changing someone else and evades questions about what they, the client, have contributed to the situation. You might notice a lot of lot of sentences beginning:

- If only they would . . .
- If only it hadn't turned out like it did . . .
- My life would be fine if only others would let me . . .

There may also be generalizations suggesting that mostly other people are getting things wrong around this client: 'They always . . .'; 'They never . . .';

plus a constant sense of weariness and disappointment. Whatever good things seem to be happening, nothing is ever quite good enough.

The next step is to *offer the client feedback*:

> Carys, I notice that in this session, as in so many others, we keep coming back to that old sore of the FD job. You've mentioned it twice in this session, just as you did in our last one. What's going on here for you?

In Carys's case, she was ahead of me. 'I must be a very annoying client because I'm always blaming someone else, aren't I?' So Carys could intellectualize her dilemma, but still could not move on.

Some clients will deny that they are contributing anything. The therapist and author Irvin Yalom suggests saying something like, 'OK let's accept that 99 per cent of this is someone else's fault. Can we work on the 1 per cent that's yours?' Along with this, it is helpful to expose the fallacy of devoting time and energy to the goal of having a better past. The past has gone and can never be rescheduled, reworked or remodelled. There is only now.

For most clients one or all of the approaches I describe here will work – one way or another. If they don't, I will have one last tactic to try: I will expose the client to my own dilemmas about how to help them. So with a client like Carys, having tried all of the above tactics without any apparent success, I might say:

> Carys, I feel at my limit here. I really want our coaching to succeed for you yet I'm feeling frustrated by my inability to help. We've tried a number of things, yet I notice you still seem attached to that original dream of the job you didn't get. What would you advise me to do?

Note that the risks here are of a client like Carys believing that I, too, am persecuting her and will be about to reject or abandon her. I will refuse to play that game, stressing my continuing support for her as well as putting half the responsibility for our relationship back on her. I know such people to be vulnerable, despite what is often an appearance of cockiness and certainty. Whenever I have taken on such clients, despite my private doubts, the coaching usually comes to an abrupt end at the point where their view of themselves as helpless victims is challenged.

Being attacked

Very, very occasionally you may find that the client is deeply upset by your conversation and attacks you and your competence. This happened to Jon, a coach still in training. He had carried out a bespoke 360-degree exercise for the client (page 123). He already knew from her boss that she was new in her post, struggling to attract the loyalty of her team. His report suggested, as tactfully as possible, how and why this might be happening. The client read the report; she raged, she shouted. She accused Jon of using flawed methodology, sneered at his careful use of language ('What do you mean *some* people thought this, *some* people thought that . . .?'). In his supervision session Jon told me that he had quickly understood that he was not the target and had managed to remain steady, despite the provocation. He described how he had used the martial arts tactic of the unexpected. He agreed with her that the methodology was flawed because it was carried out by a human being. He said he believed the report was valid nonetheless. He asked her how she might like to check it out. He volunteered to have another coach carry out the same exercise again, at no cost to the client.

He describes what happened next.

'There was a short silence. Then I said, "I don't think we can go on working together while you feel like this, I feel under attack and I have to say that it feels unfair."'

The session ended abruptly.

To Jon's surprise this client contacted him again a month later. Bravely, she had shown the report to her boss. She apologized to Jon. She and her boss had agreed that she was in the wrong job and that she could transfer back to her old post as a technical expert where she did not need to run a team.

Accountability

Accountability is a tricky concept. It can seem too much like teacher–pupil or boss–subordinate if it is done in the wrong way. It does not mean finger-wagging if the client fails to carry out their commitment. I was shocked when a close colleague told me that his hypnotherapist, someone who also claimed to be a coach, had irritably terminated the relationship because he had not carried out some small piece of 'homework' as part of his attempt to give up smoking. A client also showed me an email he had received from a previous coach, a relationship that did not survive this communication, where the coach had baldly informed her that 'If you don't do your homework I shall be very displeased'.

Accountability in coaching is totally different from boss–subordinate, teacher–pupil or parent–child accountability. It does mean that you, the coach, *hold clients to account for what they have said they wish to do to make changes*. It is their agenda and their ideas of where they want to change that is at the core but the clients design the items for accountability, not the coach and clients also design *how* they want to be held accountable. As a coach you have no attachment to whether clients have carried out their tasks/ homework. You have no stake in their doing things to please you. There is no place for value judgements or blame, as whatever has happened there will be learning in it. There may be exceptions when the client consistently fails to commit to what they have promised, in which case you will indeed need to discuss what is going on for them, but in a mature and respectful way.

Follow-up

I enjoy keeping in contact with clients between sessions and encourage phone calls, texts and emails. This can be especially useful if you and the client have focused on some important impending event in which new behaviour will be tried. If you and the client prefer not to do this, in the next session, ask: 'How did it go on those points we agreed last time?' When the client has achieved them all, congratulate them warmly and acknowledge whatever effort it will have taken to do it.

When the client has not achieved them, ask:

What got in the way?
What would you do in a different way another time?
What did you learn from not doing them?
What could help achieve them in the future?

Knowing when too far is too far

The coaching relationship is delicate: too much pressure on the client and it will fracture; too little and the coaching will feel inert. Knowing when to press and when to hold back is a matter of the finest and most split-second judgement.

Robert

Robert was a miner's son, left school at 16 and began teaching himself some of the principles of paralegal work while he worked in a solicitor's office. At the age of 40, by now an experienced solicitor, he had done brilliantly well and had become head of legal services for a local author- ity. His starting issues for the coaching we embarked on together were to bring more finesse into his managerial style – a bland, safe topic.

Soon, however, it became clear that the underlying issues were his profound lack of self-confidence and his acute social isolation. He had no friends at work and no social life. He had married his childhood sweetheart at 19 and his wife had opted to stay at home, even though they had no children. The relationship was one of mutual dependency, but at the point where Robert started the coaching he was expressing a strong wish to break out of the stifling pattern he and his wife had created: 'I want to get out at weekends, go to football, meet more people, but if I do she will feel it's a threat. She just wants me there so that we can do the garden, watch a video, just the two of us together.'

As his coach, I felt we had reached a crossroads.

JR: What do you really want?

Robert: I do want to have a better social life and one that's outside this charmed circle of just me and her.

Robert describes how this would look, sound and feel in response to the question, 'If you could have this ideal life what would be happening?'

JR: So what are the blocks to setting about this?

There is now a long pause – perhaps 12 seconds. Robert glances at me, looks tense, wrings his hands slightly and looks at his feet. Very slowly he says: 'I can't move on it. If I discuss it with her, she'll panic. It will raise the whole question of the relationship and I can't do that to her.'

What does a coach do in these circumstances with a client who has described what he wants so vividly yet also describes a total block to action? Challenge? Suggest a tiny first step? Withdraw? After a few moments more of silence, I asked how Robert felt about staying with the idea of doing nothing: 'Fine – for now', was his reply.

Later I thought long and thoroughly about this exchange, pondering whether I might have pressed him harder, but feeling in the end that it had been right to hold back. Eight weeks later, Robert called me, devastated, to tell me that totally out of the blue with no warning or previous threats, his wife had killed herself, swallowing a lethal dose of paracetamol. He discovered that she believed she had had terminal cancer (she hadn't). Robert's judgement about his wife's fragile mental state was totally correct, including a diagnosis of agoraphobia, which he had not shared with me. What he had not anticipated was how violently her feelings would implode. His weighing up of what he could cope with if he had confronted his wife was also correct.

And my judgement about what would have been too far was correct, tl
I did not have anything like all the relevant data at the time.

Subsequently, in training new coaches, I have seen how easily the coa ..s
eagerness to help can stray into too much intimacy too soon, ignoring the
warning signs from the client which say 'keep off'. When this happens, the
client's energy goes into repelling what he or she perceives as an intrusion,
rather than into learning and change. When the client tells you straightforwardly that they want you to stop – stop. Be alert to the evidence from the
client that this might be the case: small frowns, a tapping foot, looking away.
You can't go on with a task-based agenda when this happens – the pause or
the resistance becomes the agenda. Name it, saying something like, 'I notice
we seem to have hit a pause here. What's going on for you?' Then agree jointly
how to handle it.

Challenge is essential to good coaching. It is closely linked to giving information and advice, the subject of the next chapter.

10 Giving information and advice – in coaching style

Little is an absolute rule in coaching and it is not an absolute rule never to offer advice and even less never to offer a client useful information. The art is in knowing when and how to do it, the subject of this chapter.

Anwar is in a state of shock and can barely speak. His company has new owners. He has just been told that he has been fired, that he has to clear his desk and leave the next day. A financial settlement will follow. By chance, this news coincides with the day of his coaching session. His usual high levels of resilience have temporarily deserted him. The planned session has to be abandoned. Instead, he and his coach discuss the emergency measures that he can take. The coach has encountered this situation many times previously and after they have been going for about an hour, says to him calmly, firmly and very directly that he needs to call an employment law specialist whose offices are a short distance from her coaching room. He looks at her blankly.

'Why?'

'Because you need specialist advice and someone to negotiate for you and the chances are that the company is offering you less than they could and should.'

'Will you make the call for me?'

'Of course. I'll ask her to see you as soon as possible.'

Fortunately she is free to see him straight away and Anwar and his coach walk down the road together.

Thanks to this excellent lawyer's advice, Anwar achieved a 25 per cent improvement on the severance offer the company was making him. The company also paid his lawyer's fee. His comment a month later: 'I was like a zombie that day. Thank you for taking charge.'

Ruth is a Canadian working in London. She has lost her temper with a member of her team who has made a foolish mistake for the third time. She arrives at her coaching session still enraged. 'As soon as I go back, I'm telling her she's got to go,' she says. The coach realizes that Ruth may not know that UK law forbids instant dismissal unless the grounds are gross misconduct. The team member's mistakes do not amount to gross misconduct. Ruth's coach patiently explains that if she dismisses this employee in the way she plans, it will most probably result in an employment tribunal case which Ruth's company would lose. She tells Ruth that it would be extremely undesirable to follow her plan – and why.

Gemma is a doctor who has trained as a coach. She combines part-time work as a doctor with her growing coaching practice. It is a hot summer's day and she notices a black flat mole looking a little inflamed and with an irregular edge on the exposed forearm of her client. He is a busy management consultant who, as she already knows, has a dismissive attitude to his health, saying things like 'Well, we've all got to die sometime so what's the point of screening and all that crap?'

'Jamie', she says, 'I know you think that visits to doctors are just for neurotics, but what's happening to that mole on your arm?'

Jamie shrugs. 'Oh, it just itches a bit, it's nothing. Don't go all doctory on me Gemma.'

Gemma grips Jamie's arm for a closer look and feels that nothing but the most straightforward approach will work with him. She says, 'Jamie, I want you to refer yourself urgently to your own doctor. It could be nothing, but whatever it is, it needs investigating. It might be a melanoma and, if it is, it will respond to early treatment'.

Jamie stares at her. 'I've come for coaching not for medical advice' he says, smiling, but she sees a glint in his eye which could mean hostility.

'I know that. But I have a duty of care to you. Don't mess about with this Jamie. Shall I show you some melanomas on my laptop?' Swiftly she taps in a few words and silently slides the laptop to him.

A year later Jamie is a skin cancer survivor and humbly acknowledges that he probably owes his life to his coach.

All three of these examples were occasions where a classic coaching approach would have been inappropriate. Straight advice was what was needed.

What if clients ask for advice?

In general in coaching it is better to avoid giving advice (see Chapter 2) because mostly it does not work. However, coaching clients are typically mature, successful people. They are used to receiving advice and used to knowing how to put it into context, rejecting it if necessary. Even so, they are no different from every other human being in being likely to resist advice which is given heavy-handedly or inappropriately or as the coach's default. But every now and then a client will ask for advice outright:

> What do you think?

> If you were me, what would you do?

How you respond depends on the circumstances. For instance, it may be the kind of question where both you and the client know that the client could perfectly well work out the answer for themselves. If so, ask the client, respectfully, what it would do for them to know what you would do. This challenges a client's belief that the answer is 'out there' rather than in themselves. Or you could try smiling and saying, 'I could tell you what I would do, but you and I are very different people, so I'm not sure that would help. The answer you come up with yourself is the one that will work for you.' Another tactic is to say, 'I will tell you, but let's explore what ideas you have first', by which time the client has usually lost interest in hearing your advice. Some coaches will successfully avoid a direct answer by ignoring the question and going straight to a dilemma-solving technique such as identifying the options and then rating them for pluses and minuses.

Some guidelines about advice

There are occasions when it is appropriate to give advice. Here are some of the suggested conditions that need to be in place before offering it. When in doubt, I find it useful ask myself which, if any, of these guidelines might apply:

Table 10.1 Guidelines on giving advice

	Yes	No
There are clear right/wrong answers to a question the client is asking – e.g. on the legal, medical or financial position.		
It is a crisis and needs rapid action.		
The client's physical, financial or mental well-being will be in danger without having the piece of advice: you have a duty of care.		
There is physical, financial or moral danger to another person. Again, you have a duty of care.		

Table 10.1 Continued

	Yes	No

The client is not in a position to make their own decisions.

You are offering facts, not opinions.

The client has specifically asked for information and has made it clear that they will make up their own mind on how to use it.

The subject is genuinely bewildering and needs expert guidance for the client to be able to understand it. You have unquestionable expertise, rather than just another personal opinion, in the area on which the client is seeking advice.

Giving the advice is unlikely to create dependency, to humiliate or to encourage unwise optimism.

Your own motivation does not include any of the following:

a wish to impress and show off
wanting to control
being too lazy to use coaching techniques
feeling a need to pay the client back for some slight.

In dealing with what are often subtle and complex questions, think first about the facts – which are often more blurred than they seem. It is easy to get side-tracked by your own strong feelings, needs and concerns:

Kirsty

Kirsty is a coach who was sexually violated as a child. Her abuser was successfully prosecuted and served a long prison sentence. In her spare time Kirsty volunteers for a child helpline and believes strongly in the value of public punishment for abusers. In the wake of certain recent high-profile cases involving celebrities accused many years later of inappropriate sexual behaviour with children, one of Kirsty's clients suddenly tells her that she was raped by one such celebrity and does not know what she should do.

Kirsty recognizes her own immediate visceral response as unhelpful and takes several moments to compose herself. Through managing to ask some well-grounded questions she discovers that her client is hazy about detail, including dates, times and places. This puts a significantly different cast on the issue of whether or not the client should go to the police. Kirsty gives her client a brief account of her own experience and of her work with the helpline. By now she has calmed down and is able to advise the client about what might be involved in making her allegation, drawing on the training she has received for her volunteer work, and is also able to suggest a specialist advisor who can work alongside the client to help her make the decision.

Often, once you and the client start to open it out, there are many ambiguities and complexities lurking inside what may have seemed originally like a straightforward problem. There may be a difference here between so-called *simple* problems where there is an obviously right way to proceed and a *wicked* problem where for every possible course of action there is a major disadvantage. Sometimes when this happens you may have strong personal opinions which tempt you into offering advice, as in this example:

Liz (client) and John (coach)

Liz had lost her local government chief officer job because of a merger. As her coach, John had helped her come to terms with the initial shock. She had a strong commitment to public sector work, but was willing to consider alternatives. John and Liz revamped her CV/résumé and also did some interview coaching. She soon landed an offer for a well-paid job in a profit-making organization allied to her old specialism. This did wonders for her battered self-esteem, but she still felt that her heart was in the public sector and that perhaps she wanted to be a chief officer again after all. Did she want this new job or not? At an emergency coaching session she and John looked at the upsides and downsides of accepting or rejecting the job, including the possibility that in the local government sector, where severe cuts were now the norm, jobs like her old one were in short supply. She was still no clearer about whether to accept or not.

The next day she was on the phone for perhaps an hour of agonizing. 'I want you to tell me what to do', she begged. John said that he could not do that because the decision had to be hers and suggested looking at the upsides and downsides of the options once more. The core of John's dilemma was that privately he strongly felt that she should accept as it was probably the best offer she was likely to get, given the current market and her career stage.

She turned the job down.

Six months later she still did not have a permanent job and was miserably doing a series of badly-paid temporary projects. She bitterly regretted having rejected the private sector job.

Should John have 'told' Liz to accept? He, too, agonized about this, but came to the conclusion that he had been right to stick to his principles. First, there was no knowing whether she would have taken any notice of his advice. There was a strong chance that if she had accepted the job she would have been as unhappy and regretful about leaving the public sector as about her eventual decision to try to stay in it. As part of the coaching, she and John had examined all the options, including how realistic it was that she would be offered another local government job that she really wanted. It was her gamble, her life, and she made her choice.

In this case, as in all good coaching, John was clear that he was responsible *to* but not *for* the client.

Giving information

There are many points in coaching sessions where you might have information which could benefit the client. Examples might include: having helpful data about jobs in a particular sector; deep knowledge about specific techniques that you know will increase a client's chances of getting through a job interview successfully; answering questions from a client who wants to know more about the differences between management and leadership; explaining the theoretical structure of psychometric instruments, such as the Myers–Briggs Type Indicator; familiarity with frameworks and models that have proved their value to clients over and over again.

The danger is of launching into all of this information in a way that diminishes the client, bores them, drowns them in information, tells them what they already know or don't want to know. Beware especially if you have pet theories which you feel you *always* want to share with clients – for instance, a favourite analysis of leadership styles or a particular remedy for stress.

Professor Lis Paice wryly describes how this all too easily happened to her in her absorbing and candid book *New Coach* (2013). Lis is a distinguished doctor and ran a large postgraduate medical school before developing a portfolio career which includes coaching. As she describes in her book, she put herself on a coach training course only to placate a persistent colleague and to set a good example, believing that she already knew how to coach. She planned to give herself a strategic 'illness' after the end of the first day. Instead she found she knew a great deal less than she had thought, became captivated by the process and impressed by its power. Even so, as a tyro coach working towards a qualification in coaching she still found herself lured into giving what she calls 'seminars for one' with her clients, passing on her experience, regardless of whether they had asked for it or really needed it, commenting, 'I had no idea I was so inclined to pontificate until I took up coaching.' In one case, as a specialist in medical education, she enthusiastically offers the client some favourite tips for getting through the professional exam which she has assumed is the goal for the session:

> I was conscious that I was putting a lot of energy and my own personal experience into this, but she seemed to be coming with me. Once I felt we had gone as far as we could, I set her the task of developing a study plan to get that exam out of the way for once and for all.

The client returns for her next session happy and excited, only for Lis to discover that the happiness is about her ambition as a writer and that she has succeeded at last in getting a play staged, mentioned in the previous session, but that Lis had barely noticed because of her eagerness to offer advice on a topic where she felt secure as an expert. Yes, the coaching had been 'motivating' but the client had brushed aside concerns about the exam, and had in fact decided not to take it.

A protocol for giving information in coaching style

This simple protocol contains checks at every stage and will help you manoeuvre your way around these common problems.

Step 1: Ask permission

This may seem like a simple and possibly gratuitous formality, but it makes a lot of difference. It is courteous, it allows for the possibility that the client might say no.

> I've got some ideas on this that you might find useful. Would it be OK to describe them to you?

By asking, and saying it in a way that allows the client to express doubt or reluctance to hear your golden words (though few ever do) you are living the reality of the partnership.

It may also help to emphasize your expertise:

> I've been working with clients on this topic for many years and there are a few things that they've found it useful to know. Is that OK with you?

Step 2: Ask what the client already knows

One of my clients was a world-renowned authority on diet and nutrition, working part-time as he prepared for retirement. He wore his expertise lightly. After a puzzling stress fracture he had a bone scan which he was able to interpret for himself, and realized that he had osteopenia, the precursor to osteoporosis. Casually dressed and not using any of his academic and professional titles, he then had a first session with a senior hospital doctor. Unasked, she gave him a mini-lecture on diet and osteoporosis. His comment to me was, 'I knew more about the topic than she did, her advice was platitudinous and not a little out of date, but I thought she was embarrassing herself enough as it was and I couldn't be bothered to interrupt or correct her'.

Few clients are likely to be completely uninformed on any of the topics where you might offer them information. Some useful phrases here are:

> I guess you already know quite a bit about this . . .?

> I don't want to tell you stuff you already know, so give me a quick run down on your assumptions/knowledge/experience with this topic.

> You've probably already researched this on the internet, so where are you with your current thinking?

> Where are you already pretty clued up about [the topic] and where are the gaps for you?

Step 3: Ask how the client would like to get the information

Some people like to have a step-by-step explanation starting at A and finishing at Z. Some like to have the headlines first. Some only want the headlines – the detail will bore them. Some like to pause on the detail. Ask which your client would prefer.

Step 4: Use the 'drawing out then adding' approach

Many coaches have had previous careers as expert talkers – for instance, as consultants, management trainers or as managers used to giving presentations. If you fall into this category you will recognize how much you enjoy the spotlight, responding to the performance side of the work, knowing that you are fluent and articulate. Once you get going it can be hard to stop. This may tempt you into doing the same with clients, pausing for a micro-moment for a perfunctory response from the client:

> Coach: (has been talking uninterruptedly for several minutes) Have you understood that so far?
> Client: Yes. (knows this is how they are expected to answer)
> Coach: (plunges on again with another uninterrupted few minutes)
> Client: (nods wordlessly) (has most likely drifted off, tempted to start checking their phone, wonders how soon they can leave)

Instead, start as described above by asking the client what they already know, then ask which aspect of it they would be most interested in hearing about in more detail. Offer this, and then pause to ask for questions and comments, repeating the process by following the client's interests and concerns.

This is an example of how well it can work in practice:

Joanne (client) and Morgan (coach)

Joanne has recently made the transition from her job as a technical specialist to her first senior managerial role. As so many people in this position do, she is struggling to find time for thinking and planning because she is doing too much of the work she should be giving to people in her team. Her coach, Morgan, has enjoyed establishing the story so far and realizes that the core of the problem is Joanne's difficulty in delegating.

Morgan is using the 'drawing out and then adding' approach. He establishes that Joanne does know the general principles of delegation and that she has competent people reporting to her.

'So what happens when one of your people comes to you with a problem?' he asks.

Joanne describes the scene where a team member flatters her by saying, 'Joanne, you know what to do because you're the expert, I don't.' Rather than asking the team member for their own ideas, Joanne typically utters the fatal words, 'Leave it with me', thus becoming a decision bottleneck and in effect switching roles with her team member. She now has to report to him on progress, rather than the other way around.

Morgan says, 'So, Joanne, this is a very familiar problem.' He summarizes what she has said, ending by saying, 'There's a famous Harvard Business Review article on just this. It's called *Management Time: Who's t the Monkey?*[1] It's very amusing and very wise. Do you know it?'

> *Comment:* So far Joanne has set out what she already knows and does while Morgan has listened intently. He establishes whether she has already read the article. If she has not, and seems interested, he will go on to describe it.

She has not, so Morgan now gives a very brief account of the first part of the article, then stops and says: 'How far do you recognize this scene?'

Joanne is laughing and squirming at the same time. 'Totally! That's it. They bring their monkeys to me [the 'monkey' is a metaphor for the next move in any project] and then they leave the monkeys with me. No wonder I can't do anything. My office is full of other people's monkeys!'

Morgan says, 'So shall I describe what to do with the monkeys instead of you keeping them?'

Joanne nods, still smiling, and Morgan goes on to another brief explanation, ending with, 'So that's the authors' advice, but what do you think?'

> *Comment:* This conversation has been held on a basis of mutual negotiation, carefully establishing at each stage not only how much the client knows but also what it would help her to know next and how she is responding to the ideas she has heard. It has the flavour of a conversational dance rather than of a lecture with perfunctory pauses. Morgan will follow the session by emailing Joanne a link to the article along with two others on the same topic and will pick the subject up again in their next session by asking, 'What did you make of the articles I sent you?' And then, 'How far do you think you could incorporate those ideas into what you do yourself?' All of this will dismantle any resistance Joanne feels. She has not been patronized. She has been treated like an intelligent equal who can come to her own conclusions, but at the same time Morgan has fulfilled his duty to introduce her to ideas that he knows are highly likely to be able to help her solve her problem with delegation.

Step 5: Invite disagreement, acknowledge the client's autonomy

Theories and models are just that – ideas. But any of us can become overcommitted to our favourite theories and when this happens we run the risk of appearing to treat them like religious dogma: something that is true because we say it is, regardless of any evidence to the contrary or of the existence of competing ideas.

To guard against this danger, always invite the client to disagree and leave plenty of space in the conversation for the client to respond:

> This is why I think this idea/matrix/book/psychometric test is so interesting/useful – but how does it strike you?
>
> This is just one model: what holes do you see in it?
>
> How much sense does this make to you?

If you plan to send links to articles, especially on topics such as leadership where millions of words have been written with large numbers of competing theories, make it a point of principle to send more than one.

Step 6: Give several examples of how other clients have solved similar problems

Telling stories is compelling to the human brain. We like narrative and it is a lot more convincing to us than just hearing facts. Clients may be struggling with how to change their behaviour – for instance, managing anger, learning how to manage upwards, getting enough fun and leisure into their lives. Offer them several brief examples of how other clients, carefully anonymized of course, have dealt successfully with the same thing. By doing this you make it clear that there is more than one way of dealing with common problems and that you are not endorsing any single idea as the one right path.

Paula

Paula is a specialist nurse who coaches patients with an early diagnosis of pre-diabetes. She knows how important it is for her clients to understand that lifestyle changes can make all the difference and also knows how hard we can find it to change ingrained habits of shopping, cooking, eating and exercising. She may say something like:

> So let me tell you about a few of my other clients. One of them is a 67-year-old gentleman with raised glucose levels who has been able to improve everything by buying a pedometer, has steadily raised his steps target over a period of a few weeks and can now easily do 10,000 steps a day. There's another person I'm working with who is in her fifties and she's concentrated on reducing her weight. This is a priority for her, by

ruthlessly cutting down on carbs – for instance, never buying cake and biscuits so that she doesn't have them in the house and so reduces temptation, has stabilized everything for her. I've also got a much younger client who's got into the whole glucose monitoring process and has been able to work out for himself exactly what difference different foods and different types of exercise make, and he's doing really well.

But that's them. They're all different. What do you think might work for you?

Paula's comment is, 'I know there are many ways to change these habits and by offering real examples from real people who really have improved or stabilized their glucose levels, I find that my clients might tell me that none of those ideas would exactly work for them, but it's sparked something that will. And that's the whole point – not to give them my own favourite tip. This type of storytelling also raises people's levels of optimism at a time when they are often feeling low and worried.'

Managing disagreements

Most coaching conversations are good-natured and polite. They may and should contain moments of humour and intensity, but outright disagreement is rare and a straight argument even rarer. However, as coaching develops its own specialisms and niches, it is more and more likely that a client chooses you because of your known expertise, shading the boundaries between consulting and coaching (see page 20). Where this is so, there is always the lurking risk that you and the client may overtly and profoundly disagree. The most likely cause is that you are challenging some cherished belief and that you are doing so because there is a lot at stake – for instance, health, money, career – and you believe that you have a duty to raise uncomfortable issues. I have trained many hundreds of doctors as coaches where they will work either as coaches to other clinicians or as coaches to patients:

As an oncologist I frequently see patients who are afraid of chemotherapy and want to believe that various quack 'cures' are a better option. I have investigated most of the main self-ordained experts here and have yet to find one where there is a shred of scientific data to support their overblown claims. But how do I say this to the patient without being rude and dismissive or destroying hope?

It is easy to get this wrong. Clearly, I did just this some years ago with a client who was a high-profile investment banker. She was deeply unhappy with her current role, felt conspicuous as one of the few women at her level and came to me for help with her career. For our final session she was preparing for a job interview in another organization and had asked me for advice on what she should wear. I had just trained in colour and style coaching where there is a simple and attractive system for sorting people into four categories ('Colour Seasons') based on the theory that when we choose from the palette of colours that suits our eyes, skin and hair we look healthy, feel good and make shopping a whole lot easier. We agreed to devote the session to this topic. I had already noticed that she unvaryingly wore a severe black suit with a black sweater. My own view, which I never expressed, was that this was highly unflattering to her very pale skin, pale eyes and light brown hair, making her look ill and washed out, or perhaps as I privately thought, like a funeral director. At the end of the session she thanked me politely and then said with perfect composure, 'All these new colours just make me feel physically sick. I hate them. Thank you, but I won't wear any of them.'

A year later I met her at a social event. She was pleasant and friendly, told me she had got the job, thanked me for my help – and neither of us referred to the fact that she was still clad entirely in black. My guess now is that I had simply failed to notice that she was not sharing my own enthusiasm for alternative colours. I had failed to acknowledge that the whole system of analysing the colours that suit us is fallible and depends crucially on the aptitude, training, experience and judgement of the coach. Also, it is perfectly possible that as a newcomer to the craft I had got the actual diagnosis horribly wrong.

How to disagree

There is a lot to learn here from the experience of outstanding negotiators and mediators. One behaviour that they all have in common is that they listen a lot more than they talk. When they hear opinions they don't like or know to be factually wrong, they do not do what so many of us do, which is to blurt out an emotional response, brutally informing the other person that they are mistaken. Instead they do what appears to be counter-intuitive. They ask the person to say more because by doing so they will learn far more about what is going on in the other person's mind and will also preserve the relationship of trust:

> *Gary* specializes in pre-retirement coaching. He is also licensed as a financial advisor. His client, Nigel, is a 56-year-old single man about to leave employment with a modest pay-off. Nigel proposes putting this along with a cashed-in pension into a no-interest current account and leaving it there. Gary knows that this is not sensible. Instead of

saying so, he says neutrally, 'Tell me how you came to that decision, Nigel.' Nigel launches into a long speech about how stock markets can't be trusted, how he likes the idea that he can actually see his money on statements and that this makes it seem 'real'.

Gary then probes some more, asking Nigel to say what his plans are for spending the money. Nigel reveals that both his parents died in their fifties, that he believes he will not live beyond 60 himself, and also that some nameless disaster will probably soon end human life on the planet anyway, 'So what's the point of saving?'

Unlike many other executive coaches, *Leila* positively seeks out so-called *problem performers*. It is her market niche. Most of her clients are men that have been referred to her for alleged bullying. She quickly gets them to expound their assumptions about human behaviour at work and finds that almost without exception they believe profoundly that the workforce consists of slackers who cannot be trusted to work unsupervized, will only respond to threats and are motivated entirely by money. Leila listens carefully to her clients' own accounts of what has happened, knowing that these often include feelings of being persecuted rather than being the persecutor, and she summarizes their views skilfully before she does anything else.

Both these coaches have gone well past a simple rehearsal of client behaviour. They see it as essential to find out what meaning the behaviour has for the client. Gary understands that clients like Nigel are in the grip of irrational fears and have lost perspective on the difference between an implausible worry (an asteroid strike, sudden death) and a plausible worry (a stock market crash). You cannot deal with irrational fears until you know what they are. With Leila's clients their behaviour is virtually always a way of keeping assumed danger at bay. Often their world view is pessimistic; they hold rigid right/wrong views, they dread the power of their own unchecked impulses and project this on to others. With my own investment banker client I may have failed to understand that wearing black was most probably a protective shell that she donned to keep away sexist comments and to avoid looking conspicuous as one of the few women in an overtly macho world.

It is powerful to agree where you can. So Gary agrees with Nigel that the stock market is one of the most unpredictable systems in the world, that no one can forecast with complete certainty what will happen and that there is always risk when you invest. Leila agrees with her clients that some people do indeed come to work as a mechanistic way of earning money and have little commitment to their employers. She offers them the view that being a leader is stressful and will often mean that you have to take unpopular decisions.

The next step is to ask for permission to disagree:

> I've been listening carefully to what you've said. I find I can't agree with quite a lot of it. OK to offer you a different view?

> It probably won't surprise you to know that I disagree with a lot of what you've said. But I think I need permission to tell you exactly why and how!

No client is going to refuse to let you speak. You have granted them licence to talk and now they will do the same for you. This is more than just a formality: it dismantles the automatic resistance that is created when we feel we are being attacked:

> In working with Nigel, Gary first establishes how Nigel's parents died. His father drowned in a swimming accident and his mother had a rare form of cancer. Gary asks whether the cancer has a genetic component and Nigel says that it does not. He also asks what the realistic chances are of some disaster ending life on earth and finds that Nigel knows that these are small. Gary asks permission to show Nigel some alternatives to putting his money in a non-inflation-proof current account. Nigel agrees readily. Gary likes working with large colourful Post-its in unusual shapes to make choices clearer to the many of his clients who are afraid of financial data. He turns the session into a light-hearted game, splattering the table with gaudy Post-it stars, speech bubbles and diamonds, and using marker pens, shows Nigel a series of options and what each could mean in terms of risk and reward.

> Leila has long accepted that she is unlikely to change her clients' attitudes and beliefs. Instead she suggests some pragmatic alternatives based on the idea that the status quo is not an option because the client's job is at risk. She briefly summarizes some of the many research projects which show that authoritarian leadership gets short-term compliance but at a high cost. She asks her clients to do some internet research based on her suggested links and to return with their thoughts at the next session.

Whichever sets of tactics you adopt, it will pay dividends if you stress the client's right to disagree. It is also sensible to express doubts and uncertainty. For instance, where leadership behaviours are concerned there is no real consensus; opinions have varied depending on the decade in which they were formed. There are virtually no absolutely clear-cut formulae for organization behaviour where anyone can say with certainty that x behaviour will always lead to y outcome; human behaviour is simply too variable. It is sensible to acknowledge this:

> A lot of this is ambiguous and people vary in how they respond.
>
> In the end, you're the one who has to live with whatever you decide to do. I can only offer you some ideas to help you make up your mind.
>
> You will know what's best for you, but my role is to give you some challenge and some other ideas to consider.

Depending on what is involved you may feel strongly that the client or some other person in their lives will be in some kind of danger if they fail to heed whatever information you are offering them. Noticing the intensity of your own reaction will tell you that you could be over-attached to your own ideas and therefore risk their rejection. Instead, it is perfectly legitimate to express your concern, while continuing to endorse the client's right to disagree:

> I really want to help you here and I'm worried that your career is going to derail if you don't change some of the behaviour we've discussed – but in the end, only you can decide.
>
> Of course it's up to you, but my concern is that you could find yourself in a difficult situation in a year or so and I don't want that to happen to you.

Clients may benefit from all kinds of specialist help and advice, either in tandem with your coaching or serially:

Lynne

Lynne was a manager newly appointed into a senior role. Our agenda was to work on her first 100 days in her new role, but feedback indicated that she also had a problem with what her organization called 'personal impact'. Lynne's confidence issues stemmed from a childhood where she had felt socially disadvantaged as one of the few free-place children in a famous school. She had a reputation for mumbling and swallowing her words, rushing at them, apparently to get them out of the way. She and I were able to work effectively on a strategy for her first 100 days, but I referred her to a specialist coach on the speech issues. My colleague, trained as an actor and voice expert, was able to see that, along with the psychological issues, Lynne had a complex set of problems, some of them physical, with tongue and breath control. She prescribed a series of exercises which, when rigorously implemented, were able to make a significant impact on Lynne's performance at meetings and when giving presentations.

Other types of specialist help might include recommending finding a relationship counsellor where the client's marriage or partnership seems to be in trouble, fitness and weight loss experts, and a personal finance advisor for people approaching retirement. (See also how to refer a client for therapy, page 240.)

When you offer clients information in coaching-style you create a conversational dance where listening precedes talking. Understanding where it is essential not to withhold information can be liberating. Some apparently small behaviours can make all the difference: asking permission to offer information, establishing what the client already knows, pausing for reactions, asking for permission to disagree, all can have a positive impact where both client and coach will benefit.

Note

1   Republished in the November/December 1999 issue of the *Harvard Business Review*. Authors: William Oncken and Donald Wass.

11 Tears, trauma and therapy

What do you do when a client is in the grip of strong emotion? How do you know when a client needs specialist help after a traumatic experience or seems to need therapy? What do you do if a client appears to be suggesting that they could take their own life? It is inevitable that you will meet at least some of such issues in coaching and this chapter explores some possible ways of dealing with them.

Tears

We can cry with laughter – or with sadness. We can laugh with anger or with joy. Crying is just at one end of the spectrum of human emotion, and since we are dealing with the whole person in the coaching room it is inevitable that we will see tears from time to time.

Many coaches express understandable anxiety about what to do when a client cries. It is unusual for a relative stranger to break down in front of you. Also, adults may feel that crying is childish or shows that you are out of control or incompetent and can't cope. It certainly exposes the vulnerability of the person who is crying, and some clients may find it humiliating.

However, in my experience, the person who is most likely to be worried about the crying client is the coach. The reasons may be a mixture of embarrassment at seeing an apparently well-adjusted person break down, and a fear that the client may discomfit themselves then or later by their tears, regretting having shown apparent weakness. When you are in real rapport with another person emotion is catching, and some coaches describe a dread that they may join in.

As coaches we may also worry that we have in some way caused the tears through clumsy coaching. The language here is often telling: 'I made him cry', implying that it is our responsibility. But crying is one of the multitude of choices that clients make during their work with us. Coaches cannot *make* clients cry – any more than they can make them laugh, or bored, or command them to feel any other emotion. The client chooses, unconsciously perhaps, but chooses none the less. Often the coach's worry about whether the client can cope is just a way of projecting our own worry: 'Will I be able to cope with a client who cries?'

The biggest trap for a coach with a weeping client is to imagine that your role is to fix the tears. Ask yourself what message it would give your client to do anything at all which implied that their tears are not legitimate. Through their tears the client is giving you a privileged opportunity to understand more about them. Platitudinous there-thereing does not help, nor does any of the range of mumbled clichés about time healing – 'I'm sorry for your loss' or 'A good cry does you good'; all these trite comments are well-mocked in the comedian's gag, 'Sure *I feel your pain* but wouldn't you rather I did something about it?' The second biggest trap is to join in. There is a place for your own emotional reaction, but if you are crying as helplessly as your client you will be in no position to work with them effectively. You need the compassion of loving kindness, but not the over-involvement of sticky sympathy.

The most appropriate response depends on that split-second moment of judgement that only you can make:

> You're looking upset – do you want to go on?
>
> Of course you can cry – this is one place where you can.
>
> If it would help to cry, that's absolutely fine.
>
> You've been through a horrible experience, so of course you feel upset.
>
> These feelings are so strong – of course they will produce tears.
>
> Silence: sometimes you can convey empathy and acceptance simply by saying nothing, just waiting quietly and attentively or handing them a tissue.

Clients who prefer to contain their tears will stop at this point. Clients who do not, may let go and cry and will tell you later that it was exactly what they needed in order to move on:

Marie

Marie had lost her job as a result of a highly-publicized major incident in the hospital at which she was chief executive. An enquiry later exonerated her. Although in subsequent sessions we worked on how to frame her CV/résumé, how to prepare for an interview, how to network and how to settle into the new job she soon got, at our first session she wept continual, angry, hot tears as she told her story. Although I stopped many times in that session to ask her if she really wanted to go on the answer was always 'yes'. Her later reflection was:

> Letting me cry was the most amazingly healing thing. I got it out in that room in a way I couldn't do anywhere else. I couldn't worry my husband by letting him see how devastated I was

because I'm the breadwinner. I knew I just had to do that howling before I could move on. By letting me do it you conveyed far better than any words could that how I felt was legit. You conveyed that I was OK and that I would get over it.

It is always a good idea to invite clients to manage the moment with you. A possible response here is: 'Take as long as you like – tell me when you're ready to go on.'

Far from feeling that tears are an embarrassing intrusion into the coaching, to be swept out of sight as soon as possible with both coach and client conspiring in the illusion that nothing has happened, the skilled coach realizes that tears are wonderfully helpful material for the work, often revealing deeply held values and needs. Tears can often appear out of nowhere: neither you nor the client is expecting them. One useful question here is:

What triggered the tears?

Some recent answers here have been:

It's because I'm remembering my lovely grandmother. She was the only person who gave me unconditional love when I was growing up and I miss her so much even now.

Rage – unfairness! My parents made it clear to me that I had to leave home at 18. Their birthday present was a nasty cheap suitcase!

I'm thinking about how brave I was as a little girl with a squint, facing up to the bullies in my class.

Regret and guilt: that I didn't do more to help my brother. He had Down's syndrome and died when he was 13.

When I meet clients after the coaching has finished, some of them will tell me that these moments are the ones that stick in their memories as among the most helpful in the entire process and for reasons that they may not or perhaps could not have expressed at the time:

Martyn

Martyn and I worked together on and off for a number of years through a variety of jobs and roles. He remembers the moment when he wept briefly and unexpectedly and for the first and only time during one of our sessions:

> I'd suddenly fallen out of love with my job and felt overwhelmed by it. I'd been dreading bringing it up because I felt that it was important for you to see me as always on top of things. You encouraged me to name the anxiety and I took the risk of letting my emotion show. I trusted you with that and realized it was OK to fail sometimes because you accepted that it was, and you accepted me in spite of my seeing myself as a potential failure.
>
> You asked me what had set me off. Our discussion of why I felt that, and your response that it would in no way affect your view of me was one of the best moments in our work together – a real moment of learning because I realized I did not have to be a brilliant performer or totally optimistic all the time, not just with you but with anyone. We had looked together into what felt like an abyss at the time. In a weird way, crying released the anxiety and straight away afterwards I'd got it into more perspective.

Stress and mindfulness

Whether or not present day life is actually any more stressful than it was in the past is a moot point, but it is certainly true that there are new forms of stressor to plague us. We can feel hunted by our phones and emails, employment is far from secure for many people and any indiscretion is likely to be captured by 'citizen journalists' and then held up for all to see on Twitter or Facebook. 'Feeling stressed' is one of the most common issues that virtually any executive coach will see in any given week. Mindfulness has been familiar to the human species for at least 2,500 years, and probably longer, but it is having its moment of renewed attention currently with a plethora of courses and books, many of them extremely similar, as the essence of mindfulness is its deceptive simplicity.

Mindfulness is about purposefully creating an observing self which can detach you from intrusive negative thoughts about the past, present or future. It is about suspending judgement. It is about exquisite concentration on NOW: this moment, this room, this me. Through mindfulness you realize that your thoughts are just that – thoughts: they come and go and

they don't have 'reality'. By practising mindfuh
change, not through the exercise of 'willpower' bı
that overthinking can have on your choices. As a c
and learn about it yourself first.

A one-minute mindfulness exercise

Here is an ultra-simple one-minute mindfulness tast.. ....

> Choose a quiet place.
> Sit erect in an upright chair, shoulders relaxed, both feet on the ground, hands loosely in your lap.
> Keep your eyes open, but let your gaze soften.
> Breathe normally – you are not trying to do slow or 'deep' breathing. Observe your breathing: What do you notice? This may be your breath passing your nostrils, it may be that your in-breath is longer than your out-breath, or the other way around.
> Observe the rest of your body. What do you feel in your feet, hands, chest?
> You may find other thoughts intruding. If so, just think, 'Mmm ... that's interesting'.
> Observe your breath again.
> Now refocus your gaze on the rest of the room.

There is impressive evidence on the power of mindfulness, including its positive effects on cardiovascular health, its benefits for people with depression and the improvement in people's levels of resilience. Imaging has suggested that there are helpful changes in the insula, the part of the brain that is responsible for empathy, so increasing your levels of empathy will include more kindness towards yourself as well as towards others. For a readable summary of how mindfulness works and its evidence base, look at *Mindfulness: A Practical Guide to Finding Peace in a Frantic World* by Mark Williams and Danny Penman (2011).

Mindfulness is not just another technique to add to your toolkit. Your first subject should be yourself. Put yourself on a respected course, learn and practise it, and only then see whether it is something you could introduce to your clients. Many will still believe it is for people with mental health problems or is 'religious' or 'spiritual' – or 'just another relaxation technique' – and will resist. It takes effort, practice and discipline to learn and apply; most of the research on the serious benefits of mindfulness comes from studies where the subjects invested considerable time and commitment over a lengthy time period. Carole Pemberton's book, *Resilience: A Practical Guide*

ches (2014), has a chapter on mindfulness with a detailed discussion
en and how to use it with clients.

Once you have made this initial investment in your own development,
you can use the principles of mindfulness in many ways with clients, explaining how it works and offering some moments of protected tranquillity in the
session.

Sathnam

Sathnam was overwhelmed. He had diagnosed himself with the label
'Impostor syndrome', constantly worried about whether his recent
promotion had been a 'mistake' and whether he would be competent
enough to cope with the future demands of his job. We briefly discussed
mindfulness and its principles. I had noticed his hunched shoulders and
rapid, shallow breathing, feeding this back to him as a calm observation.
I suggested we should do some slow steady breathing together: a count
of seven on the in-breath and a count of eleven on the out-breath. We sat
quietly for a few minutes. I asked him what he was noticing in his body.
The answer was, 'tension in my chest'. I invited him to put his hand gently on his chest, to imagine letting the tension flow out through his arm
and hand and to concentrate on the breath. I asked him to observe his
thoughts and then to let them go, without telling me what they were,
and then to do it again – and again. This took about ten minutes of the
session. Sathnam's face relaxed, as did his shoulders. We then moved
seamlessly into a conversation about how far his fears were truly justified, how he might make more of the strengths he was bringing to the
new role, and where he did indeed have some skills gaps, as virtually all
newly appointed people do.

In all our subsequent sessions, Sathnam asked if we could repeat
this activity, telling me that 'having those few moments of special stillness is just so great' and that he was also committed to putting himself
on a mindfulness course to learn more.

Habitual weepers

Recently I was at a celebratory gathering where there were many generations. By chance I witnessed the following. Two toddlers tumbled at much
the same time, as toddlers do, on the unforgiving surface of a garden path.
The girl toddler bawled and her granny rushed to her, cuddling and soothing.

The bawling continued for some time. The boy toddler bawled and his granny rushed to him, picked him up briskly, inspected his knees and said, 'Oh well, be brave!' – at which he stopped crying. One observation is not evidence as I well know, but there is no doubt that in Western societies it is mostly considered acceptable for girls to cry and unacceptable for boys. Girls may learn that crying keeps danger at bay and creates sympathy. Boys may suppress necessary emotion because they learn that that crying attracts contempt as weakness.

I did once have an ambassador client who found it difficult to contain emotion – for instance, at ceremonial events when the national anthem was played – though mostly he was still able to do it. But he is the only man who has ever brought me the issue of how to manage emotion in public, whereas countless women clients have asked for help on this question. The more senior they become, the more it seems that their propensity to give way to tears can become a career-limiting issue.

These women will cry easily and often in coaching sessions. The crying will not be full-on sobbing, just eyes filling with tears and an immediate need for a tissue. Your role as their coach may be to notice how often this happens and, with the client's assent, to explore its history and function in the client's life. Where such clients ask for help because they know it is becoming a problem, I have asked them to monitor first where, when and how the tears happen. When they report back, the circumstances usually involve what the client interprets as a personal attack, but on discussion it seems that all that had happened was a mildly negative comment from a colleague. Clients can learn that although they will claim that the tears are uncontrollable, it is possible to see crying as a choice and that there is always a microsecond between the stimulus (the apparent criticism) and the response (to cry or not to cry). It is also a revelation to many to realize that, far from creating sympathy, others may view the tears as the sign of a fatal flaw:

Beatrix

Beatrix was part of the executive team in one division of a German bank. A German national herself, she said, 'You British think you invented the stiff upper lip, but believe me in Germany it's much worse, and it's harder for a woman.' The immediate trigger for coaching was that Beatrix had cried and had then rushed out of the room during an important meeting with a regulator. Her boss had been horrified, telling her that this was but the latest in a series of such events and that if she was not tough enough for the banking world, then maybe she should rethink her career. Beatrix was indignant: 'I know he wouldn't say that to a man. It's already hard enough for a woman in banking – you have to be twice as good to get anywhere.'

When I collected feedback for Beatrix by interviewing her colleagues, she learnt that while there was immense respect for her other leadership qualities, most of them found her crying dismaying, distracting and sometimes manipulative. They did not see it, as she did herself, as a sign of her humanity and as an allowable weakness. Whether or not it was unfair or sexist then seemed less important than learning how it could be controlled.

With Beatrix, as with other clients, the solution was to learn some cognitive approaches first – for instance, to understand rationally that she was not helpless in the grip of emotion and that she was not necessarily the target of other people's comments – and even if she was, then that there might be some valuable feedback in it that it could be worth exploring. It can help to acquire skills for managing such moments. Something as simple as taking a deep breath or learning some powerful distraction techniques is often all that is needed.

Traumatized clients

To live our lives with reasonable confidence we have to assume that the world is a safe, predictable place. Essentially we believe in our own value and right to exist. All of this is overturned in psychological trauma: an event or series of events where the client experiences feeling out of control and chronically unsafe. Their assumptions about justice, personal safety, health or cause and effect are often replaced by the confusion of betrayal and bewilderment. They may feel exhausted, powerless and needy. Feelings of being essentially a good person may be replaced by feelings of being essentially a bad person because 'bad things only happen to bad people'. In effect, they feel that their psychological contract with the world around them has been breached.

Enter this area only if you are confident, experienced and know the boundaries of your own skill. In fact you may be thinking that this is exactly the sort of territory in which any coach should think twice. The immediate response may indeed be to feel alarmed and frightened by the extent of the client's distress: *This is too much – I'm out of my depth*. When, on mature reflection, you trust that feeling, you must strongly encourage the client to consult a specialist in this area. In fact, see your task as coaching the client around the issue of finding specialist help. Be suspicious, equally, of over-eagerness to get involved because you are enjoying the drama of it all without necessarily having the skills and awareness that you need.

It is obviously true that there are many potential snares. You may be deluding yourself about your levels of skill. You may meddle with techniques which you only quarter understand. The client may endow you with skills and knowledge which you do not in fact have. You may make a mess of it.

However, there is a case for not backing away in terror. The client may previously have been stable and functioning well and is not feeling overwhelmed by the trauma – this may be so, even when whatever has happened has been real tragedy. If the client has chosen you as the person who can help them, then until proved otherwise, you might assume that you can. The client may also believe that there is no other obvious source of help (but you should note that this is probably not true, and one of your roles could be to refer them to additional helpers). The client may make this choice because you might have worked with them over a long period of time and there is a high level of trust and liking between you. All of the above may be especially appropriate if the traumatic incident occurs while you are in the middle of a coaching programme and you know enough and have had sufficient training to deal with what the client brings.

As you build your experience, all of this may happen more often than you expect. Examples from my own practice include a diplomat unexpectedly caught up in offering consular services to British survivors of a major natural disaster which had happened while he was on holiday in the same country, a senior partner whose stress levels got well out of control when his accountancy firm was formally investigated in the aftermath of a political scandal, and a medical director whose personal reputation was seriously compromised by crisis events in his hospital. There are also all those clients, too many to list, who suddenly lost their jobs in the aftermath of a merger or a redundancy programme. The examples described here are those of obvious crisis and trauma, but you will meet much milder versions of the same phenomena on a more frequent basis: the abrupt discovery of a major health problem, a partner who suddenly leaves, a son or daughter who develops a drug problem, a career-threatening episode, and so on.

These are the symptoms to look out for:

- *Flashbacks*: Reliving an event as if it is happening all over again, often triggered by an innocent reminder from someone else, or from seeing a single word in a newspaper.
- *Nightmares and poor sleep*: For instance, waking early and finding it impossible to get back to sleep.

- *Numbing and avoidance*: A client who had been attacked by a mugger a few metres from her own home talked of feeling 'hollowed out'. Another client described being separated from the experience, as if he was in a film where he was somehow outside the whole traumatic event in which he had been involved. Seeing himself on the television news added to this feeling.
- *Intrusive negative thoughts*: Imagining catastrophe; ruminating about the worst possibilities. For instance, the medical director client imagined scenes of public disgrace where he was summarily ejected from his hospital with his belongings in a bin bag, struck off the medical register, his pension denied him and a hostile article about him in every newspaper.
- *Survivor guilt*: Where the client has survived an incident in which others have lost their jobs, been injured or killed – after an initial period of euphoria, there can be feelings of unworthiness and guilt. *Why me? Could I have done more? Was I selfish? Am I a coward?*
- *Preoccupation with 'if onlys' and 'what ifs'*: The accountancy client, whose reputation was at risk, repeatedly went over the events leading up to the crisis, asking himself what would have happened if only he had not done or said particular things.
- *High levels of arousal*: Jumpiness, irritability, hyper-vigilance, rapid heartbeat, sweating.

These are difficult phenomena to deal with. At their most extreme, they are properly described as post-traumatic stress disorder (PTSD). It is not surprising that clients will report anxiety and depression along with loss of appetite. Using alcohol, sexual promiscuity, tobacco or drugs as a way of seeking to anaesthetize against the distress is also common.

You will find reliable guidance given by the psychological trauma specialists, the Centre for Crisis Psychology, as published in the classic book by Peter Hodgkinson and Michael Stewart (1998). Essentially this is that an empathetic but directive and structured approach, sustained over a period of time, is what will work. The directive approach is justified by the helplessness that such clients report. Temporarily, they are not in the resourceful state in which coaching will work. There will be an educative element to it where you will be in the role of teacher with a client. Tell the client that this is what they will experience and ask for their consent to it. (For more on this see Chapter 10.)

Tactics that work

When my own clients have been caught up in traumatic events, I have used a number of standard coaching interventions with them – for instance, identifying what they need from me, asking carefully structured coaching questions, and listening empathetically to the replies. All may work in the right circumstances.

Normalizing the client's reactions is helpful – for instance, through explaining the change cycle (page 160). You might refer them to self-help sources in books or on the internet as you would with other problems, so in this case encourage them to read the pamphlet on PTSD by Martina Mueller of the Oxford Cognitive Therapy Centre (2007).

It may be valuable to reconstruct the whole story with the client, concentrating on its factual aspects first and creating the environment where the strong feelings that this will create can be accepted and contained: be wary of assuring the client that you 'understand'. You don't and can't 'understand' because you have not been through the experience, though what you can say with truth is how their story is affecting you. When my accountancy client was describing his dread of what the investigators would find, and his fear of humiliating collapse during the process of being interviewed, I said something like, 'This sounds so difficult and I can see the hurt and stress it's causing you. Just listening to your story, I'm feeling some of that tension and anxiety.'

Where you notice that the client is avoiding facing their fears, it can help to fill in any missing factual elements: for instance, the client who had been mugged had somehow got to the point where she believed that her assailant had followed her for weeks, marking her down for attack. Discovering, through reading court accounts, that it had actually been a stupid, random and opportunistic crime, was a vital part of her recovery.

Teaching de-arousal techniques such as steady diaphragmatic breathing and classic muscular relaxation will usually offer rapid ways of calming down, as will teaching techniques which show the client how to interrupt negative ruminating – for instance, through physical or mental distraction. When you notice flawed logic you can respectfully and firmly question it: so, for instance, a client whose son had drowned had come to believe that 'Anyone close to me could be in danger'. From this, he had rapidly moved to, 'It will be bad luck to be near me so I'd better keep away from everyone.' Challenging the grossly faulty generalizations here was enormously helpful to this client's adjustment. (For more on spotting these patterns, see page 172.) Many clients can also benefit from developing a self-designed programme of simple physical activity to be followed every day. Other tactics that work will include sending the client a relaxation recording to play on one of their devices before going to sleep, and suggesting the value of keeping a daily journal of the positive aspects of whatever is happening – for instance, the levels of support and sympathy they are receiving from others in their lives.

Where the problems seem overwhelming, then your role should probably be to strongly encourage the client to consult their doctor and to consider a short-term recourse to medication as a way of managing the worst symptoms. At the same time, you might recommend trauma specialists who can deploy techniques such as progressive desensitization, helping people to re-enter situations where they have developed phobic responses.

These are not one-off interventions. If you find yourself in this position, consider being prepared to offer telephone and email support on a no-limits basis and to follow up through a structured process over as many weeks as are needed, agreed with your client, but only if, again, you are experienced and confident of your skills.

Developmental disorders

Over my two and a half decades as a coach I have probably worked with at least 15 clients who were somewhere on the autistic spectrum. In most cases my 'diagnosis' is a speculative one made with hindsight. However, these clients – and all but one were men – typically presented with similar issues, and all had been referred by someone else – usually in the context of organizational change. More recently, as the stigma of autism seems to be fading, several clients have identified themselves as being 'on the spectrum', in one case telling me that autism ran in his family and that he knew that the diagnosis explained much about his own behaviour.

Some of the signs that a client may have a form of mild autism, such as Asperger's syndrome, might include difficulty with eye contact and over-formal speech patterns: for instance, never using an elision but saying *should not* rather than *shouldn't*, or speaking using the passive tense and in convoluted sentences. Another set of such symptoms includes repetitive body movements such as mild finger-flapping or foot-tapping which the client finds it hard to control, plus reported problems in creating rapport and making emotional contact with colleagues, along with a reputation for eccentricity. Physical clumsiness may also be an issue: I remember one such client repeatedly stumbling as he came into the room and later managing to bang his head against our front door as he left; another spilt his coffee in all but one of his sessions. You may occasionally also encounter inflexibility about time-management – for instance, insisting on particular routines. The client's skills may be concentrated on a restricted spectrum plus intense resistance to change, and extreme and obsessive interest in hobbies which involve counting and collecting. I remember one such client whose overwhelming commitment to a minor local football club came a long way before the needs of his job, his health, his wife or his children.

Any of these behaviours could have other origins, but the more of them that are present, the more likely it is that you should consider whether autism is part of the explanation. All of my own clients who might have fallen into this category were intelligent and articulate people at senior levels in their organizations. Most were in what seemed to be viable partner relationships and had children. Often they had been able to sustain their jobs, typically specialist roles in IT or finance, in a protected pocket of the organization, until a change had dislodged them. The coaching probably had limited success. Mostly it was about closely offered feedback, and in some cases frank teaching about social interaction – for instance, learning the importance of eye ͘n-tact or of asking social questions of others, and how to sustain this effec͘

A suspicion that your client has some kind of developmental con͘ this kind is not a reason for refusing the assignment, but it may b͘ for understanding that the coaching will need to have a different ͘ pace. It will also be important to be realistic, with the client ͘ nization, about what the coaching might achieve. Now that ͘ as Asperger's syndrome are better recognized and the assoc͘ intense than it was, we might increasingly expect clients ͘ tions to let us know that this is what we are jointly up ag͘

Understanding common psychotherapeu͘ psychiatric conditions

As a coach you do need a working knowledge of common psychological and psychiatric problems. For instance, I have had several clients whose extreme fluctuations in mood might possibly have been mild versions of bipolar disorder. One such client, a chief executive, was eventually removed from her post most probably because her grandiose plans for her organization, her casual lack of interest in their practicality, and her sudden plummets in energy and optimism came to be seen as far too risky.

There may be occasional clients who can benefit from specialist help and others where you may notice a need for it but decide not to raise it with the client:

Kamila

Kamila was a client who had a perfectly conventional list of performance-related work problems, many of them to do with her perfectionism and lack of self-confidence. At the outset of her coaching programme she had said that having a major tidying up of her apartment was one of her goals. When we had worked successfully through most of her list, I commented mildly that the tidier apartment had been consistently avoided as a topic. Kamila tentatively said a little more, revealing that she was hoarding thousands of newspapers and feeling unable to invite anyone into her home as a result. This did a lot to explain the social isolation of which she had complained. Knowing that such excessive hoarding was a classic symptom of obsessive compulsive disorder (OCD), that it often accompanied just the perfectionism and lack of confidence that Kamila had described and that hoarders with OCD are often reluctant to seek treatment, I left it at that, feeling, rightly or wrongly, that I did not have permission to go further.

Where OCD is concerned, I notice that many clients will now casually describe themselves or others as 'a little bit OCD'. Normally this merely means that the person concerned likes to manage detail and routine scrupulously. Since I know from first-hand experience with several sufferers that this is not at all what is involved in the infinitely distressing actual OCD, I usually challenge this phrase.

It is not at all uncommon to find that some clients have partners with serious mental health problems – for instance, delusional states of one kind or another. One such client was secretly followed into work by her husband, convinced that she was merely pretending to be a manager in her organization and was actually working for MI5. Another was in the grip of paranoid obsessions, believing that their TV had personal messages for her and that the water supply to their flat was being poisoned. Problems of dementia in ageing parents, and the troubling behaviour associated with some forms of it, are extremely common.

The anguish all of this causes to those who love them is beyond agonizing, and it seems that it is often too painful for discussion anywhere but in the privacy of the coaching room. Your role here is to allow the client to explore their feelings and also to consider what action, if any, they need to take. Again, you may be able to suggest specialist sources of advice. So with one client whose husband was very ill, in the grip of a long-running psychotic episode, but was refusing treatment, I was able to suggest she booked herself a conversation with a fellow coach who is also a consultant psychiatrist. This coach accepted the brief on the understanding that he could not prescribe treatment for the husband without seeing him as a patient, but that he could and did work with my client on ways to manage interactions with her husband.

Be ultra careful in how you enter this arena because it is fraught with tripping points. Classifying and labelling psychiatric disorders is controversial even among the professionals dealing with mentally ill people. Richard P. Bentall, a professor of clinical psychology, has written a jauntily iconoclastic book *Doctoring the Mind: Why Psychiatric Treatments Fail* (2010) about the way the pharmaceutical industry has taken over treatments based on what he says is the myth that mental illness has a physical basis. He writes:

> My own view is that most psychiatric diagnoses are about as scientifically meaningful as star signs, a diagnostic system which is similarly employed to describe people and predict what will happen to them, and which enjoys a wide following despite compelling scientific evidence that it is useless.
>
> (Beutall, 2010, page 110)

So we should consider ourselves warned.

Suicide

One of the worst moments of my coaching career was the Sunday afternoon some years ago when a client called me on my mobile. I give my number freely to clients: no one has ever abused it. It has to be an emergency, especially if the call comes at a weekend. The client's call was to say in a cheerful voice, totally at odds with what he was about to tell me, that he had just woken up from a sleep which he had intended to be his last: he had taken a large overdose of prescription painkillers, hoping to die, but here he was, alive. I was beyond shocked: numbed, incoherent, appalled. This lovely man had certainly described unhappiness – but suicidal despair? At first I did not think so. Later, I realized that perhaps he had, but expressed so subtly that it might just as well have been in code. Somehow I managed to do and say what I later realized was the right thing, telling him that he was mistaken to say that no one would miss him – I was among the many who would miss him – that he absolutely had to promise me that he would contact his family doctor for an emergency psychiatric referral at 8am the next day (he did), that he should flush away any remaining pills, that I would be in constant touch and available at any point and that I could listen without time limits to anything that he wanted to say about how he was feeling, as well as texting him the number of a free telephone befriending service for people who felt suicidal.

I was frightened by this episode: it appeared to have come out of the blue from a charming, successful, sociable, well-adjusted client. I put myself on a suicide prevention training course for a charity staffed by volunteers, realizing early on that being one of their volunteers was not for me. But from this training I learnt that many of my assumptions about suicide were wrong. Since doing this training I have also realized how common suicide is and how often it touches so many people's lives. The longer your coaching career continues, the more likely it is that you will encounter it either directly in clients or because someone in their family or friendship circle has taken their own life or is threatening to do so.

Now I am alert to the language of potential suicide either when spoken directly to me or when it is reported by clients who are telling me about someone close to them: 'My life seems meaningless'; 'Sometimes I think I want to die'; 'What's the point of life when there's so much cruelty and despair in the world?' Rather than running away from these statements and ignoring them out of fear that by naming them as *suicidal*, even if just to myself, I will make suicide more likely, I trust the research which shows that this is not the case. I now understand how often suicide is condemned, wrongly, as 'selfish'. I also understand that people who attempt or who do it are experiencing the sharply distorted perception which means that they are blind to the impact that their act will have on friends and family.

When people make vague hints or outright assertions which might indicate a suicidal intention, I stop and I explore. I ask what people mean by these statements and ask what lies behind them. I break the taboo, asking, 'Where do you hurt?' and 'How can I help?' I learnt on my course that when people express the wish to take their own lives they may not actually wish to die, only to end what feels like unendurable pain, but getting my tongue around sentences like 'So how dead do you want to be – totally or just a bit?' or to explore whether or not people had actually made a plan to take their own lives was unbelievably difficult.

There are a number of myths about suicide that are not helpful. One is that an unsuccessful attempt is merely a *cry for help* and therefore not serious, just a trivial bid for attention. Any suicide attempt is serious and should be seen as a *cry of pain*. Whether or not people are doing it to draw attention to their problems is irrelevant. They have taken a drastic step which may indeed have resulted in their death and a first attempt makes it more likely that it will be followed by another. It is also untrue that it is impossible to prevent suicide. Some suicides are planned intricately and secretly without the slightest hint to anyone around them, but many happen opportunistically and could be prevented by the right kind of intervention.

You may work with clients who are struggling with the aftermath of a suicide. I have worked with several clients who discovered as adults that they had been told lies about the death of a parent and that the parent had taken their own life. One such client told me that the discovery was 'like a snowstorm that never settles'. I have worked with countless others where there had been a suicide in the family. Feelings of anger and betrayal, the perpetual question 'Why?' to which there can never be an answer – all these add to the anguish of bereavement. Margaret Atwood describes it perfectly in her novel *The Blind Assassin* (2000):

> Curiosity is not our only motive: Love or grief or despair or hatred is what drives us on. We'll spy relentlessly on the dead: we'll open their letters; we'll read their journals; we'll go through their trash, hoping

for a hint, a final word, an explanation, for those who have deserted us – who've left us holding the bag, which is often a good deal emptier than we'd supposed.

If you search *suicide aftermath* on your browser you will find many websites which are helpful. To learn more about this tricky subject, you might read *Cry of Pain: Understanding Suicide and the Suicidal Mind* by Professor Mark Williams (2014), a thorough, subtle, readable and deeply compassionate exploration of the psychology of suicide.

When might a client need psychotherapy?

There is no universal way to pinpoint when a coaching client needs psychotherapy. One overall behaviour which often does seem to point to severe psychological difficulties is that the intensity of the client's response seems out of proportion to the stimulus.

You may see any number of the common patterns where it seems that therapy might be helpful. The most noticeable might be that the client cries – frequently, intensely and uncontrollably – or returns over and over again to one relationship, typically with a parent, parent-figure or sibling. This may be especially the case where a bereavement has never been acknowledged and worked through. Sometimes, one major fear appears to dominate the client's life: for instance, abandonment, ever-present dread of complete catastrophe, rejection, loss of control. Another form of the same symptom is when the client has constant worries about their own and others' health, interpreting every small symptom as life threatening.

Look out for signs that there may be some difficulty if, when the client tells their life story, it features a major trauma. Examples from my own practice include: living through a major house fire; being the apparent cause of the death of a sibling; childhood as a refugee; a mother leaving children behind after moving into a new relationship; being the survivor of childhood abuse; having had and having recovered from a childhood cancer; an entirely unanticipated divorce after a long marriage; the theft and destruction of a PhD thesis by a trusted colleague. Where the client is unable to move on from one incident you will notice that everything seems to be seen through the prism of that event. Typically the event will involve loss of some kind.

In these cases you may spot that the client frequently resorts to 'If only . . .'

- he/she/they would change
- that hadn't happened
- I hadn't done that

- I wasn't the way I am
- I didn't look the way I do

It is relatively rare for executive coaching clients to present with more serious problems, but it can happen. The client may have such problems but hesitate to reveal them, worried that despite your promise of confidentiality, their apparently shameful secret might be exposed. They may understand perfectly well that you are not a therapist and therefore could not be expected to deal effectively with the issue. The need for therapy may be more obvious when the client describes symptoms of frequent mental dysfunction which intrude significantly into everyday life: for instance, depression, anxiety, panic attacks, agoraphobia or OCD, or where the client engages in substance misuse: drink, eating problems, drugs. Even more rarely you may encounter clients who have other kinds of addiction – for instance to gambling, compulsive risk-taking or sexual promiscuity.

It may be useful to remember the acronym **PIPO**, which stands for

Persistent distress in the client – unable to stop crying, never-ending feelings of sadness.

Intrusive impact on their lives.

Physical symptoms: palpitations, sweating, problems with appetite.

Out of control emotion: frequent threats to harm themselves or others.

Note that all of this behaviour could have other, more innocent explanations, and many of us might consider ourselves perfectly mentally healthy while subject to a few of such symptoms occasionally. But the more of such symptoms that are present in a client, and the more long-lasting they are, the more likely it is that you are in therapeutic territory. Overall, probably the most important single indicator is your own feeling that *you are out of your depth* or that *something is wrong*. Trust that feeling and listen to your worries – but don't panic too soon. I believe we should stop searching for a non-existent boundary with therapy. It is, and always will be, grey, and as you gain in experience, confidence and skill it will most probably become greyer. As well as trusting your own feelings and judgement, trust your clients. If they believe you can help them, they are probably right.

Handling the conversation about referral

As coaches, we need to accept that few clients are likely to take up the therapy option, even it is clear to you and maybe also to them, that they could benefit from it. The difficulties of finding a suitable therapist, the feelings of shame still associated with needing it, the hope that the misery may go away all on its own, the fear of change, the cost and the poor reputation that some therapy has – these may all deter a client from pursuing it. None of this should prevent you making the suggestion when you feel it is right. In the UK, primary care physicians are always the first and best point of contact for mental health issues. Here, your coaching will be about how the client can find specialist help, rather than working directly on the issues.

Tell the client that you feel at the limits of your skills. Beware of appearing to blame them for their problem. Stress your respect for the client and your desire to help. Explain the differences between psychotherapy and coaching, describe how psychotherapy can help, and then ask for the client's reaction. You might point out that you do not have to be 'mad' to benefit from therapy any more than you have to be 'stupid' to benefit from education. Some clients will shrink in horror at the idea; some may politely nod and encourage you to go on. You may be able to suggest some possible therapists or to coach the client around how to find the right person, including consulting their family doctor. There may be no reason to end the coaching relationship – you may be able to continue in parallel with a therapist, or alternatively you and the client might agree to resume after he or she has had therapeutic help.

Coaching clients may often present with varying kinds of psychological distress. The art is in building skills in the range of interventions you can use yourself at the same time as knowing when it is essential to refer the client to other professionals.

12 Bringing pace and interest to the session

When I listen to recordings of other people's coaching sessions as their supervisor, I am an eavesdropper after the event in a different role and for a different purpose from either of the two players. Even so, with some coaches, I find that my attention drifts off with the soporific drone of the discussion. I long for some action, some change of pace and, yes, some drama. Everything in my experience tells me that this will make for better learning. Sitting still for two hours of the same kind of question and answer can be deeply dull. Sometimes coach and client seem stuck in a kind of talking trance and all the life seems to have drained out of the conversation. Have my own sessions sometimes had this quality? Of course! When appropriate, there are many techniques that can accelerate learning as well as providing the change of pace that is the focus of this chapter. Most of them involve deliberate changes of action, or point of view, or of using non-verbal techniques.

Overtly managing the time

It helps to make the principles of pace and timing explicit to clients. I always have a clock just over the client's right shoulder, meaning that I can glance at it covertly, and am also expert at reading the client's watch upside down. I provide an exactly matching clock for the client to see just behind my right shoulder. Even so, I sometimes do a certain amount of pantomime time management. This could involve rolling back my sleeve to look at my watch, or saying out loud, 'Now what time do we have left?' and then glancing at the clock, as well as agreeing a rough schedule for each of the items on the client's list at the outset of the session. It can also help to draw attention to the need for a change of pace by saying something like, 'We've spent a long time on that rather heavy and sobering topic. How about we go now to your lighter one?'

A two-hour session often has an energy dip after 90 minutes. At that point you might say, 'So we've got half an hour left. What would be the best use of that time for you?' If a session has run out of steam altogether, never prolong it for the sake of finishing exactly at two hours, or whatever your allotted time is. Be prepared to suggest ending early, or to spend the remaining minutes in overtly social chat.

In the first session (see Annex 1), as part of your contracting conversation, you might like to ask the client how they feel about the proposed length of the session. For some people, two hours of sitting still is agonizing. So when I met a young client whose presenting issue was how to cope with the many stresses of competing at elite level in his sport, I noticed that his right foot was busy waggling throughout our first 15 minutes. Creating a little pause in the conversation, I said, 'So, Ed, I notice that your right foot seems to have a life of its own. What's that about?' His reply was, 'I'm feeling anxious right now and also I've never been able to sit still without wriggling but I'm trying to be polite.' This led to a productive discussion about how to manage our sessions so that we built in frequent breaks, did some of our sessions outside as walks, and worked in 90-minute instead of 120-minute blocks.

Changing the physical pace

Sometimes the simplest interventions are the best. Stopping halfway through a session and suggesting another cup of tea will often revitalize a flagging session. Similarly, suggesting a quick stand-up and physical stretch can be useful.

Depending on the weather and the location of your coaching room, a walk can also be a way of adding pace and variety to the session. I was working with a client on a longer-term programme whose aim was to establish himself as a self-employed consultant in his field. At the time of the session he had, only a few hours before, returned to London from San Francisco. It was a luminously sunny, fiery July day. About ten minutes in, he suddenly said, 'Jenny, I just can't concentrate. It's no good – I'm hot, jet-lagged and distracted.' Within moments we were out of the office and had set off on a walk around the attractive buildings and surrounding gardens of one of the ancient Inns of Court, a few minutes away from what was then my office in central London. We kept going on a circular route for the best part of 90 minutes. Possibly this was one of our best sessions. There is often something to be said for a conversation where you are side by side instead of face-to-face – there may be more candour because you are outside in a pleasant place and released from the relentlessness of the eye contact involved in a conventional conversation.

Brainstorming

At some point in the coaching programme virtually all clients describe feeling stuck. The 'stuckness' will be around finding a more satisfactory solution to a long-standing problem than the solutions the client has already thought of. The client is clear about the goal, maybe thanks to your expert clarification and questioning, but cannot identify how to get there. Typically, the client has gone round and round the same thought processes without coming up with an answer that feels right:

> My weight gain has got out of hand, but I hate exercise and I know that diets just make you fatter in the long term.

> We can't afford to move out of our company's premises, but they're so shabby and unsatisfactory and in completely the wrong location.

Brainstorming[1] is a simple but powerful approach to generating ideas. Where you have been longing to offer ideas, this is one legitimate place where you can do it. However, you have to stick to the rules, the most important of which is that while you are in the idea-generating stage, no evaluation of any kind is permitted: no raised eyebrows, sighs, self-censoring of the 'Oh, that's a stupid idea so I'm not going to say it' sort. This rule applies equally to you and to the client. Brainstorming only works if you say whatever comes into your head without editing.

How to do it

First you ask the client's permission:

> It might be useful to brainstorm some ideas here. Is that OK?

Next, get clarity around the question. It needs to be reduced to something simple and straightforward, normally a question beginning 'How can I . . . ?', or 'What ways could there be of . . . ?'

Now you explain the rules. A lot of people think they know what brainstorming is, but in practice they often start evaluating the ideas as soon as they have been uttered – the self-defeating habit that brainstorming is designed to prevent. Explain that, at this stage, any idea, however silly, outrageous or off-the-wall, is welcome. All ideas will be written down: ideally on a flip chart. Standing up while you do this seems to help because, again, it breaks the trance of the seated conversation. Encourage humour, wildness and silliness. You explain that you will be giving yourself permission to join in because this is not advice, only idea-generation.

When the ideas have clearly been exhausted, turn to a fresh sheet of paper and ask the client what criteria they will use to evaluate the ideas. Now you are back in strictly coach-mode. The criteria will normally cover areas such as practicality, cost, fit with the client's core values, time, realism, likely impact on relationships – and so on.

Put the two sheets of paper side by side, hand the client a pen in a different colour and ask them to highlight any of the brainstormed ideas that look interesting enough to explore further. Review these ideas against the list of criteria and move to action in the usual way.

Alan

Alan enjoys good food and wine. He hates exercise because he says he was 'the class fat boy' at school and fended off jibes from other boys by clowning about being fat. He also loathes being fat and has recently become even fatter: 'I went to Marks & Spencer to buy a suit and found that they didn't do Size Huge.' Along with a number of goals relating to his leadership style, one of Alan's goals for his coaching is to lose 30 pounds. He frequently has to represent his organization on television and he describes himself as acutely embarrassed to be so obviously overweight: 'I'm not a good advertisement for us looking the way I do.' Additionally, he has some underlying anxiety about health. His father died young of heart disease and Alan has a nagging fear that he might also suffer premature death.

His goal is to find a way of permanently sustaining increased fitness and weight loss by making changes in his lifestyle. He knows every diet: 'You name it, I've tried it.' He also knows that long-term successful weight loss is about steady, undramatic shedding of pounds and that this comes from eating less and exercising more.

His coach suggests brainstorming. The question is, 'What exercise could I do that will help me lose weight, get and stay fit?'

Ideas generated by both Alan and his coach include: scuba diving, jazz dancing, entering for the London Marathon, walking to work every day, cycling, swimming, taking the stairs instead of the lift to his apartment, joining a gym, getting a personal trainer, doing pilates, buying a home treadmill – and many more. And what were the criteria he would use to judge any of these ideas? Alan is clear: it has to be something that involves other people – probably something 'blokeish'. It has to be competitive, he has to be in charge of it and, strange as it may seem for a self-labelled 'lazy' person, it has to involve the major effort of running because cross-country running was the only sport he ever enjoyed at school. A moment later Alan makes a hurrumphing noise. None of the brainstormed ideas is quite right on its own. However, he has had a moment of epiphany. He now knows exactly what he is going to do.

This is because he starts and then organizes the 'Big Bellies Running Club' for other 'blokes' at his workplace. Running a total of 20 miles a week in a London park at lunchtime with a pack of other men suited him just fine. Perhaps he could have got there with another sort of discussion, but there was something about the pace and fun of the brainstorm that, for him, as with so many other clients, freed up his thinking.

Empty chair techniques

These approaches appear in a number of different therapeutic traditions, but most particularly they are associated with Fritz Perls of the Gestalt school, and are also invaluable for coaching.

Essentially they all work on the same assumption: physically altering your point of view and seeing things from a literally different angle can bring worthwhile insights and can lead to changed behaviour. All 'empty chair' exercises work on the same principles. You set up an empty chair identical to the one the client is sitting in. You ask the client to move, to sit in the empty chair, and to imagine that they are looking at themselves from another viewpoint.

The Meta Mirror

Probably the most useful versions of empty chair work involve a relationship that is problematical in some way. It need not be a relationship that is in crisis; it could be one that is already healthy but could be even better. A more important criterion is that the present and future state of the relationship should matter. Typically the coach will then ask the client to be the other person, to imagine their feelings as the other person, and to look through the other person's eyes at him or herself.

One classic exercise is the Meta Mirror where you set up two empty chairs and ask the client to pass through four stages:

> **Stage 1**: Invite the client to be 'themselves', looking at the other chair and imaging the person sitting opposite them. You ask the client: 'How do you feel about this person?'

> **Stage 2**: Invite the client to swap chairs. Say, 'Now you are the other person looking at an imagined version of yourself sitting in the other chair.' The coach asks: 'How do you feel about [your client's name]?' Encourage the client to reply as if they are the person with whom they are in the relationship.

> **Stage 3**: Now ask the client to stand up a few metres away and look at the two empty chairs imagining both people (the client and the other person) sitting there. Tell the client they are now in the most resourceful version of themselves. Ask the client: 'What strikes you about this relationship from this distance?'

> **Stage 4:** Either move even further away, or return to the original seating and coach around whatever emerges.

The Meta Mirror asks a client to enter into a state of maximum empathy with another person. By physically moving around, the client changes the physical and mental dynamic – and gains new insights and energy. The movement of the exercise also enables the client to see significant relationships from different perspectives – literally looking at them from another point of view.[2]

There is no way of verifying the accuracy of our perceptions of what the imagined other person in the chair is feeling unless we check with them later – which some clients do – but the insights from the perspective of the other chair are often unnervingly close. Most of us *can* actually access the cues others give us about their feelings towards us in the right circumstances, and this is what empty chair activities can provide. Perhaps most valuable of all, it allows us to understand and experience how we are contributing to the problems in a relationship.

There are many variants of empty chair techniques. They can be introduced simply and spontaneously and take little time. Here are some examples:

Sonia

Sonia feels puzzled about how to speak up sooner at meetings. Her coach sets up the two chairs, explains the protocol and says, 'In the other chair I want you to imagine the part of you that wants to be confident and extroverted at meetings versus the more restrained person you feel you normally are . . . Get up from your own chair and sit in the more confident Sonia's chair. Now tell me how you feel.' [Later] 'What advice would you give the more restrained Sonia about what she could do differently?'

Brian

Brian is in a dilemma about which career path to choose. He has two good offers and feels paralysed by the responsibility of making the decision. His coach explains the exercise and invites Brian to sit in one chair at a time, imagining he is in each of the jobs, exploring how it feels.

An even simpler variant is one where the client is puzzled or troubled about the behaviour of another person in their lives. As ever, remind the client that you cannot work on the other person, only on the person you have in the room. Ask them to stand up and look at their empty chair. 'Imagine you are other person looking at yourself. What would you see?' Most clients will at least some insight into their impact on others by doing this.

Changing your physical point of view can be an even simpler process. My coaching room has three identical chairs and a small round table. I began to notice that many clients were gravitating to the same chair in every session. With one client where this had happened, I suggested that he sat in a different chair. As an invariably kind and courteous man he always wrote me a little email thank you after every session. The one after this session said:

> Thank you for that session. It felt different and that was helpful – you got me out of the Leukaemia Chair!

This was a reference to the two sessions we had spent discussing the devastating news that his younger daughter had been diagnosed with leukaemia, his overwhelming anger and sense of injustice, his pain at the prospect of the treatments she would have to endure and his worry that, because he was so profoundly upset, he would not be able to support her. Changing the chair had changed the physical point of view and that had helped with a mental reframing as well. Since then I frequently change where I sit myself as it is just as easy for the coach to become stuck in a point of view as it is for the client. In the summer I may also invite the client to sit on the leafy terrace outside my usual room, where the view is different again.

'Pebbles'

Another way of working on relationship issues is to ask the client to identify the 'system' in which they are operating by representing it through a set of physical objects.[3] On a shelf easily to hand in my coaching room, I keep a bowl of pebbles of different shapes and sizes. They are nothing special – no polishing or 'crystal magic' is involved – in fact I chose them somewhat carelessly and impatiently from a beach visit.

Here is how to do it:

Invite the client to pick pebbles which represent him or herself and the other important people involved. They can use a nearby tabletop as the base – or the floor, if they prefer. The task is to arrange the pebbles so that they visually represent the nature of the relationships. Physically handling the pebbles, choosing the right size or colour for the 'people', is something that clients usually enjoy. Now ask:

> Which pebble represents whom?

> Tell me why you chose the various pebbles you did to represent them (e.g. differences in size, colour and shape).

Tell me what the distances between them represent to you.

Are these people looking at each other or facing away?

You've put yourself [wherever]. Tell me what your thinking is there.

How does it feel looking at this system?

In relation to the pebble representing yourself, how does that feel?

Then, depending on how the client has answered, invite the client to rearrange the pebbles so that the pattern (system) feels more comfortable, and then to talk you through the whole thing again.

Then ask:

So what needs to happen to make this improved system a reality?

Tiffany

Tiffany was in the first weeks of her first chief executive role. She described the experience as being like scaling a mountain without any of the correct equipment or team support. We explored what that might mean for her through the Clean Language approach (page 107) and what emerged was that the new job meant she had moved to a new country, had lost her network of close friends and neighbours, had to make a relationship with a seemingly prickly new boss, and had inherited an organization where her executive team was far less competent than she had realized, with one of its members immediately going off sick and another lodging a grievance against her. At the same time she was without her husband because he had stayed behind to sort out the sale of their house. She chose a small round pebble to represent herself and placed it slightly off-centre on the table. She arranged pebbles representing each of her team with two of the six facing away from her. Her boss was placed nearest her and was the biggest of the pebbles. Her husband and former friends were on the extreme edge, her husband facing towards her, the friends facing away. These were her comments on the exercise:

'It was stark doing this, but it brought home to me like possibly nothing else could, that I was socially and professionally isolated. That poor little round pebble! I felt sorry for it. I understood immediately that my feelings of incompetence and of being out of control could only increase unless I changed my attitudes and behaviours. When you asked me 'ange the pebbles so that they represented a more satisfying arrangement, and I did, I felt better straight away. You will remember that I also introduced some new pebbles, one of which was a PA, as I did not have this vital role filled at the time and I'd let the vacancy drift. I also realized that I had been invited to join a pan-European chief executive "academy" and that this would give me support and challenge from peers. I added more pebbles close to me to represent the new friends I needed to make – people who had nothing to do with my work, and another one to represent an as yet unknown personal trainer who could make sure that I got exercise back into my life. It was a brilliant insight. I felt better immediately and it was the start of planning a whole set of new approaches.'

Note that this activity does not 'cure' the problems. What it does do is to highlight what they are and to create motivation for change. In Tiffany's case it was an important platform for the work we continued over several months.

Guided visualizations

One of the many amazing aspects of the human brain is its ability to use imagination. It seems as if the brain does not distinguish too readily between imagined and real – a disadvantage when we dwell on our fears, an advantage when we create a positive alternative because we are then laying down the new neural pathways that could lead to different beliefs and behaviour. If you are attracted to this approach, you will want to develop your own script, but all of the many variants of such scripts have the same core elements:

You ask for permission and briefly explain the benefits. If clients are dubious, don't press it: it's not right for everyone. You ask clients to enter a light trance state. Some coaches prefer not to name it as such because of the poor reputation of stage hypnosis. If you believe a client will resist if you name it as *trance*, then don't. I do because I also explain that trance is a commonplace human experience. We can all enter it at will and often enter it involuntarily – for instance, when driving on a monotonous motorway or going for a lengthy jog. The state is characterized by unawareness of time passing or of the intrusive effects of the physical environment. Churchgoers will enter it through prayer or meditation, and you could well experience the same state at a concert. The theory is that when you are in a light trance your mind is more open to suggestion, and all current research on the brain suggests that this is so. You reassure clients that they are in control at all times and invite them to enter the state through physical relaxation and closed eyes. This leads to a matching mental quieting. Your voice remains low, gentle and monotonous. You are aiming for a pleasant drone. You speak slowly, using linking words like *and* . . . or *so* . . . You use only positive suggestion: so, for instance, you would say 'You feel calm' rather than 'You don't feel tense'. (Saying the word 'tense' invites tension because what the mind focuses on is what expands.) You build the content around what the client needs as a result of asking the right questions. This enables you to create the specific content that will help.

All visualizations start with settling the client into a calm state by asking them to get comfortable and close their eyes.

A sample script

Get yourself comfortable in your chair. Sit without anything crossed – no crossed legs, feet or arms. If you'd like a cushion to support your neck, that's fine.

First, let's establish some relaxed, steady breathing. Take a deep breath in from below your waist and feel your lungs filling and expanding and pushing outwards. Hold for a few moments; now let the breath out and feel your chest going in again. The out-breath is going to be much longer than the in-breath. Take the in-breath with your mouth closed and breathe the out-breath out slowly and steadily through an open mouth. (Do several such breaths with the client, counting slowly with each breath.)

Close your eyes and let your body relax.

First let your feet go floppy – let them feel as if they are completely free. Unclench any muscles that may have tightened in your toes. Wiggle the toes and let them relax.

Now do the same with your legs. Let the knees flop and now your thighs. Let your legs feel loose and very relaxed. They may start to feel heavy – if they do, that's fine. They may tingle a little and feel warm.

Now let your hands go loose. Shake out the fingers a little and let them relax so that they feel floppy. And now feel them getting heavy. And now the same with your arms. Let them get heavy and feel very, very relaxed. They may feel warm and tingly. If they do, that's fine.

Keep the breathing slow and steady, breathing in . . . and then out . . . in . . . and then out. (Time this with the client's breathing, matching it with your own.)

And now your shoulders. Let them drop so that the muscles are soft and floppy. And now your neck. Let go of any tension in it. Now the same with your chest and stomach. And let the centre of your body relax. Feel a soft, warm feeling creeping through your whole body.

And now your face. Feel the facial muscles relaxing so that your skin is smooth. Let the muscles around your mouth go soft and floppy. And do the same with the muscles in your forehead.

Feel your whole body relaxing, your breathing slowing and your heart-beat steadying to a quiet, steady, relaxed beat. And feel whole, feel well, feel relaxed.

And now I'm going to ask you to imagine yourself in a pleasant place. It could be a real place that's special to you or an imaginary one. Call up how this place feels to you and the sensations it creates in your body to know that you're there . . . remember or imagine the sounds you can hear . . . and the views you can see. Enjoy all these sensations . . . Relax – even more deeply – and let go while you experience yourself in this place . . .

Where you take it after this depends on what the client wants to achieve. I have used it myself in a number of ways and also collected these examples from fellow coaches:

Client situation	*Coach response*
Chronically nervous before a job interview.	Suggests client imagines themselves in the interview room, totally calm but alert, doing well; sees and hears the interviewers responding positively.
Now divorced from physically and mentally abusive husband, but still haunted by fear of him.	Coach asked client to imagine how the ex-husband looked. Response was that he was like an outsize goblin. Coach suggested shrinking him down to garden gnome size. Then asked what client would like to do with him. Answer: 'Stuff him at the back of XY Garden Centre where no one can find him.'
Afraid of speaking up at a large meeting.	Suggests client imagines the room, places herself in the best position to catch the eye of the meeting chair, sees self performing in a sparkling and confident manner.
A patient at a dental clinic who has chronic facial pain as a result of a dentist-inflicted accidental injury. Pain cannot be cured by any known means.	Coach is a doctor (but not a specialist in dental problems). Over eight sessions coach invites client to tell her what the pain looks like. Answer: 'A giant crab whose claws are stuck into her check from the outside.' Coach suggests shrinking the crab and diminishing the grip of the claws. Session by session the pain lessened to manageable levels.

Afraid of the future; perplexed by how to find life purpose.	Invited client to imagine life five years on; to see a friendly, confident figure approaching – their future self – and to listen to what this self had to say.
Wanted to give up smoking; had tried patches, going cold turkey, willpower.	Created scenario where client is exposed to all the situations where she usually smoked (as described by client) and sees and experiences herself happily untempted by cigarettes.
Could not get to sleep easily; client described 'racing thoughts'.	Coach and client discussed general preparation for sleep tactics, including avoiding stimulants, cooling the bedroom down, reading a pleasant book. Coach taught client progressive relaxation techniques first, including how to control breathing, and then did the visualization.

Stephen

I came for coaching with what now seems like a laughably mundane request: I wanted to know how to influence my boss, the chief executive, and how to get a better grip on my job which was specifically like a sort of bag-carrier role for him. He needed someone like me to smooth his path, write his speeches, make sure his flights were booked, deal with the press – and so on. When I did this visualization, I saw myself very clearly five years ahead. The other people with me were my wife and young children.

At the time of doing the exercise, I didn't have a wife, only a girl-friend, and I definitely didn't have any children! I was also aware in the visualization of how I was earning a living. I saw myself directly running a major part of the organization and running it in a particular way – very differently from the bullying standard leadership style I saw around me every day. It was a complete wake-up call. I suddenly felt I had been wasting my time in a highly paid but totally pointless backroom job, frittering away my energy in a playboy bachelor life – and this wasn't what I wanted at all. The advice from my future self was: 'Get real, mate!'

The coaching took a completely different slant as a result of that activity. Five years later I am on my way to that senior job. I real-ized how much I loved my then girlfriend and how mad I would be to lose her. We married within a year and have one and a half of the two children I saw in that meditation. I refuse to do the 12-hour days I see my colleagues working – getting a proper work–life balance is important, and I'm not going to put any of that at risk again.

These are powerful activities. They can work better than anything else in the right place and with the right client. Don't necessarily expect one iteration to be enough. The doctor-coach dealing with facial pain, for instance, did a version of the visualization every time she and the patient met. You might also record the visualization and then email it to the client so that he or she can play it as many times as they wish.

Using technology

Technology now makes it easy to use all kinds of aids in a session. I always have my iPad to hand in a coaching session and the awe-inspiring range of apps is a constant source of useful ideas. So, for instance, I have a drawing app which I use to invite clients to make drawings or notes which they can then email to themselves. I use TED.com with clients who need help on speaking at conferences or in the boardroom and which get away from the grinding boredom of most PowerPoint presentations. There are many apps which allow you to record your own voice, and some which will turn this into text. So clients can experiment with voice and style if they wish. I also use the brilliant 3D Brain app to explain brain functioning to clients (see page 70).

My fellow coach, Dr Amy Iversen, describes here how she uses video recording with clients:

> As a coach, I have found this invaluable as a way of allowing clients access to the 'meta-stance' – to see themselves as others see them. Clients can discover for themselves how they really look (clothes, make-up, facial expressions, their posture and gait), how they speak (voice, accent, tone, inflection, vocabulary), and how they come across (greeting, handshake, general demeanour).
>
> I have found it a powerful tool in two ways. The first is that it can help a client to bring into awareness something important which they may not have noticed, and can subsequently address (e.g. a tendency to avoid eye contact, or to interrupt). This can be powerful information for clients who are preparing for interviews, exams, or assuming a new leadership role in which they need to influence others.

Often just watching the video together and using some
questions brings up some really powerful reflection; allowin\
to do this in the third person and inviting them to 'watch this l
are watching a video of someone you don't know works even better
(e.g. What do you notice about this woman?).

The second is that it can help clients who have become very
concerned or preoccupied about a certain aspect of their appearance
and behaviour to get real-time feedback on just how important this
feature is to the average person who meets them. In this case, the client
and I produce a short video and some stills and construct together
a survey of questions that the client would like to ask of others.
I recently worked with a client who had started antidepressants and
was concerned that he came across as 'drugged up', to the extent
that he was turning down opportunities to speak in public. With his
permission, 100 volunteers were emailed a short video clip of him
speaking and were invited to comment on his appearance, with
specific reference to whether they had noticed anything unusual
about his voice and face. Evidence that not a single one noticed anything abnormal provided powerful new information for the client and
enabled him to move forward.

Role play

Role play is another invaluable way of accelerating learning as well as of
introducing a change of pace into the conversation. Some people have embarrassing experiences of role play from courses, where they claim that the arti-
ficiality of the exercise has created their extreme aversion for the method.
Usually they are referring to staged and artificial scenarios where people who
are not actors have to act. This is why it is probably safer not to label the
activity 'role play', but just to do it without giving it a label at all.

Role play means that the client rehearses or revisits an important conversation. Normally the client 'plays' him or herself – and you 'play' the other
person – though you can also use the technique to reverse roles where you
play the client.

Some clients seem unable to move past their usual ways of behaving.
Some cannot see how others see them. Role play is a safe way to experiment.
Where you have grown the trust between you, clients can make themselves
vulnerable without feeling that they will lose face if they get it wrong, and
it also gives you opportunities for feedback to the client. Role play is an
effective way of rehearsing for a challenging conversation that clients
describe as being on their agenda soon, and also a powerful way of reviewing a
difficult conversation in the recent past. Role play is invaluable for those

clients who describe many different people behaving in much the same way to them. In such cases it is one of the ways for clients to find out that the response we get is as much to do with us as with the other person. For the same reason it is useful for clients who come to coaching hoping to change another person. Role play is a way of finding out that the only way to change another person is to change ourselves first, and it is often useful to remind clients of that old cliché: *Behaviour breeds behaviour.*

How to do it

No real acting ability is required for role play to be successful, but it does help if you are able to change your own normal pace and delivery to become a little like the person you are playing.

Ask for a briefing:

> What kind of a person is this?
> What do they look like?
> How old are they?
> How do they typically respond when x or y happens?
> Tell me about a situation where there was a difficulty – give me some of the dialogue.

This briefing need not be extensive – a minute or two is all that is necessary.

Now say: 'OK, let's assume I'm the other person, and you're back in that situation. So you said . . . ?'

You then respond as you have been briefed the person would typically respond. Let the conversation run for a few minutes – or for however long seems useful. Three minutes is usually enough.

Debriefing

Role play has no purpose without the debrief. Ask the client for permission to give them feedback.

- Ask for the client's view on how it went first; log how accurate the client's self-perception seems to be and explore any over-modesty or unrealistic self-acclaim later.
- Ask how like real life the role play was. Usually clients will tell you that the way it went was exactly like the real life incident went or could go. They will often say: 'You must know this person – you're just like him/her!' The later learning to be gleaned from this observation is that the client's typical behaviour is shaping the response they are typically getting.

- Tell clients how it felt to be on the other end of their style. You are not analysing here – just noticing and trusting your own emotional responses.
- Be very specific. You are looking here to feed back your micro as well as your macro observations, your objective as well as your subjective impressions, so you will need to note these while the role play is happening. Nothing is too small to be noticed and fed back. The objective impressions are likely to include posture, voice, facial expression, language and so on:

> When you started telling me about the project being at risk, you leant forward and raised your voice. I felt you were really authoritative at that point, but only a moment later your voice dropped and I noticed you put your hand slightly over your mouth.

- Your subjective impressions are about the impact of the behaviour on you. To do this you imagine yourself in that person's shoes. Use 'I' all the time: 'When you did/said this . . . the effect it had on me was . . .':

> So at first when you were looking authoritative I felt wary, but later at that point where your voice dropped and you put your hand over your mouth I felt certain you would back down. The impact on me was that I felt if I hung in there I could get you to agree to what I wanted.

- Ask what the client would like to change or experiment with.

Always do a rerun if the role play has not gone well, to give the client the chance to experience success. Look for all the small and large gains which will tell you that the client is beginning to learn how to behave in a different way.

Role play as practice

A role play may last just a few minutes and be introduced with little fuss and no labelling. Alternatively there are circumstances where it can be usefully extended. These will include areas such as job interview coaching, preparing to face the media and learning to enhance presentation skills.

Gareth

Getting on shortlists was easy for Gareth, but landing a chief executive job eluded him. After four failures in quick succession, he realized he needed help. First, we worked on how he mentally approached the interview process. From his language, it was clear that he saw it as the equivalent of an academic examination:

JR: What is an interview like for you?
Gareth: It's a viva – it reminds me of the verbal grilling I had to go through to get my PhD.
JR: So you see it as a place to demonstrate your knowledge?

Gareth needed to learn that a job interview is a social and not an academic event. Interviewers would most probably take his knowledge for granted. Displaying it at such length was not answering the main question that potential employers had in their minds, which is always, 'What would it be like working with this candidate?'

Together we worked on a new set of skills for job interviews, this time emphasizing the social aspects of the interview situation as well as his leadership experience and skills, his approach to influencing, his motivation for wanting the job, and so on. There are only about eight core questions that can ever be asked in a job interview and we set about practising how to answer all of them. Working in five-minute blocks, I took the role of interviewer and he gave practice answers. Then we debriefed the answers with feedback from me, sometimes using video recordings. This way Gareth could see for himself how he was coming across. His own ruthlessly honest feedback, seen through the dispassionate lens of the camera, was all he really needed: 'I look too cocky there', or 'I seem a lot more confident when I sit up', or 'I'm more convincing when I answer the question more briefly and directly', and 'I seem like a nicer person when I smile.' Within two months Gareth had the chief executive job he wanted, has moved on successfully once more and is now a well-known figure in his sector.

For clients like Gareth, already very senior, it can take courage to make yourself vulnerable enough to come forward for help. *Talking* about the interview may be useful so far as it goes, but only practice will really make it clear what the blocks are and how they might be overcome.

Similarly, a surprising number of clients describe themselves as handicapped by lack of social confidence. Inside their organizations, or in structured situations where they can feel in control, everything is fine. Put them in a room of strangers without the carapace of their role and status and they can freeze. Here, again, identifying from observation (this could be a homework assignment) or discussion of how socially confident people behave in such situations is the starting point, followed by bite-sized chunks of practice and feedback.

Shadowing

There is usually a strong case for seeing the client at least once on his or her home territory. When you do this, you meet the rest of the cast, people the client mentions who otherwise will remain vividly described but fantasy figures to you.

Shadowing means that clients invite you to accompany them for a day or half day, being with them as unobtrusively as possible. The idea is to see clients in their own setting. In this way you will get to see how they interact with others at the same time as getting a first-hand taste of the organization's culture. Virtually all clients forget how weird the organization seemed when they first joined it – they have become immune to its funny little ways. However, you will notice. Feeding this back, along with everything else you notice, can be an invaluable source of learning. It takes a brave client to do this, but you may find that a surprising number of clients are up for it.

Explain the benefits for the client. Discuss how the client will explain your presence to others. Total openness is really the only option. Most clients can see that their visible willingness to be open to such a high degree of feedback models exactly the behaviour that most organizations need so badly. Far from appearing 'weak', such clients appear robust and confident.

Be clear with the client – and others – that your role is observer. Encourage the client to negotiate both permission and confidentiality boundaries with the colleagues who will be present during the day. Telling such colleagues that the spotlight is on the client, not on them, is usually enough to assuage any fears about being judged by the coach. Ask the client on what he/she needs particularly to have feedback. Typical choices would be: delegating and briefing conversations; running meetings; interactions with a PA; time management; decision-making. Leave plenty of time at the end of the shadowing (typically a half day) for feedback and discussion.

You may be able to organize some shadowing within a normal coaching session, depending on the client's issues. Here is an example of a coach who came up with an unusual piece of improvised shadowing by seizing the moment with style and humour through a perfect piece of provocation (page 195):

Ravi

Ravi grew up in a big family, but described himself as chronically shy. Self-consciousness was the hallmark of his interaction with others when they were not part of his close circle of family or friends. In spite of his striking good looks, Ravi found it impossible to initiate conversations, so at the conferences, which were an increasingly important part of his professional life, he lurked on the perimeter of the room feeling miserable. Ravi's goal was to build his capacity to network confidently, and this meant learning how to take the initiative with people he didn't know.

Ravi's coach seized the moment, knowing that her coaching room was in an area surrounded by crowded sandwich bars. It was coming up to lunchtime. Ravi's challenge was the following:

Coach: Ravi, I challenge you to collect the lunch orders from others in the office, to go into six different sandwich bars, striking up a conversation in each with a complete stranger. It doesn't matter how banal the conversation is – it can be about the weather, the food, the sandwich bar – anything at all. I will be by your side, giving you feedback and encouragement on each one. I expect you to flirt whether you're talking to a man or a woman.

Ravi: (utterly taken aback) You are a very wicked woman! Is this what my company is paying all this money for?

Coach: (shrugging) Yes – dreadful isn't it. Don't tell them, will you?

Ravi: What will my wife say?

Coach: Tell her the company paid this crazy woman to teach you how to flirt with other women.

Ravi: (helpless laughter) OK, I'll do just that.

After recovering from his shock, Ravi accepted, collected the orders from the somewhat bemused office staff and set off with his coach trotting at his side. At each stage, his coach gave him encouragement and some further tips – for instance, about his eye contact (sometimes avoided), his smile (dazzling when he used it), and asking him questions about what was working and what wasn't. The effect was astonishing. Within 20 minutes Ravi had discovered not only that he could overcome 30 years of waiting for others to speak first, but that he actually enjoyed it because of the response he got.

Observing

When you visit a client's premises, observe everything. Notice the state of the building: what is on the walls, the condition of the restrooms, the kind of food in the restaurant and how it is set out. Notice how you are treated as a visitor. Notice what surprises or impresses you. For instance, making a visit to a training college for one of our uniformed services, I began to understand more about how my clients would be likely behave.

The college was in the middle of soft and verdant countryside, but I was received by a uniformed guard. The grounds were crowded with people, most of them men, smartly turned out in full uniform, including hats. The noisy canteen was set out with long refectory tables topped by a high table with linen table napkins – a striking contrast to the cheap paper versions supplied for everyone else. The food was wholesome, plentiful and definitely in the school dinner mode. I was received with immense and elaborate courtesy by everyone and treated as an honoured guest. There was an easy camaraderie to life in this organization – a hugely supportive network of colleagues who enjoyed spending time together. Hierarchy, clarity about roles, rules, and a smart appearance were also vital factors in the culture. The more senior you were, the more physically comfortable your life was likely to be, perhaps as a straight and visible reward for the notably stringent responsibilities for command you were expected to bear uncomplainingly. I understood that to appear to be threatening the camaraderie in such an organization would be difficult and painful. So, for instance, when one of my clients faced the ultra-tough challenge of having to investigate fellow officers, I immediately knew something of what courage and steadfastness this would take.

In general the way I think about any coaching session has been affected by my earlier career as a television producer. In any programme the producer knows that it is important to start with something that will grab the attention of the audience. This needs to be followed by subtle or overt changes in pace throughout the programme. There need to be fast parts and slow parts, points where there is laughter and places where there is room for sadness or thoughtfulness, light and shade, long sequences followed by short ones. Even the simplest kind of DJ-driven radio show will alternate fast music with slow, sweet ballad with upbeat cheeriness. Understanding that the same principles apply to any coaching session will immeasurably help both you and your client.

Notes

1   I am assured by mental health professionals that this word is politically correct. That is a relief because the clumsy suggested alternative *thought shower* is repellent.

2   There is a full description of this technique in Phil Hayes' (2006) book *NLP Coaching*. If you use your search engine for Meta Mirror Demonstration you may also find some recorded examples, but I have to say that most of the examples I have seen have left me unimpressed.

3   There is a coaching and group work technique called Constellations which has a faint resemblance to what I describe here and which arose out of a particular approach to family therapy. I am not a believer in Constellation Theory, which claims that just 'representing' The System (always written with initial caps) somehow has magical powers to change it. 'Systems' in Constellation Theory allegedly also have mystical memories going back many generations, even without anyone in the current System knowing anything about it. Amazing, rapid resolutions are allegedly possible. You will find words and phrases such as *ancestor worship, phenomenological, The Knowing Field, existential, morphic resonance,* used to describe what allegedly happens. Some people for whom I have considerable respect believe in this theory. The more I investigated it, the more it sounded like a load of old hogwash to me, but then I may be too much of a rationalist and a sceptic for my own good. If you Google Constellations Theory you will find plenty of websites offering training. For a more sceptical view, go to skepdic.com/ hellinger.html.

13 Practising professionally

Coaching is a new profession. This chapter looks at what issues the professional coach needs to take into account and how some of those issues might be resolved.

Ethics

Coaching may present you with a number of dilemmas, none with easy, obvious solutions. There are few, if any, absolutes.

What alerts you to the presence of a dilemma? First, there could be a gut feeling that something, somewhere, is making you uneasy. Or there could be the knowledge that if whatever it was appeared in a newspaper, it would at the very least be embarrassing and hard to defend. Another symptom could be discomfort at the thought of having to endorse it to a person whose moral judgement you respect and whose good opinion you prize. There may be the knowledge that a client's proposed action is against the law or a realization that you may be infringing a stated (or implicit) value for you.

Dilemmas may concern priorities. Some possible candidates might be: 'truth' versus 'sensitivity'; individual versus organizational need; organization versus community; business versus environment; short-term versus long-term impact; financial versus client need. Dilemmas may also occur when you are working with clients who propose action based on religious, cultural or political beliefs which turn out to be radically different from your own.

Dilemmas in action

The chief executive of a company with whom you want to build business has set up a coaching programme for one of his team. He accepts that you will not be able to give any feedback direct to him. However, he asks you to let him know if the person terminates the coaching or fails to turn up for a session.

You are coaching a client and gathering 360-degree feedback on him from ten people nominated by him through focused, structured interviews. You discover that all his colleagues appear to be extremely critical of him. The more you probe for some positive features and behaviour, the more detail pours out about the poor esteem in which his colleagues hold him.

You are working with a number of board-level individuals in an organization. You are approached by their most significant competitor to undertake a similar programme.

Two candidates for the same job have approached you, both of them clients in different organizations – and in different organizations again from the one with the vacancy.

The client's boss and sponsor calls you to say that the client is not changing fast enough and hints that the client could be a candidate for the sack. Is this privileged information – or should you pass it on to the client?

You feel uneasy about taking on the client, you don't really like working with people of his profession/age/background or with the issues he describes wanting to tackle, but you need the money and adding his company to your client list would give you prestige.

A client confesses to something illegal or to private knowledge of a crime.

A client threatens harm to him or herself or others.

It is perfectly possible that different coaches would respond in different but equally acceptable ways to these dilemmas.

Where organizations ask for progress reports on a client as an absolute condition of the assignment, it is sensible to refuse. Such a progress report will be valueless because the real evidence of change is in the daily way the client actually does their work. As coaches we do not witness this, so how could we judge our clients' performance? Equally importantly, it is impossible to create trust if the client believes that the coaching is about *assessment* – a completely different process. Even where the client's boss has made the apparently bland request to confirm the client's attendance, in its mild way, this amounts to coercion. It is usually better to suggest that client and boss agree between themselves how to satisfy the boss's perfectly understandable need to know what is going on.

It is difficult to work with direct competitor organizations simultaneously because it is inevitable that commercially sensitive information will be part of the coaching, so there is potentially a conflict of interest. If you could not be a coach to two competing football teams simultaneously, it is hard to see how you could coach two candidates for the same job. When unexpectedly faced with this dilemma recently I consulted both clients, without of course telling them the name of their rival. One candidate told me he was 'perfectly relaxed about it and may the best man (*sic*) win'. The other told me, a trifle unconvincingly, that she would live with whatever I decided. My decision was to recommend a colleague for the candidate I had coached previously, and to go with the woman candidate with whom I had an active coaching relationship. In discussing it later, she confessed that she would have felt 'very hurt but concealed it' if I had chosen to coach both of them.

Where you have personally collected feedback for a client, and this feedback unequivocally shows how much the client is disliked by colleagues, you have a duty to convey it to the client. It is patronizing to assume that the client will be unable to handle such feedback. The art is to write and then debrief it in a way that the client can hear, without warping the essential truth of the messages.

Working across cultures

As coaching has accelerated its already rapid growth, it has spread beyond the countries which had its first and most enthusiastic supporters. As a coach you may work with ex-pats in your own or another country. You may be an ex-pat yourself, working with people speaking your mother tongue but not necessarily as their first language. Where this is the case you will be involved in *cross-cultural* coaching.

You will already know that national cultures differ hugely, but it can still be a surprise to meet these differences in action. So Bobbie, an American coach working in Dubai for US-owned companies, was shocked that some of her Saudi clients would not shake her hand. Brookes, another American coach was training a group of eager learners in Shanghai on how to become coaches in their organizations and found that his biggest difficulty was their assumption, only gradually uncovered, that coaching was a synonym for mentoring, by which they meant giving advice but doing it very politely, followed by what he felt was their over-deference to him as an 'expert'. In my own work with British ambassadors I have found that, seasoned diplomats though they all are, they can still be surprised by deep-rooted differences in attitudes to work held by their locally employed staff, even in neighbouring European countries: for instance, that being asked to work over a weekend in an emergency or to travel on a Sunday evening might be received with hostility because family life is considered sacrosanct.

It may be especially important to look out for these differences when you assume that a common language or an apparently common cultural heritage means that you share assumptions. Language differences can be subtle, so the use of intensifiers like *very, remarkably, fantastically* [something] or modifiers like *quite, rather* [something] may have different underlying meanings in different English-speaking countries. Similarly, a British coach working with a German, Danish or Dutch client needs to remember that British tact and circumlocution could be misunderstood in countries where being direct is the norm. A German client working in London once gave me these examples of how feedback conversations can be misinterpreted on both sides:

British boss says	Actually means	German team member interprets as
It's probably my fault because I didn't explain it properly.	It was your fault, I'm just being polite.	Great! It was not my fault.
This needs a little bit of work.	It needs wholesale revision.	It's fine – just a few small changes.

Transatlantic coaching may be vulnerable to the same misunderstandings. The old saw about *two nations divided by a common language* is so true. If you are a British coach working with US clients or vice versa, learn the vocabulary and beware of embarrassing yourself because you don't know that many innocent-seeming words can have radically different meanings, often with a sexual subtext. Here are just some of them:

> *Bum, fag, fanny, shag, pants, period, spunk, slash, rubber, solicitor, knocked up, vest, restroom, bathroom, underwear.*

I have learnt the hard way that if I am supervising/mentoring a coach from another country, whose conversational English is good, I might still expect limited understanding of the casual idioms that I use without a second thought with a native British-English speaker.

There may be subtle differences in expectations about coaching. So in some African countries it would be considered rude to get down to the gritty business of goal-setting too soon: you would be expected to spend significant time at the beginning of a session in mutual enquiry about family and health, whereas in other cultures these topics would be off limits and it would be regarded as impertinent and inappropriate to ask about them at all. In some Asian cultures, a senior executive coach might be expected to dispense expertise and advice in a way that a European or North American coach could find uncomfortable. The writer and coach Phillipe Rosinski has written compellingly on cultural issues and offers a framework for alerting you to how differences may play out – for instance, in attitudes to time management, to family obligations, or to people's sense of individual responsibility. You can read a crisp digest in his article (2011) for the *International Journal of Coaching in Organizations.*

Multicultural issues

Multicultural issues are no easier. With unstoppable current global migration added to earlier arrivals in most Western countries, we may frequently be working with clients where the country and culture of origin of their parents and grandparents is a substantial force in their lives, even when the client has been born in your own country. For certain you will need *multicultural intelligence*: awareness of your own cultural conditioning, curiosity about other cultures and acute linguistic awareness.

Multiculturalism can seem like a tricky topic. You may hesitate to raise issues that jar your own moral compass out of fear of seeming 'racist'. 'Multiculturalism' may bring you up short against rifts that cannot be concealed. We may not always realize, for instance, that coaching is essentially based on the values of Western democracies and it is obvious that many parts of the world do not share our assumptions here. A pleasant Nigerian acquaintance once asked me for informal coaching where his problem was how to tell a gay colleague that he would go to Hell if he continued to be in a homosexual relationship. A woman coach I was supervising brought me the dilemma of how to react when a self-styled 'devoutly Muslim' client wanted to discuss how he could persuade his British wife to go with him to Saudi Arabia where he had been offered a job. Taking his wife to Saudi implied her leading a highly restricted life. For instance, she would not be able to drive because if she had done so, and the car had broken down, this would involve being alone with a man. This coach said dryly, 'It did not seem to have occurred to him that as a "devout Muslim" he was alone in a room with a woman – me!' A French client who had asked me for interview coaching said that the job, as a senior bankruptcy specialist for a US hedge fund, could potentially involve enforcing the assets of a whole (probably very poor) country. A client originally from mainland China, but now working for a US company, told me that he wanted help on how to get around the directive from bosses to consult his staff on an important issue regarding their future.

Are we being First World-centric, racist, or unduly self-righteous and pompous to hesitate over such challenges? Are we being guilty of narrow-minded thinking? Should we work with clients on issues like these if we profoundly disagree with the moral basis of the dilemma? My own answer to these questions is 'No': refusing and respectfully explaining why seems to be the only option. You may want to consider where you would draw the line yourself on such issues, and your conclusions may be different from mine.

The limits of confidentiality

It is crucial to explore what confidentiality means in practice, and especially to discuss it thoroughly where there is a third party – for instance, the client's boss. Where a boss tells you privately that a client's future in the organization is at risk, encourage the boss to be open with the client rather than making you collusive in an uncomfortable secret. At the beginning of the coaching I explain to clients that confidentiality is not a blank cheque. In the unlikely event of clients confessing to something illegal or dangerous to themselves or others, I forewarn them that confidentiality rules would not apply. My policy here is that I would always try to persuade clients to take appropriate action themselves, but if they refused I would do whatever I thought to be right, alerting the appropriate people or authorities while simultaneously doing everything I could to preserve the dignity of the client. I have very occasionally had to act on this principle, and it is never comfortable. Ask yourself: *Is this against the law? Could someone be harmed if I fail to act?*

At a coaching conference, one coach brought up the issue of a woman client, originally from sub-Saharan Africa, but now working in a senior UK health service role. The client's dilemma was that her husband was proposing to take their two daughters 'home' during the long summer break for 'cutting' – female genital mutilation (FGM) – on the grounds that this was the only way they would be considered 'clean' when it came to arranging their marriages. FGM is against the law in the UK. As this coach commented, breaking into tears as she did so:

> My own horror of this practice was one thing. My client shared it because she had been 'cut' as a child herself, but felt helpless against the powerful family dynamics in which she lived. But my duty seemed clear. I knew I had to act to protect the children. I told the client that I felt I had to inform social services and to do so immediately. I knew my action could expose my client to harm if it came out that she was the one who had triggered it, albeit through me, and I had no way of knowing how effectively social services and the police would protect her. Although I knew I had done the right thing, I still felt I had betrayed the client, and of course never worked with her again. And I had not explained at the outset of the coaching that confidentiality had limits. It was a hard way to learn that lesson.

Guidelines about confidentiality can be fuzzy when clients bring you a dilemma like this one:

> Helen notices that a colleague smells strongly of whisky throughout the day and is making repeated mistakes with his work. She likes him, their relationship goes back a long way, and she knows that he is having marital problems. His work has a direct bearing on public safety issues. Helen has no actual evidence that he is drinking at work – only that he always has a small vacuum flask on his desk from which he takes repeated sips. She has raised it with him, and

he denies that the flask contains alcohol or that he has a drinking problem. She is perplexed about her responsibility. Helen says that she would struggle with feelings of guilt if she brings the issue to their joint boss, yet knows that it will be increasingly difficult to stand by and do nothing. As Helen describes the issue, her coach also feels a sense of foreboding. If Helen does not act, what is the coach's responsibility?

The coaching around an issue like this needs to identify what the actual evidence is, and to pinpoint what the moral and personal dilemma for the client is before moving on to which part of it might be the client's personal responsibility. You may have strong views on the moral issues, but what you as the coach would do is a different question. What is important is to work with the client on what will happen if they do nothing, and then on what the advantages and disadvantages are of any of the various options – and, only then, what your own responsibility is as the coach.

Common sense should override any over-exaggerated concerns about confidentiality. For instance, an employment tribunal ruled against the Citizens Advice Bureau (CAB) which had sacked a staff member for having called a doctor when a client described having taken a potentially fatal overdose. This saved the client's life. It is hard to see how such action could be 'wrong' or 'unethical'. CAB policy dictated that the proper course of action was to refer to a senior manager who would then consult a committee. CAB justified the sacking on the grounds that the staff member had made an 'irrational emotional error'. The tribunal had no difficulty in deciding that this judgement was 'ridiculous'.

Ethical guidelines

Ethical guidelines make explicit what may be assumed and therefore be misleading. Most of the national and international coaching bodies such as the International Coach Federation (ICF), the Association of Professional Executive Coaches and Supervisors (APECS), and the European Mentoring and Coaching Council (EMCC), have codes of ethics which involve protecting the public reputation of coaching, treating clients at all times with respect, protecting their confidentiality, avoiding any hint of exploitation in the relationship, being scrupulous about boundaries and keeping up to date with training and supervision. You can consult their websites for details – for instance, www.apecs.org.

The legal situation on coaching is unclear and at the time of writing has not been tested in the courts, but there are any number of possibilities. The risks are low but they still exist. For instance, a client could claim that you did not deliver the positive benefits you promised and, if you refused to refund their fee, might pursue a claim to recover it. A client could allege that you broke confidentiality and that this had a palpably negative impact on them and their career, suing you for damages. You should note that informed consent is not a concept recognized in UK law. 'Duty of care' is also difficult to specify: what standard does it have to be and who would define it? You might be called as a witness by an organization in an employment tribunal defending themselves against an accusation of unfair dismissal by pointing out that they had hired you to help the client and that therefore they had done everything they reasonably could. The client's response might be that your help was not helpful. This is why you must keep notes as the judicial view is that if nothing has been recorded of a session, then, to all intents and purposes, it did not happen. Coaching confidentiality is not protected in law and your notes could be subpoenaed, a good reason for making sure that they are always immaculate.

All of this makes it essential to have professional indemnity insurance. It is not expensive if you buy it through a coaching membership organization, most of whom have recommended suppliers of insurance and who understand what coaching is.

Putting it into perspective

Although our ethical dilemmas as coaches are real enough they do pale by comparison with the dilemmas that I have heard from clients who work in medicine, nursing and social work. Although it can indeed happen, we very rarely work with life and death issues as so many people in these professions do. We do not have to act on whether, for instance, a young woman with a learning disability has the capacity to decide that she does not want to be sterilized, as is her parents' wish. We never have to judge whether a terminally ill patient's desire for a hastened death should be granted, nor whether to apply for a court order to override the wishes of devoutly religious parents who have refused a life-saving blood transfusion for their child – and so many more. For this, maybe, we should be grateful.

Supervision and coach-mentoring

What is the purpose of supervision

Ethical guidelines for coaches usually endorse the value and necessity of receiving supervision. Coaches need supervisors, often described in the US as *coach-mentors*. But what is supervision *for*? Looking at the coaching literature you will see two different purposes described, and each comes from a different discipline of origin. The first purpose is that supervision is a process where coaches can *develop self-awareness* about their current practice. This comes from the therapeutic tradition where, in virtually all types of therapy, a practitioner is required to have another and usually more senior therapist as a supervisor and sometimes to be in therapy as well. The second purpose is that supervision is intended to *protect the coach's clients and to be a guarantee of quality*. This assumption descends directly from some types of therapy but also from social work, the profession of origin of several of the most influential writers and teachers on coaching supervision.

In social work settings a manager is working within a formal legal framework and will hold frequent supervision sessions with their direct reports to follow up on casework and spot problems before they become messes. Clients for social work are most often vulnerable people with multiple socio-medical problems. This is radically different from the situation in coaching where the great majority of coaches are working with mature, stable clients. Coaches typically do not have bosses in the traditional sense because they work independently, in micro-firms or as associates. These coaches combine coaching with other ways of earning a living, such as facilitation and training. Supervision has to be a conscious purchase triggered by the coach and paid for out of fee income.

In social work there are sanctions for failure to protect vulnerable people and a supervisor is held to account along with the practitioner. In coaching supervision there are no sanctions. If you were to object to the tricky questions that your supervisor asks, then you can just change supervisor with no one any the wiser. Can you imagine a situation where an organization or client sues a supervisor for not ensuring that the coach did a good job? Of course not. This is because the supervisor in coaching has a moral but absolutely no formal authority or responsibility.

I cannot see how supervision *guarantees* either the quality of the coaching process or protection for the client. How would a supervisor know for certain that a coach was acting improperly? And to whom would they report it if they did? Whether supervision works depends at least partially on the honesty and self-awareness of the supervisee. A dishonest or un-self-aware supervisee could, in theory, fool a credulous supervisor. A supervisor is also assumed to have access to greater wisdom and experience, but there is no certainty that this is the case.

This confusion of purposes persists in the coaching world. Peter Hawkins' paper (2006) for the Chartered Institute of Personnel and Development (CIPD) showed that while coaches wanted skills development and to achieve 'aha!' moments from supervision, buyers of coaching wanted client protection, quality control, and assurance that the concerns of the organization would be addressed through the coaching.

It seems vital to endorse the idea that supervision promotes self-awareness and, at the same time, it is difficult to see how it can possibly protect clients except very indirectly.

How supervision works

Supervision ideally enables three closely related processes to happen.

First, it enables us to spot our patterns. Since as coaches we work in isolation, it is all too easy to develop blind spots which prevent us understanding what is happening in the relationship, hearing what the client is saying, or seeing how we are contributing to any triumphs and difficulties ourselves. Next, it gives us the chance to deepen our understanding of coach–client dynamics, looking at what is happening in the relationship, and raising self-awareness about our own responses to clients. Finally, supervision can offer much needed support. Coaches work alone. Coaching is 'emotional labour' and like any such work it can be exhausting, troubling, exhilarating. Coaching also raises many ethical dilemmas which are difficult to discuss with people who are not fellow coaching professionals. Supervision may be the one place where you can explore this material without fear of being judged or told what to do.

In her book on supervision, Julie Hay (2007) defines three levels of supervision, equating roughly to your levels of experience:

1 *Normative* applies to the beginner level, and here the supervisor is in effect extending the training of the coach by providing benchmark standards. The supervisor may also be an assessor and the supervision sessions may have an openly directive style.

2 *Formative* supervision may be appropriate when your experience is more extensive, but here again a more experienced coach/supervisor may offer advice and direct feedback. The aim is greater self-awareness and greater understanding of the psychological patterns that may play out in coaching, as well as offering unconditional support.

3 *Supportive* supervision has more of a peer–peer flavour and is suitable for more senior and experienced coaches. The role here is to exchange reflections, for the supervisor to spot patterns that the coach may be missing, and to provide a place where the coach can discuss how their own personal issues may be getting in the way of delivering excellent coaching.

Supervision is normally useful at more frequent intervals when you are in training, or a relatively new coach, than it is when you are more experienced. However, there is also a good case for supervision when you are very experienced indeed. The long-serving coach may need supervision to guard against potential jadedness or complacency. For instance, a coach who becomes invested in being a *clever* coach may urgently require challenge and refreshment.

Burn out and rust out

Look out for either burn out (super-stress) or rust out (boredom). Clients notice these signs, possibly before you will. Any incongruity between what we claim and how a client actually experiences us is immediately apparent. Such signs might include feeling messianic – you can save your clients from their own failings, you feel wonderfully insightful all of the time as well as boasting about your expertise as a coach. Watch out if you fail to experience at least a quiver of apprehension before meeting new clients or find that you believe that you know exactly what clients are going to say long before they open their mouths. You may also notice signs of boredom and irritation with your clients, or feeling a restless search for new gizmos, 'tricks' and 'techniques' to jazz up your coaching and to keep tedium at bay.

These dangers can be overcome by applying some realism and common sense and discussing them openly with a supervisor. It is also invaluable to have an experienced practitioner with whom to discuss difficulties and achievements. It is not a guarantee of perfect practice, but it may make poor practice a lot less likely. You may also decide to move on from coaching. If so, there is no shame in acknowledging that you and coaching have to part company, for whatever reason.

Supervisor styles

Barbara Moyes (2009) found from her literature review, and then from her own intensive qualitative study, that there was a wide range of methods and assumptions among the 12 practising supervisors she interviewed in depth. They differed especially over how far it was appropriate for a supervisor to take on the formal 'power' role of educating and challenging, rather than assuming that supervision had to be essentially non-directive.

In my own professional circle I see many variants on the role. There are people who take a psychodynamic view of supervision with a lot of emphasis on interpretation, transference and counter-transference (page 47) including in the supervisor–supervisee relationship; others combine a place where the coach can talk about anything they like with personal life as well as professional issues on the agenda, and yet others who offer business development mentoring along with discussion on the coach's casebook.

Getting best value from a supervision session

Choose your supervisor carefully, explore their beliefs about the purpose of supervision and ask how they typically run a session. Liking and mutual respect are important. Be clear about what you need from supervision and ask about their own coaching experience. It takes about 1000 hours of practice to handle the range of everyday coaching situations and about 3000 hours to be equipped to work with virtually any client. Regardless of the actual amount of experience, it probably takes at least a chronological year to become reasonably adept as a coach and another three or four years to operate competently with any client most of the time. This is the level at which you would be acceptable as a supervisor with another coach because 3000 hours of coaching and several years of practice imply a successful coach with a high level of repeat business based on word-of-mouth recommendations. It is an open question whether excellence and experience as a coach automatically means excellence as a supervisor as the role is different, but at least it is a start.

Training and qualifications to become a supervisor are now available in the UK – but again, as with coaching itself, there is little regulation or standardizing and most providers are their own judges on the quality of their work. There are coaches who are attracted to these courses because, they argue, it is another qualification which will help distinguish them in a crowded marketplace. Some providers of supervision training will accept people with negligible coaching experience, including people who have yet to complete a basic coaching qualification. It is hard to see what such a supervisor could add, other than empathetic listening, when their own coaching experience is so minimal.

Notice your own reactions to the supervision sessions. It is highly probable that you will be feeling apprehension combined with excitement, pleasurable anticipation and interest. This is useful – it reminds us that our clients make themselves vulnerable in their work with us. Similarly, in order to get value out of a supervision session, we also make ourselves vulnerable by being willing to own up to doubts and mistakes and to receiving feedback.

Concentrate on you and your coaching style. There is only you and your supervisor – you are the raw material, not your clients. There is a danger that supervision becomes an arena where the supervisor second guesses the supervisee on what he or should ideally have done in a client session, subtly asserting their own superiority as a coach, thus undermining the supervisee.

The question should be, 'My dilemma with this client is x', not 'This client's problem is y.'

Good questions for supervision sessions include:

> Which clients am I finding it most enjoyable to work with? What does that say about me?
> What is the best/worst coaching moment that has occurred since we last met?

What ethical issues are troubling me?

Where have I got stuck with clients recently?

What dilemmas am I facing (with particular clients, or in general)?

What issues do I find recurring with my clients? What might this suggest I am noticing or ignoring? What does that say about me and my practice?

Which skills and techniques do I find easy? Which am I avoiding?

What feedback have I had from my clients? How should I be addressing the themes that come out of this feedback?

How am I developing as a coach?

Alternatives to a paid supervisor can work well. These will include a co-coaching arrangement with another coach or a group meeting where coaches will take it in turns to explore their issues, in learning set style. Some groups usefully do live coaching with each other for review and feedback. This is another invaluable way to benchmark your practice and to get thoughtful feedback from people in the same business.

Being realistic about supervision

There is much talk about the virtues of supervision in coaching circles, but what do coaches actually do about getting supervision? Some coaching associations suggest a ratio of one supervision session for every 25 hours of coaching. That seems high. In my own case, since on average I give 12 hours of coaching in a week of part-time working, I would need to be employing a supervisor every two weeks – but of course I do not. When they have to pay for it out of fee income, coaches seem to buy carefully and sparingly, hoping perhaps to make a little supervision go a long way. A coach who still has to build a thriving caseload may avoid supervision altogether, feeling that it is unaffordable, even though their need for it may be considerable.

There is a striking absence of research into coaching supervision. At the time of writing, there is no research into how many practising coaches actually buy supervision, how often they buy, or what they pay. There is no research which can compare the commercial success and competence of coaches who buy supervision with the success and competence of those who do not. The research on its effectiveness is anecdotal and is mostly based on small, self-selecting samples.

I am troubled by some of the inflated claims made for supervision. We need to remember that most supervision is just two people in a room talking about the work one has done when the other was not present and where there is no formally shared accountability. I have worked with seven different supervisors in my coaching career. All have contributed something different to my own development, but what they have in common is that they increased my feelings of *prudent confidence*. I have heard many other coaches describe the same thing and have heard it at first-hand from my own supervisees. But does a more prudently confident coach do better work? We assume that this is so, but it is hard to prove. For instance, I was faced once with giving a coaching session, the fourth in a series of seven, to one of the most challenging clients of my entire coaching career, a person profoundly damaged by the tragedy of her history, given to shouting, screaming, crying and other kinds of troubling behaviour in the sessions and openly acknowledging that she needed therapy as well as coaching. I was quailing inside at the prospect of working with her and actively considering terminating the relationship. Luckily, I had a supervision phone call with my then supervisor, Julia Vaughan Smith, immediately prior to the session with the client. Julia listened quietly, steadied me down, reminding me of what it was probably possible and not possible to do with this client, encouraging me to be clear about boundaries. In this way I entered the session calmly grounded and with a lot more focus than would have been likely without it. But did it mean I did better coaching and, if so, how much better? I really don't know and I think it would be impossible to prove one way or the other.

In general, supervision is one part – an important one when done rigorously – of the continuing professional development to which all of us need to commit. We may need it in different ways and at differing levels of frequency at different stages of our coaching careers. We also need to seek out other forms of development such as training to update our skills and qualifications, attending conferences and workshops, reading, and simple networking with other coaches.

Getting evidence and feedback

It is good practice to invite a third party to run a simple emailed questionnaire for you with clients who have completed their coaching. Ask them for feedback on how useful the coaching has been, what changes they have made in their lives as a result of the coaching and any suggestions they have about what you might do to improve your effectiveness. For some ideas on how to do this, see my (2006) book, *Developing a Coaching Business*. The reason for asking a third party to perform this service is that you will get more truthful answers that go beyond conventional politeness. Where you work for a coaching firm, it is essential to conduct such client surveys from time to time. If you work independently, you may be able to offer a mutual exchange service with another coach.

Keeping notes

As a coach, you absolutely must keep and file notes on each client. The focus in these notes is on the client, not on you. A professional coach spends time before a session reviewing notes from the earlier sessions as a way of getting in the right frame of mind to work with a client.

Should you make notes during the session? These are the various arguments for and against:

Taking notes during the session

For	*Against*
It is a reliable way of remembering what the client has said and of recording details accurately.	You may find you have jotted down inessentials, or have written notes that are too full to be read quickly next time.
It looks as if you are taking the client seriously.	The client may wonder what you are writing.
You don't have to spend time later reconstructing the conversation.	You have to break eye contact with the client in order to write; the notebook forms a barrier between you.

Making notes after the session

For	*Against*
You can concentrate wholly on the client.	You may forget some of what has been said or remember it inaccurately.
There is no barrier between you.	Not taking notes can worry the client who may think you are likely to forget vital details.
Writing the notes later makes it easy to edit down to the essentials.	You have to spend time after the client has left writing up the notes.
It sharpens your listening skills when you know you are going to have to write up your notes later.	Your listening skills may not be as good as you think they are.

If you coach by phone, you may be able to have the best of both worlds – though be aware that there is a temptation to write down a jumble of everything the client says, which may or may not make sense later.

Keep notes short and simple. Keep judgements out of them – limit what you write to the factual and descriptive and always write notes in a way that

; you if they were seen by clients – which clients have the
ney are stored in a computer. Tell a trusted colleague how
ne notes if, for any reason, you are unable to run a session
cess to your notes when you are not in your office. It is best
the client's contact details separate from the actual notes of
his enables a PA or admin assistant to contact a client without
breaking confidentiality by accessing session notes.

A on r two-page bulleted list is usually enough, recording the client's name, invoicing details, the date, the client's presenting issues, any reading material you supplied or psychometrics used, action points for the client, action points for you.

Some coaches follow up a session by sending an email to clients with their notes from the session. I don't recommend this. It is the client's job to make their own notes.

Training and development for coaches

Training can make a substantial difference. It can offer a framework for understanding and assessing what you are doing, feedback on how you are doing it and the chance to swap bright ideas with other participants. Furthermore, with the coaching market saturated with coaches, all claiming equal expertise, corporate clients are now insisting on qualifications.

More and more providers are entering the coach-training field, many of them of dubious merit. Some providers do not actually coach at all – they just train coaches – so it is hard to see how they are keeping their own practice up to date or on what basis they think they can advise beginners.

Open/distance learning

There are many ways in which training can now be delivered: by open/ distance learning, by webinars where there could be many dozens of learners on the line with one tutor. These methods are a great deal cheaper for the provider than doing the same thing face-to-face. Where pre-prepared materials are concerned, once the development money has been recovered, there is far less cost than there is with face-to-face training. With open learning materials you can work at your own time and pace. As with any kind of learning delivered at a distance, everything depends on the quality of the materials. Some of this is deplorable, some excellent. Technology now makes it possible to see examples of actual coaching, right/wrong ways of coping with common problems, and this can bring theoretical concepts to life. You can study the theory by reading and then reporting on it via the internet. Chat rooms, blogs and specialist discussion groups can offer learner support. Blended learning can work in the right place and for the right purpose. However, coaching is a complex and subtle skill. It is difficult to acquire such a skill from watching a video or reading a book. You can read descriptions of coaching and watch others do it, but until you actually do it yourself and get closely observed feedback, you may have no idea what your actual standard is and whether you are going to find it easy or difficult to acquire the skills you need.

The most effective training for coaches is often about challenging ingrained poor practice as well as finessing an already sound style. Without that instant individual feedback from a practice partner or experienced tutor, bad habits can become chronic handicaps, simply because they are never challenged. This is the kind of thing that would be hard to spot when you are one of 30 people in a webinar, viewing a DVD, or just reading a few pages on a website.

In choosing a training provider, these guidelines may help you reject the charlatans and identify the quality providers:

- Look for realism and modesty in what providers say about their training. Anyone promising that they can turn you into a fully-fledged coach within a few short days will be misleading you. A training course starts, rather than ends, the process of growing as a coach. Beware particularly of that exclamatory text which offers amazing discounts if you buy NOW!
- 'Free' workshops often turn out to involve paying substantial sums for essential workbooks plus accommodation, so investigate before booking.
- Look for a low ratio of participants to tutors: 1:10 is about the maximum that can be guaranteed to provide enough individual attention.
- The best providers are also successful practising coaches with a demonstrable track record. Ask how many years of successful practice as coaches the actual course tutors have.
- Beware of coaching based principally on any one theory or school of thought. Coaching works best as an eclectic and pragmatic art.
- There should be a high ratio of practice to lecturing and an emphasis on personal feedback.
- Accreditation should fit within a national or international framework – be suspicious of any that do not.

Accreditation/credentialing

Assessment of your actual coaching through observation or recordings should be at the heart of any accreditation process, rather than writing essays or asking your clients to fill in a questionnaire about you, useful though these processes can also be as backup to the main question: 'How good a coach are you?' This coaching should be based on your work with an actual client, not just another participant on your course. Some training providers accredit students solely on the basis of a 'dissertation'. Interesting and challenging though this no doubt is, it does not prove anything about their likely quality as coaches. You could write a brilliant essay about coaching and be a terrible coach, or be a brilliant coach and be unable to write an essay about it.

The greater the potential for danger to life, limb, soul and pocket, the more important this issue becomes. The key question is accountability. Professions where there is tightly-administered accountability include medicine and its allied professions, the law, religion, architecture, accountancy and flying. In these cases, *licensing*, which can include active re-registration and continuous additional training (now compulsory in some professions), controls access to the profession.

To have real control over quality there would need to be a national or international body – say the equivalent of the various institutes in financial services. To be effective, these bodies need the power to control entry to the profession, backed by law as well as with money to set and test standards. Crucially they would also need consensus on what constitutes a good outcome of a professional intervention, plus a complaints mechanism and accountability procedure with teeth – to discipline and, if necessary, expel miscreants. (You should note that this is notoriously difficult and time-consuming even in highly regulated professions like medicine and nursing.) Along with this they would need public support and agreement that the profession is important enough to be worth controlling – that is, it has the potential to do significant harm as well as good – plus the support of all practitioners and staff to administer all the above.

There is no national or international body which can deliver all of this at the moment. The existing accrediting mechanisms do not and cannot control access to the coaching profession. This is easy. Anyone can call themselves a coach regardless of whether they have been trained or hold a coaching qualification. There is no effective means of disciplining a coach who has been accredited but who is guilty of a professional misdemeanour, because there is no way to prevent a poor coach from continuing to practise.

An excellent coach has *wisdom* and *skill*. Real success as a coach is the result of a great many hours of practice with real clients and commitment to continuing professional development, rather than the accumulation of factual knowledge which can be tested fairly straightforwardly through an exam, as in professions such as accountancy or the law, though knowledge of underpinning theory is also vital and will deepen your awareness of the origins, benefits and limitations of many of the ideas on which coaching is built.

Does coaching work?

Many coaches have an anxiety they will only express in private: Does coaching really work? And if it does, why and how? If we fail to take any of the credit for the apparent successes of our clients, we do not honour the coaching process. If we take it all, we do not honour our clients. It is an infrequently discussed danger of coaching that we can be overkeen to see our clients 'succeed' as a way of proving to ourselves and others that we add value. For instance, if you coach a client for a job interview, how much of the credit can you claim if that client gets the job?

Coaching is, or certainly should be, a voluntary process. So any clients who seek coaching could be different in some way from clients who do not – for instance, they may already be more self-aware and probably therefore already more successful. This makes it difficult to compare a coaching cohort with a control group unless there is also a large waiting list group. Knowledge and skill may also leak from individuals getting coaching in an organization to individuals who are not – in fact, we have to hope that it does. Few organizations conduct any kind of evaluation before a coaching programme begins, so it is usually impossible to assess how much change there has been in an individual, let alone in the organization.

Success in work or in life is never down to any one factor. There are usually far too many variables to be able to say for certain that it was the coaching that made the difference. For instance, in any large-scale coaching project there are not only many clients, but also many different coaches. It may be impossible to establish how much of the success or failure of the coaching was because of the strengths and weaknesses of any individual coach.

Enjoyment of the coaching does not necessarily correlate with behaviour change. It is relatively easy to assess the immediate impact of the coaching by asking the client for feedback on each session/coach: valuable for the coach, but not necessarily for the organization. All of this is complicated by the fact that so much of the research into coaching has been conducted by enthusiasts, often the very same enthusiasts who have been involved in the coaching.

Concern with measurement may also lead to attempts to measure the only things that can be measured. Dismayingly often, these are the most trivial things. For instance, you can easily measure how many sessions any individual client attended, but how far does this tell you whether or not that client had value from the process?

Return on investment

Some attention has been given to whether the investment in coaching can actually be measured financially through calculating return on investment (ROI).

One neat way of calculating ROI has been developed by the Ohio-based company Sherpa Coaching. This still involves an element of inspired guesswork, but you might like to try it with the help of a willing client.

Step 1	Estimate the total value of resolving an issue – or the costs involved in *not* resolving it. *Example:* client retained two of his most talented staff, both of whom had been in danger of leaving. Coaching had concentrated on how to remotivate them through redesigning their jobs and managing them in a different way. Avoided recruitment costs and disruption to business. **Benefit: £110,000**
Step 2	Multiply the sum you arrived at in Step 1 by the percentage you and the client attribute to the coaching: let's say this is 50% = **£55,000** (half of £110,000)
Step 3	How confident are you both in the accuracy of Steps 1 and 2? Let's say the answer is that you are 80% confident. **Adjusted total benefit: £44,000** (80% of £55,000)
Step 4	Subtract the cost of coaching: (£6000) **Net benefit: £38,000** (£44,000 – £6000)
Step 5	To calculate ROI, divide the net benefit by the cost of coaching and turn into a percentage. In this case: £44,000/£6,000 x 100 = 633% **ROI = 633%**

In other words, this was a substantial return on investment.

As a coach, there are a number of actions you can take to ensure that there are answers to the legitimate concerns of the commissioning organization about how its money is being spent. Ensure that the goal-setting process gets enough time at the outset of the coaching and in every session (see Chapter 7) and make your goals measurable as far as possible, involving the boss in the goal setting where appropriate. Make every effort to link business results with the relationship and skills issues and ask for feedback all the time on how the client is progressing towards achieving these results. Ask what and how the coaching is contributing and, when you are involved in a large-scale project, look for ways to build evaluation in from the start.

Other measures of coaching success

Trying to measure ROI has many limitations. Most importantly it can underestimate the importance of team effort, making it difficult to attribute any benefits to coaching alone. In their book *Managing Coaching at Work* (2011), Jackie Keddy and Clive Johnson make the point that in looking to assess the impact of coaching, the *balance of probabilities* approach adopted in civil law is more sensible than looking for the absolute proof demanded in a criminal case. Their suggestions, in a whole chapter devoted to this subject, include openly facing ambiguity in the evidence as well as using a number of methods to track what they call *impact chains* – that is, the organizational effect of coaching which goes beyond the individuals involved.

It seems beyond doubt now, after many hundreds of studies, that coaching has multiple benefits for organizations. In their impressive meta-analysis involving an extensive literature search and a ruthless exclusion of any studies that did not conform to their own definitions of coaching, Tim Theeboom (2013) and his colleagues looked for evidence that coaching could affect performance, well-being and skills. Their conclusions were, with many caveats, that:

> The results show that coaching has significant positive benefits on performance and skills, well-being, coping, work attitudes and goal-directed self-regulation. In general, our meta-analytic findings indicate that coaching is an effective tool for improving the functioning of individuals in organizations.

It is important to have such objective evidence because every coach is asked for it one way or another by potential clients. But in the end, the evidence you accumulate for yourself will probably matter more. Much of this will be about elements that are intangible and therefore hard to measure. Recently I was at a joyful event held to celebrate the launch of a book on coaching. There was a light touch on my shoulder and then a big hug. It was a former client who had come to me as chief executive of an organization facing radical change and with her own job in danger. Although she had always been an enthusiastic, hardworking and appreciative client, I had never realized how much the coaching had mattered to her. I treasure her warm and generous words, which were:

> You gave me the only safe space in my life at the time. Coaching allowed me to face my worst fears and to work out for myself what I wanted and needed to do. The tipping point was when we began to explore the complications in my personal life as well as everything that was so challenging at work, and I realized that I could stop being that one-dimensional character 'The chief executive' and just be me: the all-round person. Something important shifted for me. I was able to make difficult decisions calmly – for me and for my organization – and to make a smooth transition in my career.

Coaching still has a long way to go as a profession. The word *coach* may be on its way to becoming a vague term, much like its close cousin *consultant* – a word that often conceals a temporarily stalled career. While, in practice – and longer term – the market decides who is an excellent coach and who is a dabbling amateur, this may not be immediately apparent to those doing the hiring. Making what contribution we can to continued professionalism is a duty we all share.

14 Beyond technique

I see you

I am here

(West African greeting – and reply)

Now that coaching has become a popular intervention in organizations, I find that I am often working with 'coaching divorcees'. These are executive coaching clients who have already had one coaching relationship that has not worked out. Discussing what had happened has been a humbling experience, reminding me of how difficult it can be to be the kind of excellent coach we would all aspire to be and wondering how often any of my own former clients would tell similar stories of disillusionment. Every one of the coaches concerned had already been through an initial selection protocol, either by a tendering process or as part of a framework agreement. I know from talking to some of the disappointed HR people who hired them that their track record appeared impressive. If they had been required to describe what they could do at a 'beauty parade' they had talked it up well.

There's a pattern in these failed coaching assignments and it's this: all the coaches involved were over-reliant on 'techniques':

> *Coach A* held her sessions in a branch of the busy sandwich chain Pret a Manger, so there was a total lack of privacy. She then insisted on beginning the process with two minutes of deep breathing, asking the client to close her eyes. This must have been entertaining for Pret's other customers, even if it was acutely embarrassing for the client.

> *Coach B* was enchanted by NLP techniques and seemed to believe that visualizing was the solution to every problem. He asked the client – and this was in the first ten minutes of the first session – to imagine himself standing under a waterfall where 'all your past mistakes and confusions will be washed away'. That coach had perhaps missed his vocation as an evangelical preacher. Later on in the same session he asked the client to imagine his future life spread out in front of him and to take a step into it. The client's comment: 'I didn't really know what he was talking about and I couldn't do it – felt stupid'.

Coach C ignored his client's account of how unconfident and exposed she felt in her largely male-dominated organization and suggested that she rehearsed a challenging presentation by pretending that she was a man. 'I couldn't be vulnerable with him' said this client, with remarkable restraint.

Coach D spent the two sessions she conducted with the client giving him mini-lectures, with no apparent irony, on 'Listening'.

From the direct accounts given soberly and in a generous spirit, mostly of puzzlement by these and other clients, it is clear that this sort of coach believes that 'techniques' will solve every client problem. When the techniques don't work, these coaches have no underpinning psychological knowledge or insight and therefore nowhere else to go.

This is the paradox: you have to learn technique in order to bypass it. The same is true of learning to act, to play a sport or a musical instrument. In acting you have to acquire and then go past methods to get to the meaning of the text. To inspire the orchestra, a conductor has to be an accomplished musicologist before going beyond what is simply written in the score. A jazz musician must acquire a thorough grasp of musical technique before being able to improvise successfully.

To be a coach you have to learn the techniques in order to discover where they fit into real learning and change. This learning can only happen in the crucible of the coach–client relationship. This is because the coaching client is not an *object* to be worked on but a *subject* to be worked with by another human being. The Viennese philosopher and writer Martin Buber, whose ideas have had considerable impact on Gestalt therapy, wrote astutely:

> The deciding reality is the therapist, not the methods. Without methods one is dilettante. I am for methods, but just in order to use them not to believe in them. Although no doctor can do without a typology, he knows that at a certain moment the incomparable person of the patient stands before the incomparable person of the doctor; he throws away as much of his typology as he can and accepts this unforeseeable thing that goes on between therapist and patient.
>
> (Hycner and Jacobs 1995: 17)

Yourself: your own best instrument

In general, as a coach, your best instrument is yourself. You will need all the tools and techniques and many others described in this book, but if you cannot use your authentic self, you will be consistently disappointed in the work you do.

As with so much else in coaching, this is the central paradox. You have to be fully present, yet not intrude too much. You have to bring the full force of your personality into the coaching room, yet it must never overwhelm the client. You have to know all the techniques, yet restrain yourself from using them except when they are totally appropriate. You have to be able to form a relationship of intimacy with the client, yet it must never cross the boundary into a friendship while the coaching is continuing. You have to be vigilant about yourself and your own interventions while simultaneously maintaining a high level of alertness to everything the client says and does. You have to keep a degree of control over the overall process, yet allow the client to take control as well. The end result of coaching is about feeling and acting in a more powerful way, yet, to work, both coach and client have to stay together in powerlessness.

One way to think about it is to accept that if you see yourself as *doing coaching*, it will be far harder than just *being a coach*. Doing coaching is intrinsically stressful because you are trying so hard, whereas being a coach is easier and more fluid because you trust the process.

The place of insight

It matters as a coach to have psychological insight. Feeling that you have useful insight into others is probably one of the main reasons that people become coaches. Insight is closely linked to curiosity about people, another important qualification for being a coach.

However, it is also important to keep the question of insight in proportion. Mind reading is an inexact art. There are two principles here. First, the best and most valuable insight to have is into yourself. Second, it is far more important for the client to have insight into themselves than for you to do so. This quote from Carl Jung's book *Modern Man in Search of a Soul* (2001) says it all:

> Nothing is more unbearable for the patient than to be always understood. It is relatively unimportant whether the psychotherapist understands or not, but everything hangs on the patient doing so.

Also, while you are searching for insights, you will be distracted from your main task of listening at Levels 2 and 3 (page 38) to your client. You will be worrying about yourself and how to ask *clever* questions. The point about coaching is to ask *wise*, not clever questions, and to keep out of the client's way.

This means that you do not have to labour to make connections for the client. Instead, say 'What connections do you see between x and y?' You do not have to read a client's motivation. Instead, say 'What was your motivation then?' You do not have to grasp all the content of the client's issues – effort spent on trying to discern all the nuances will tend to draw the client's effort into helping you understand what they already understand. This will pull you away from *experiencing* what the client is telling you – a better emphasis. You do not have to offer insights to the client. Instead, say 'What insight do you have now into that incident?' Or you can ask 'What learning did you gain from that?' – another way of asking the same question.

This does not prevent you from having insights – sometimes a coach will experience an intuitive moment when an insight appears which is potentially useful to the client. My rule here is that I try never to present it to the client as a profound truth. Instead, I might say something like, 'Can I offer you a potential insight here? It may or may not be right, but it's occurred to me that . . .' – and then I describe my insight. 'How does that seem to you?' If you are wrong, the client can then tell you so. If you are right, then the client has the benefit of your ideas.

Often, insights that seem inspired and brilliant to the coach are about the coach's gratification and rarely have meaning to the client. What seems clever to the coach is often blindingly simple to the client, whereas the insights and connections that clients make for themselves are part of what coaching is all about.

Letting go of the need to be right

The heart of my own approach to coaching is to let go of the need to be right and to let go equally of the need to find solutions for the client, and then to knit those beliefs into every interaction with them. Time and again I see coaches of all levels of experience dutifully mouth the words about *partnership* or about not giving advice to their clients but then getting overwhelmed with anxiety when they see the client struggling or not apparently making what the coach considers to be 'progress'. The inevitable result is that the coach slowly but surely begins to do most of the work in the session and the client's energy drains away. An even more exaggerated version of the same phenomenon is where, in their need to feel useful, the coach begins to lecture or, in some cases, hector the client. You don't know what is best for the client. You don't need to be right. The client does not need to leave every session with a neatly packaged action plan or a list of ticked boxes. Sometimes clients choose confusion, caution, inactivity and procrastination. Sometimes just thinking is enough. The client is the one who will live with or without the solution, and that is always their choice.

Being centred

As a coach, you need to be as centred as possible. This means that your own concerns and anxieties have to be banished during a coaching session. This is challenging, but it is a state to strive for. If you are not centred, you will find intrusive worries affecting your behaviour and therefore your effectiveness with your client. These might be thoughts and feelings such as:

> Am I good enough? Am I asking clever enough questions?
> I don't like this client.
> I'm afraid of this client.
> I'm too important to be working with a junior/young/not very bright client like this.
> I need to take control to prove who's in charge here.
> – and so on.

One way of putting this is that there is a spectrum of possible places to be during a coaching session. At one end is the anxious, defended, protected ego, described by Thomas Crane in his book, *The Heart of Coaching* (1998), as 'Fortress Me'; at the other is the centred person who can stay relaxed and alert. Fortress Me is self-conscious rather than self-aware, critical and judgemental rather than accepting and discerning, arrogant rather than self-confident, spiteful rather than inquisitive, and controlling rather than adaptable. Fortress Me tries to be perfect. The centred coach will accept good enough as the norm, but with the aim of keeping on learning. The paradox is that you cannot really have the aim of *doing* brilliant coaching without a self-serving element creeping into your work, though you can have the aim of *being* an excellent coach.

There is no one right way. Each coach has to find their path. Experienced coaches find that any or all of these help: meditation, mindfulness, prayer, yoga, listening to music, moderate physical exercise such as walking, dancing, cycling, jogging or swimming, when the mind can be suspended.

Most of the world's great religions are about releasing the grip of the ego on the personality. You do not need to subscribe to any of them to find your own path, but as a coach you do need to be able to detach yourself from your ego, to set your own needs aside, and to listen deeply and non-judgementally.

> We meet ourselves time and again in a thousand disguises on the path of life.

> (Carl Jung)

In the West African greeting I quoted at the beginning of this chapter, there is a wonderful acknowledgement of the importance of two people meeting and seeing – really seeing each other; being present – and being fully present. That is what the best coaching is all about.

Annex 1:   The first session: a template

This is a basic template that you might find useful.

In advance

The 'Look-See' or 'chemistry' conversation: 30 minutes

Many clients like to shop around for a coach so you may have a conversation before meeting where the client is assessing whether or not you are the most suitable of the coaches he or she is considering. If this has not happened naturally, call the client beforehand to introduce yourself. See this as entirely a two-way conversation which models the partnership that will be established during the coaching; it is a test of compatibility *not* a sample coaching conversation. Make it clear to the client, very respectfully, that it is about making a mutual decision to work together: you are choosing the client as much as they are choosing you.

Your role is to facilitate this conversation, starting not with a sales pitch about how wonderful you and coaching are, but to establish what the immediate trigger for coaching has been, what else the client might have tried, what other experience of coaching, mentoring or therapy they have had and what worked or what didn't. Then you will go on to what they want to get out of a coaching programme and what they are looking for in a coach. Ask them what has aroused their interest in you specifically. Turn the second half of the conversation over to the client where they question you. It would be normal in this conversation for the client to ask you about your general approach, where you will meet, frequency of meetings, how long the sessions will be and fees. (There is much more on this in my book *Developing a Coaching Business* (2006)).

Be prepared to end the relationship at this stage if you cannot satisfactorily resolve any problems or misconceptions, suggesting another coach if that feels appropriate.

Other advance preparation

Some coaches like to send the client a simple workbook with well-known exercises such as The Life Scan Wheel (page 148) or a summary of achievements and goals still left to achieve. If you do this you will need to build the debrief into the first session. These notes assume that you have not sent these materials in advance. There is no one right way – it comes down to what you feel comfortable with and what you find works for you.

Alert the client by email to the fact that the first session is different because it is about creating the framework for what will follow. You may want to say that it is the only one that will follow a set format. Ask clients to bring any recent feedback, for instance, 360-degree feedback, performance appraisal documents, their CV/résumé and results of previously taken psychometrics.

Ask the client to fill in a personal information sheet with their contact details and to email it to you in advance.

These notes assume a 90-minute session

The welcome: 5 minutes

Most clients will feel at least a little nervous: be alert to the signs of this – for instance, a slightly flushed face or mild sweating. The journey may have been more difficult and have taken longer than they anticipated and they may be flustered. Welcome the client warmly, ask them how their journey was. Offer tea, coffee (including decaffeinated versions), water, herbal drinks. Show the client where the loo/bathroom is. Take their coat and hang it up. Show them where you will be working.

A quick recap on why the client wants coaching: 5 minutes

Recap briefly on what you know about why the client is coming for coaching and ask them to do the same. Say that you will return in much more detail to this later and interrupt them respectfully if they launch into a long account of he-said, she-said, assuring them that there will be time for this later in the session.

Contracting: 6–10 minutes

Say again, very briefly, that this session will have a different shape and feel from what follows and explain why.

In effect you will recontract every time you meet the client, but the first session is especially important. This part of the conversation is not an excuse for a mini-lecture on what coaching is as it is essentially a two-way discussion where, as in every session that follows, you draw out material from the client. Ask how clients see coaching – most will be clear that it is not the same as training, mentoring or therapy. Offer your own brief comments with any additional explanation of your own approach, if necessary.

Discuss how the coaching partnership is different from other kinds of one-to-one work. Ask for successful examples of coaching from the client's experience, even if it has been informal, and discuss the implications for how they would like to be coached.

Ask the client: 'What do you need to know about me?' Many clients are curious about how you have come to be a coach and may also want to know what your training and experience is. Keep your own autobiographical details short.

Explain accountability (page 202), emphasizing that it is not conventional boss–subordinate or teacher–pupil accountability.

Discuss roles and responsibilities: for instance that the client brings the agenda, while your own role is to ask the questions and to offer comment.

Talk about confidentiality and your approach to it. Ask the client for their concerns: most have at least some – for instance, will you ever mention that they are a client to a third party? (normally the answer will be 'no'). Explain your practice on note-taking. If you do take notes while the client is present, offer the client the chance to see them at the end of the session. Discuss what you will each do if the coaching does not seem to be working for either or both sides.

Explain your cancellation policy. Agree frequency, session-length and method for coaching – for instance, whether or not you are available by phone, text and email between sessions, whether you will meet face-to-face or conduct the coaching by phone or Skype.

Autobiography: 15–30 minutes (pages 117)

Ask the client for a brief account of the significant events in their lives, starting from early childhood, explaining why you are asking: that early life shapes who we become as adults, most especially our beliefs about ourselves and the world around us. Ask for connections to their primary reason for coming to coaching.

The Life Scan Wheel (page 148): 10 minutes

Explain its purpose and ask the client to fill it in if you have not sent it in advance. Coach the client through the way they have filled it in. This will normally generate more goals for the coaching.

Reviewing previous development experiences: 10–15 minutes

Ask the client what other development experiences they have had – e.g. many clients have already undergone 360-degree feedback, though not necessarily recently or with a high-quality instrument. Ask what psychometric instruments they have experienced and what learning they have taken from them. Many will become vague at this point – essentially any impact has been minimal and the lessons forgotten. If clients have brought feedback with them, ask to read it – or make a copy to read later. If the client has sent it in advance, which is much better, review it together.

Discuss tools and techniques that could help the client reach his or her goals – for instance, additional 360-degree feedback, retaking or taking the MBTI™ and the FIRO-B™. Agree the cost implications of any of these approaches – for instance, the telephone version of 360-degree adds major costs.

Raise the question of involving the client's line manager in creating input from the organization on what it wants from the coaching (page 143). If the client feels that this would be interesting and appropriate, discuss how you propose doing it and any cost implications.

Overall goal-setting: 20 minutes (Chapter 7)

Discuss the professional and organizational needs that will form the basis of the coaching. Return to the Life Scan Wheel discussion, and ask whether anything that emerged here should be added to the list of goals for the whole programme. If the goals seem too extensive or too modest for the programme you have initially agreed, now is the time to discuss recontracting.

Feedback: 3–5 minutes

Ask for feedback on how this session has gone

Mechanics: 3 minutes

Agree times and dates for the next two sessions. If you have agreed to do psychometrics, explain the protocol and ask the client to complete the questionnaires before the next session. Check invoicing details. Show the client out.

After the session

Write up your notes straight away. File them in a safe and secure place immediately. Email the client confirming the arrangements you have made on the number of sessions, fees and dates, plus any other promised material. If you have agreed to invoice all or part of the fee in advance, send the invoice with this email.

Doubts

If the session has revealed doubts about whether you have a genuine client – for instance, someone who feels that coaching has been dumped on them or who consistently blames others for the mess they are in – be prepared to end the relationship at this point. Never go past the opening session without such doubts being resolved.

Short coaching programmes

It is increasingly common for organizations to offer coaching as a follow-up to a leadership development programme. Sometimes the coaching on offer is limited to two or three sessions and it would not be unusual for the organization to suggest or to insist upon a format of their own – for instance, debriefing psychometrics or concentrating on action plans emerging from the development programme.

The shorter the coaching programme, the less appropriate it is to have a fully-fledged 'intake' session of the sort described here. It is still possible with an abbreviated coaching programme to give the first session a slightly different slant from what follows by using a truncated version of the classic format – for instance, using the Life Scan Wheel so that personal goals can be added to those generated by organizational concerns. But you will have to be pragmatic and judge what will work for each client and each organization, given the limited time available.

Annex 2:   Coaching by phone

Technology has made it possible to coach and be coached anywhere in the world. Coach and client no longer need to be in the same physical space. What are the plusses and minuses of coaching this way? How do you make it work?

The case for

Phone coaching has its fervent adherents, especially in the US where one recent survey estimated that 45 per cent of coaching is delivered by this means. Where geographical distances are considerable, this may be the only practical way that a client can get access to the high-quality coach of their choice, sometimes believing, maybe wrongly, that there are no locally based coaches who are up to the task. Making a date is simpler and more time-efficient because no one has to travel; coach and client can each be at home or at their desks, so it is possible to have shorter coaching sessions at more frequent intervals and this may be an advantage, creating more intensity and energy.

Enthusiasts for phone coaching claim that excluding the visual element also excludes distractions and, in some cases, stops either coach or client making stereotyped judgements based on prejudice. The argument goes that since you can't see each other, all you are doing is listening to words, so the coaching has an essential 'purity': some people will claim that you get a heightened sense of subtle underlying meanings when you are just listening and not distracted by the other person's physical presence.

The challenges

Given the choice, almost all clients and coaches prefer face-to-face encounters. This is because you experience each other more fully when you are actually together: you see shifts of body language, changes in energy, expression and facial colour or small variations in eye contact. Rapport is easier and the lack of it is also easier to spot. For some kinds of coaching – for instance, preparation for a job interview, presentation skills or problems associated with personal impact – phone coaching is much more limiting and video links are a crude substitute.

It is hard to do a lengthy session by phone: an hour seems to be the maximum that either coach or client can tolerate and this may be too short to get into the issues fully.

Time zone differences can be tiresome. There may be misunderstandings about whose time you are referencing when you set up the call – this is especially risky where there are only one or two hours of time difference between countries, when the start of summer/winter time is different in different countries, or where the 24-hour clock is used in one country but not in the other. There may be only a few hours when your working days coincide, but even then it may mean that one of you is battling against end-of-the-day fatigue or else having to get out of bed unusually early. Technological glitches are fewer than they used to be but can still be annoying: that tiresome echo on a mobile/cell phone, a poor-quality line, sound that fades in and out, or if you are using a video system, a picture that judders. Sometimes it may feel as if there is something too casual about phone coaching – it may lack the seriousness of effort associated with having to make a date to meet in person. A client who would never be late for an actual meeting may allow themselves to be late for a phone call.There may be greater security and privacy risks with phone coaching: one of my own diplomat clients told me wearily to assume that our conversations were being bugged, despite speaking on what was allegedly a secure line.

The ease of setting up a phone call may tempt either side into incomplete barriers against intrusion – for instance, from children banging on the door, dogs barking, noise from colleagues or frankly sloppy attention to confidentiality – for instance, talking on a train. When clients are fitting their coaching sessions inside a busy day, they can seem rattled, subtly or overtly distracted – for instance, by incoming emails or colleagues who barge into their room.

When you can't see the client, handling pauses can be problematical. You ask a question and there appears to be a long blank at the other end: Has the line gone down? Is the client still there? Probably you have asked a great question and the client is thinking, but without visual clues you may rush to fill the gap with words. At the same time you will also need, judging it very carefully, to work harder to keep the momentum going, possibly by doing a little more summarizing than you would if you were face-to-face, and certainly making more uh-huhs and other minimal noises to show that you are still present.

Where you and your client are using a language that is a foreign tongue to one or both or you, a phone conversation can be more effortful because accents can be more difficult to follow and there are no helpful visual clues to make meaning clearer.

Making it work

- Contract carefully and have a candid discussion about how to make the most of the advantages and minimize the disadvantages. Stress the importance to the client of having a quiet space where there will be no interruptions or eavesdroppers and where they have turned off their email.

* Agree who will call whom and have back-up numbers available in case there is some technological mishap. It would be normal for the client to call the coach but, if it is the other way around, subscribe to a scheme where you can make cheap calls to anywhere in the world.

* Double check the time of the call, clarifying any confusions created by time zone differences, e.g. 'You'll call me at 1400 BST, 1500 your time.'

* If at all possible have at least one face-to-face meeting to start the process off: this can make a lot of difference to the ease of the conversation later on in the coaching programme.

* In theory, if you are working by phone, and not Skype, Facetime or a video-conferencing system, then you could do the coaching wearing your pyjamas or even stark naked. You could – but it is better not to. Dress for work; be at your usual desk but with your email turned off; sit up and be as attentive as you would if the client were in front of you.

* Prepare for the conversation as carefully as you would for meeting face-to-face: read your notes from previous sessions, make sure you have no distractions and that you are in a place where you can talk freely. During the session, plan to be interruption free. Beware tapping on your computer, filling a kettle, slurping drinks, shushing a dog or a child, scribbling or rustling papers: the client will hear and may assume, correctly, that you are giving less than 100 per cent attention. Make notes after the session, not during it.

* Use hands-free equipment and suggest the client does the same, using a mobile/cell phone with earbuds. It is tiring to keep clutching a phone. Don't use the speakerphone option and discourage your client from using it. The amplification may threaten the privacy of the conversation; speakerphones also pick up ambient sound, making nuances of speech more difficult to hear because of intrusion from background noise.

* You may need to speak a little more slowly than usual and may have to ask your client to do the same.

* Empathy may need to be expressed verbally when the client cannot see your encouraging nods: expect to do this more frequently than you might if face-to-face. So, for instance, you might say, 'I know you can't see me at the moment, but I'm smiling'.

* Watch out for habits such as repeatedly saying 'OK': these verbal tics are more noticeable on the phone than they are in person.

* Beware of filling what could be a productive silence with too much nervous chatter, though sometimes you may need to explain your

own silence, for instance by saying, 'I've gone quiet here because I need some thinking time.' It will also pay to check out what emotional resonance any issue has for the client: this is easy either to miss or to over-interpret when you don't have the client in front of you.

- It may be more important to email the client after a phone session than it would be for one where you have been face-to-face, for instance suggesting some online links that the client might like to follow up, to pick up on the themes of the session and to express your enthusiasm for your mutual work.

But really. . .

But really, in the end all the usual principles apply. These are more important than any specific elements associated with doing it by virtual means. There is no 'mystery technique' associated with phone coaching. The same good coaching practice is essential: creating and maintaining rapport, setting goals, asking incisive questions, summarizing, prompting action points and managing the flow of the session.

Bibliography and further reading

Anderson, M. (2003) *Bottom Line Organizational Development*. Oxford: Butterworth-Heinemann.

Ariely, D. (2008) *Predictably Irrational*. London: Harper Collins.

Atwood, M. (2000) *The Blind Assassin*. Toronto: McClelland & Stewart.

Bandler, R. and Grinder, J. (1979) *Frogs into Princes*. Moab, UT: Real People Press.

Bandler, R. and Grinder, J. (1982) *Reframing*. Moab, UT: Real People Press.

Bandura, A. (1997) *Self-efficacy: The Exercise of Control*. New York: Freeman.

Bentall, R.B. (2010) *Doctoring the Mind: Why Psychiatric Treatments Fail*. London: Penguin.

Berglas, S. (2002) The very real dangers of executive coaching, *Harvard Business Review*, June.

Berne, E. (1964) *Games People Play*. London: Penguin.

Berne, E. (1975) *What Do You Do After You Say Hello?* London: Corgi.

Bevan, J. (2002) *The Rise and Fall of Marks & Spencer*. London: Profile Books.

Block, P. (1981) *Flawless Consulting*. San Diego, CA: Pfeiffer.

Bluckert, P. (2006) *Psychological Dimensions of Executive Coaching*. Maidenhead: Open University Press.

Bridges, W. (1991) *Managing Transitions*. Reading, MA: Addison-Wesley.

Briggs Myers, I. and Myers, P. (1980) *Gifts Differing*. Palo Alto, CA: Consulting Psychologists Press.

Brockbank. A. and McGill, I. (2006) *Facilitating Reflective Learning through Mentoring and Coaching*. London: Kogan Page.

Brockbank, A. and McGill, I. (2013) *Coaching with Empathy*. Maidenhead: Open University Press.

Brown, P. and Brown, V. (2012) *Neuropsychology for Coaches: Understanding the Basics*. Maidenhead: Open University Press.

Bryce, L. (2002) *The Coach*. London: Judy Piatkus Publishers.

Carson, R. (1987) *Taming Your Gremlin: A Guide to Enjoying Yourself*. London: Harper and Row.

Casement, P. (1985) *On Learning from the Patient*. London: Tavistock Publications.

Clarkson, P. (1995) *The Therapeutic Relationship*. London: Whurr Publishers.

Cockman, P., Evans, B. and Reynolds, P. (1999) *Consulting for Real People*. Maidenhead: McGraw-Hill.

Covey, S.R. (1992) *The Seven Habits of Highly Effective People*. London: Simon and Schuster.

Crane, T. (1998) *The Heart of Coaching*. San Diego, CA: FTA Press.

Csikszentmihalyi, M. (1990) *The Psychology of Optimal Experience*. New York: Harper & Row.

Csikszentmihalyi, M. (2003) *Good Business: Flow, Leadership and the Making of Meaning*. New York: Viking.

Doidge, N. (2007) *The Brain that Changes Itself*. New York, NY: Penguin.

Egan, G. (1998) *The Skilled Helper*, 6th edn. New York: Brooks Cole.

Elkins, D. (2007) Empirically supported treatment: the deconstruction of a myth, *Journal of Humanistic Psychology*, 47(4): 474–500.

Farrelly, F. and Brandsma, J. (1974) *Provocative Therapy*. Capitola, CA: Meta Publications.

Farwagi, P.L. (1998) *The Life Balance Programme*. London: Orion Publishing Group.

Feltham, C. and Horton, I. (eds) (2000) *Handbook of Counselling and Psychotherapy*. London: Sage Publications.

Flaherty, J. (1999) *Coaching: Evoking Excellence in Others*. Oxford: Butterworth-Heinemann.

Frankl, V. (1959) *Man's Search for Meaning*. New York: Pocket Books.

Gallwey, T. (2000) *The Inner Game of Work*. London: Orion Publishing Group.

Griffin, J. and Tyrell, I. (2004) *Human Givens*. Chalvington, Sussex: HG Publishing.

Goleman, D., Boyatzis, R. and McKee, A. (2002) *The New Leaders*. London: Little, Brown.

Harris, T.A. (1973) *I'm OK – You're OK*. London: Pan Books.

Harvey, J. (1988) Eichmann in the Organization, in *The Abilene Paradox*. Lexington, MA: Lexington Books.

Hawkins, P. (2006) *Coaching Supervision: Maximising the Potential of Coaching*. London: CIPD.

Hawkins, P. (2012) *Creating a Coaching Culture*. Maidenhead: Open University Press.

Hay, J. (2007) *Reflective Practice and Supervision for Coaches*. Maidenhead: Open University Press.

Hayes, P. (2006) *NLP Coaching*. Maidenhead: Open University Press.

Hazler, R.J. and Barwick, N. (2001) *The Therapeutic Environment*. Buckingham: Open University Press.

Hycner, R. and Jacobs, L. (1995) *The Healing Relationship in Gestalt Therapy*. Highland, NY: The Gestalt Journal Press.

Hodgkinson, P. and Stewart, M. (1998) *Coping With Catastrophe*. London: Routledge.

Jackman, J. and Strober, M. (2003) Fear of feedback, *Harvard Business Review*, April.

Jung, C.G. (1923) *Psychological Types*. New York: Harcourt Brace.

Jung, C.G. (1963) *Memories, Dreams, Reflections*. London: Fontana.

Jung, C.G. (2001) *Modern Man in Search of a Soul* (classics edn). London: Routledge.

Kahneman, D. (2011) *Thinking, Fast and Slow*. New York: Penguin Group.

Keagan, R. and Lahey, L. (2009) *Immunity to Change*. Boston, MA: Harvard Business Press.

Keddy, J. and Johnson, C. (2011) *Managing Coaching at Work*. London: Kogan Page.

Kellaway, L. (2005) *Who Moved My Blackberry?* London: Penguin.

Kline, N. (1999) *Time to Think*. London: Ward Lock.

Kübler-Ross, E. (1997) *On Death and Dying*. New York: Touchstone.

Levitin, D J (2014) *The Organized Mind: Thinking Straight in the World of Information Overload*. New York: Penguin Random House.

Lewin, K. (1935) *A Dynamic Theory of Personality*. New York: McGraw-Hill.

Lewin, K. (1948) *Resolving Social Conflicts: Selected Papers on Group Dynamics*, edited by Gertrude Lewin. New York: Harper and Row.

Lewis, T., Amini, F. and Lannon, R. (2001) *A General Theory of Love*. New York: Vintage Books.

Locke, E.A. and Latham, G.P. (1990) *A Theory of Goal-setting and Task Performance*. Englewood Cliffs, NJ: Prentice Hall.

Luft, J. (1970) *Group Processes: An Introduction to Group Dynamics*. Palo Alto, CA: National Press Books.

McGilchrist, I. (2009) *The Master and His Emissary: The Divided Brain and the Making of the Western World*. New Haven, CT: Yale University Press.

McLelland, D.C. (1985) *Human Motivation*. Chicago, IL: Scott, Foresman.

Martel, Y. (2002) *Life of Pi*. Edinburgh: Canongate Books.

Masson, J. (1990) *Against Therapy*. London: Fontana.

Mearns, D. (2003) *Developing Person-centred Counselling*, 2nd edn. London: Sage Publications.

Mearns, D. and Thorne, B. (1999) *Person-centred Counselling in Action*. London: Sage Publications.

Moyes, B. (2009) Literature review of coaching supervision, *International Coaching Psychology Review*, 4(2): 160–71.

Mueller, M. (2007) *Recovering from PTSD*. Oxford: Oxford Cognitive Therapy Centre.

O'Neill, M.B. (2000) *Executive Coaching with Backbone and Heart*. San Francisco, CA: Jossey-Bass.

Orbach, S. (1999) *The Impossibility of Sex*. Harmondsworth: Allen Lane, The Penguin Press.

Paice, L. (2013) *New Coach: Reflections from a Learning Journey*. Maidenhead: Open University Press.

Palmer, H. and Brown, P. (1998) *The Enneagram Advantage: Putting the Nine Personality Types to Work in the Office*. New York: Harmony Books.

Pemberton, C. (2014) *Resilience: A Practical Guide for Coaches*. Maidenhead: Open University Press.

Persl, F. (1967) *Gestalt Therapy Verbatim*. LaFayette, CA: Real People Press.

Peters, S. (2011) *The Chimp Paradox*. London: Vermilion, Random House.

Prochaska, J.O., Norcross, J. and DiClemente, C. (2007) *Changing for Good*. New York: HarperCollins.

Rock, D. (2008) SCARF: A brain-based model for collaborating with and influencing others, *NeuroLeadership Journal*, 1: 1–9.

Rogers, C.R. (1951) *Client-centered Therapy: Its Current Practice, Implications and Theory*. Boston, MA: Houghton Mifflin.

Rogers, C.R. (1980) *A Way of Being*. Boston, MA: Houghton Mifflin.

Rogers, J. (2007) *Adults Learning*, 5th edn. Maidenhead: Open University Press.

Rogers, J. (2006) *Developing a Coaching Business*. Maidenhead: Open University Press.

Rogers, J. (2010) *Facilitating Groups*. Maidenhead: Open University Press.

Rogers, J. (2011) *Job Interview Success: Be Your Own Coach*. Maidenhead: McGraw-Hill.

Rogers, J. (2006) *Sixteen Personality Types at Work in Organizations*. London: Management Futures; Milton Keynes: ASK Europe.

Rogers, J. with Whittleworth, K. and Gilbert, A. (2012) *Manager as Coach: The New Way to Get Results*. Maidenhead: McGraw-Hill Education.

Rosinski, P. (2011) Global coaching for organizational development, *International Journal of Coaching in Organizations*, 30(8): 49.

Samuels, A. (1985) *Jung and the Post-Jungians*. London: Routledge.

Schein, E.H. (2006) *Career Anchors: Self Assessment*, 3rd edn. New York: Pfeiffer.

Schutz, W. (1984) *The Truth Option*. Berkeley, CA: Ten Speed Press.

Schutz, W. (1989) *Profound Simplicity*. San Diego, CA: WSA Bantam.

Schwartz, J.M. (1996) *Brain Lock*. New York: Regan Books.

Scoular, A. (2011) *FT Guide to Business Coaching*. London: Prentice-Hall

Senge, P. (1994) *The Fifth Discipline Field Book*. London: Nicolas Brealy Publishing.

Siegel, D. (2010) *Mindsight*. Oxford: Oneworld.

Stacey, R.D. (1996) *Strategic Management and Organizational Dynamics*, 2nd edn. London: Pitman Publishing.

Stoltenberg, C.D. and Delworth, U. (1987) *Supervising Counselors and Therapists: A Developmental Approach*. San Francisco, CA: Jossey-Bass.

Sullivan, W. and Rees, J. (2008) *Clean Language: Revealing Metaphors and Opening Minds*. Carmarthen: Crown House Publishing.

Theeboom, T., Beersma, B. and van Vianen, A.E.M. (2013). Does coaching work? A meta-analysis on the effects of coaching on individual level outcomes in an organizational context, *Journal of Positive Psychology*, 9(1): 1–18.

Tolle, E. (2001) *The Power of Now*. London: Hodder and Stoughton.

Ward, P. (1997) *360-degree Feedback*. London: Institute of Personnel and Development.

Waterman, J. and Rogers, J. (1997) *An Introduction to the FIRO-B*. Oxford: Oxford Psychologists Press.

Whitmore, J. (1996) *Coaching for Performance*, 2nd edn. London: Nicholas Brealey Publishing.

Whitworth, L., Kimsey-House, H. and Sandahl, P. (1998) *Co-active Coaching*. Palo Alto, CA: Davies Black Publishing.

Williams, M. (2014) *Cry of Pain: Understanding Suicide and the Suicidal Mind*. London: Piatkus.

Williams, M. and Penman, D. (2011) *Mindfulness: A Practical Guide to Finding Peace in a Frantic World*. London: Piatkus.

Wildflower, L. and Brennan, D. (2011) *The Handbook of Knowledge-Based Coaching: From Theory into Practice*. San Francisco, CA: Jossey-Bass.

Wildflower, L. (2013) *The Hidden History of Coaching*. Maidenhead: Open University Press.

Yalom, I.D. (1991) *Love's Executioner and Other Tales of Psychotherapy*. Harmondsworth: Penguin Books.
Yalom, I.D. (2002) *The Gift of Therapy*. London: Judy Piatkus Publishing.
Zinsser, W. (2006) *On Writing Well: The Classic Guide to Writing*, 7th edn. New York: Harper Collins.

Contact details

For feedback on this book, or for information about training courses, email Jenny@ JennyRogersCoaching.com

Index

Resilience
A practical guide for coaches

Carole Pemberton

ISBN: 978-0-335-26374-5 (Paperback)
eBook: 978-0-335-26375-2
2015

Resilience: A Guide for Coaches is based on the author's experience as an expert executive and career coach. Inspired by her own research with individuals who have lost their resilience; it provides key insights from psychology, case study evidence and tools for coaches to work with on resilience issues.

Practicing or training coaches can gain:

- An understanding of what resilience is, and what separates it from burnout and trauma
- A range of approaches that they can use in working with resilience issues
- A better understanding of the their own resilience

www.openup.co.uk

Manager as Coach
The new way to get results

Rogers, Whittleworth and Gilbert

ISBN: 9780077140182 (Paperback)
eBook: 9780077140199
2012

How do you manage performance?

If you come across as too directive you may get a reputation for harshness.
If you are too nice you risk being known as gullible and easily
outmanoeuvred. Neither approach works.

'Employee engagement' is the magical ingredient: it makes staff genuinely
committed, creating excellent work. Few organizations actually achieve it,
though all say they want it. Coaching is the most reliable way of producing
it.

Manager as Coach challenges many of the traditional assumptions about
what works in management and shows you, step by step, how to be a
brilliant manager and get fantastic results:

    Reduce your stress
    Develop employees' key skills
    Create a culture of engagement
    Improve bottom line results

www.mheducation.co.uk

OPEN UNIVERSITY PRESS
McGraw - Hill Education

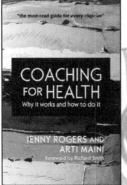

Coaching for Health

Jenny Rogers and Arti Maini

ISBN: 9780335262304 (Paperback)
eBook: 9780335262311
2016

This book has a radical new message for any clinician: through coaching you reduce your own stress and you get far better outcomes for patients. Coaching for health' means creating a different relationship in consultations, asking a different kind of question and giving information in a different way. It goes beyond what is usually meant by 'patient-centred practice'. It will work with virtually any patient. When you take a coaching approach the chances are that your patients gain confidence in managing their own health, reduce the number of appointments they request, are less likely to need emergency admissions and are more likely to take their medication.

Coaching is not just a technique that you switch on and off, it is a wholly different mindset. Coaching for Health explains the rationale for a coaching approach and gives pragmatic step by step help on how to do it.

The authors - one an executive coach, one a doctor - write from their extensive, collective experience. Having trained many hundreds of clinicians in coaching skills, Jenny Rogers and Arti Maini have seen firsthand how transformational it can be to use in practice.

www.mheducation.co.uk